UP TILL NOW

UP TILL NOW

THE AUTOBIOGRAPHY

WILLIAM SHATNER

with David Fisher

**THORNDIKE
WINDSOR
PARAGON**

LIBRARY OF CONGRESS CATALOGING-IN-PUBLICATION DATA

Shatner, William.
   Up till now : the autobiography / by William Shatner ; with David Fisher. — Large print ed.
    p. cm.
   ISBN-13: 978-1-4104-0869-3 (lg. print : hardcover : alk. paper)
   ISBN-10: 1-4104-0869-8 (lg. print : hardcover : alk. paper)
   1. Shatner, William. 2. Actors — Canada — Biography. 3. Large type books. I. Fisher, David. II. Title.
PN2308.S52A3 2008b
792.02'8092—dc22
[B]   2008017277

BRITISH LIBRARY CATALOGUING-IN-PUBLICATION DATA AVAILABLE

Published in 2008 in the U.S. by arrangement with St. Martin's Press, LLC.
Published in 2009 in the U.K. by arrangement with Pan Macmillan Ltd.

U.K. Hardcover: 978 1 408 41345 6 (Windsor Large Print)
U.K. Softcover: 978 1 408 41346 3 (Paragon Large Print)

Printed in the United States of America
1 2 3 4 5 6 7 12 11 10 09 08

I've written several books and many other things, and always cherished the dedication. In fact, one can riffle through my life based on the various people or, indeed, events that surrounded my time on this planet. But up to now, I have never acknowledged my father and my mother . . . my dear, hardworking, caring, loving dad, and my funny, frustrated, gentle mother. All that I am or might've been is their due. I bow with great humility in their direction.

ACKNOWLEDGMENTS

Without the love of my wife, Elizabeth, and daughters, Leslie, Lisbeth, and Melanie, there would be no book.

I'd would also like to acknowledge David Fisher, who turns out to be not only a wonderful writer and listener but a dear soul, as well. Blowing away some of the mists of memory, in his company, was an honor, as always.

And we would also like to express our gratitude to those members of the Shatner family and the many friends and associates who so willingly and enthusiastically gave their time and memories to help us create this personal portrait. We also deeply appreciate the efforts of our agent, Carmen La Via of the Fifi Oscard Agency; our publisher, Tom Dunne; our editor, Peter Joseph, and all of those truly supportive professionals at Thomas Dunne Books at St. Martin's Press. This book would not have been possible without the work of Suzanne Copitzky and her staff at the Karmen Executive Center, and the hospitality of dear friends Eli and Noa Attia and George and Kathy Hicker.

David Fisher would simply like to express his love and his appreciation to his wife, Laura Stevens, who makes even the hard days wonderful.

ONE

I was going to begin my autobiography this way:

Call me . . . Captain James T. Kirk or Sergeant T.J. Hooker or Denny Crane Denny Crane or *Twilight Zone* plane passenger Bob Wilson or the Big Giant Head or Henry V or the Priceline Negotiator or . . .

Well, that's the problem, isn't it? I've been a working actor for more than half a century and I've played so many different roles on the stage, on television, and in the movies that it would be impossible to focus on just one of them. Besides, my career as an actor is only part of my story, so I realized I couldn't begin this book that way.

Then I decided I was going to start this book by telling the story of my memorable meeting with Koko the gorilla:

In 1988, to help the Gorilla Foundation

encourage Californians to contribute to its Endangered Species Campaign, I was permitted to visit Koko the gorilla in her quarters. Koko was an extraordinary animal who had learned to communicate with human beings. She was able to sign more than six hundred words, but more impressively, as her handlers told me, she understood the meaning of those words. She knew the signs for *water* and for *bird* and the first time she saw a duck landing on a lake she signed *water bird.* That displayed a synthesis of knowledge. So you see, she was obviously very intelligent. I was allowed to go into her compound, to enter a room with her all alone. As I walked into that room I was reminded that she was an imposing, powerful animal; smaller gorillas have been known to tear off men's arms in anger. I am not often afraid, but truthfully I was frightened.

There is a form of acting that teaches: feel it and say it, and that feeling will be revealed through your words. The English form is quite different: say it and then you feel it. To deal with my fear of this magnificent animal as I got closer and closer to her I found myself saying, "I love you, Koko. I love you." I said it earnestly and honestly and I looked directly in her eyes as I spoke. I crouched over a little to show submission, moving forward rather than backward to show I was not afraid. Over and over I repeated, "I love you, Koko, I love you." And as I said it, I began to feel that love. Finally I stopped directly in front of her and looked into her deep brown eyes and saw her furrowed brow and her enormous hands. I love you, Koko.

And with that she reached out and grabbed me by my balls. And looked me right in the eyes. After a slight pause — in a substantially higher voice — I tried to repeat, "I love you, Koko." Obviously these words had more significance than a few seconds earlier.

Her handler, standing just outside the room, said, "Stand very still. She wants you to go to her bedroom." So I stood very still because I did not want to go to her bedroom. I think it is fair to say that few people in history have ever stood as still as I did at that moment. Meanwhile, in the adjoining compound a young gorilla who they hoped would mate with Koko was pounding on the door like a jealous husband. There I was, caught in the eternal triangle, with a gorilla holding on to my rapidly shrinking scrotum. Eventually she got bored . . .

Starting this book with that story would enable me to inform the reader that it's not

11

going to be limited to my professional career, that it will also include stories about all the extraordinary opportunities I've been given to explore the world. I'd discuss all the amazing experiences I've had, from that dark night in Africa when I pursued a wild elephant to the afternoon a helicopter left me more alone than I'd ever been in my life on top of a twenty-thousand-foot-high glacier, and even to that memorable moment when I saw aliens in the desert. And it would also demonstrate that there are going to be a lot of laughs in this book, most of them at my expense. But then I realized that people know me primarily from the work I've done as an actor, so that wouldn't be effective as a beginning. So I decided not to begin that way either.

Then I had a great idea. I was going to start the book by quoting the lyrics to a song I'd written about the truly tragic death by drowning of my beautiful wife, Nerine Shatner:

My love was supposed to protect her
It didn't
My love was supposed to heal her
It didn't
You had said don't leave me

12

And I begged you not to leave me
We did

Opening the book that way would be so meaningful to me, beginning with the great tragedy of my life. And it would immediately let readers know that this is to be a truthful book. But it would also be such a sad beginning, when my life has been filled with so much joy. And of course, I'm not known for my singing; in fact there are those who believe my performance of "Lucy in the Sky with Diamonds" may be the worst version of a Beatles song ever recorded. Not me — of course. And this is such a personal story that it needs to be told in its entirety, so certainly I couldn't begin my book that way.

There is one extremely well-known phrase that I definitely decided I would not use to begin this book:

"Beam me up, Scotty."

In fact, I am determined that this phrase will not appear anywhere in this book.

The beginning, I knew, needed to catch the interest of the reader within a few words, to engage their curiosity, to make them wonder, perhaps, what the hell is he talking about? Which led to:

I arrived in New York City for the first time in my life in an Indian outrigger canoe,

13

having paddled all the way from Montreal . . .

I liked that, but it didn't seem to convey the essence of my life. Somehow it seemed too gimmicky, too clever, so I knew I couldn't use that. Maybe later in the first chapter, I decided.

It occurred to me that perhaps I should open this book with a description of the day I took my beautiful horse, Sultan's Great Day, for his final walk in the pasture. Oh my, you should have seen him in his world-championship days. I'm telling you, this was the most magnificent stallion you've ever seen. I'm not kidding about that. Really, people were in awe of his presence. They would look at him and . . .

I would use that beginning to tell you about my passions, the passions that have made all the difference in my life. The passions that I've spent my life pursuing: the love of a beautiful woman, the love for my family, the love for my craft, my art, the need to experience every aspect of life. Sometimes I'm amazed to realize that I live today with the vestiges of my priorities as a young man, the desire to act, the need to be loved, the pleasures of a great meal, a great laugh, and enduring companionship.

But simply telling you about my passions

— even my passion for horses and dogs — seemed far too somber an opening.

Perhaps, I thought, I should start this book by being glib, by exposing my quirky sense of humor to the readers. Make them laugh at the very beginning by quoting a newspaper story about one of the more unusual things I've ever done:

(AP) 1/17/2006 Actor William Shatner agreed on Monday to sell his kidney stone for $75,000 to an online casino. The money will go to Habitat for Humanity. "This takes organ donors to a new height, or perhaps a new low," said Shatner. The auction price includes the surgical stent and string used to permit passage of the stone.

According to Shatner, the kidney stone was so big, "[Y]ou'd want to wear it on your finger. If you subjected it to extreme heat, it might turn out to be a diamond . . ."

While that beginning certainly would be humorous, it just seemed too frivolous to start that way. Instead, it occurred to me that the opening of this book should be thoughtful, it should be about my life. How much more sincere could I be about the life I've had than using words written by David

E. Kelley for the character I play on *Boston Legal,* Denny Crane Denny Crane:

Evening: Crane and Shore on the balcony outside Crane's office

Crane Alan Shore believes man has a soul. Stop the presses.

Shore Don't you believe it? Can this be all there is? And if so . . . have we not wasted . . .

Crane I haven't wasted a second. I've enjoyed my ride, all of it.

Shore But will it have truly counted for something?

Crane You've heard the old joke, Alan. Man shows up at the pearly gates, sees this guy in a pinstripe suit, briefcase, cigar, prancing about, he says to St. Peter, "Who the hell is that?" St. Peter says, "Oh that's just God. Thinks he's Denny Crane."

Shore What would you do, Denny, if you actually met God one day?

Crane I dunno. Probably take him fishing.

For a brief time I had decided this was the perfect way to open this book. Then it occurred to me, let Denny Crane write his own book! Finally, inspiration struck! I had what I believed would be a unique and perfect opening:

Are you tired of paying full price for this

book? Well, you don't have to. You can buy as many copies of it as you like — and you name the price! That's right, you name the price you want to pay. At Priceline.com it's as simple as that. Here's the way . . .

Opening this book like that would be funny, yet accurate, as many people know me from my work representing various companies, such as Priceline.com. And if we also could sell a few more copies of this book, well, I didn't think St. Martin's would object. And if Priceline was approached properly by my agent, perhaps they might even be willing to purchase the rights to the opening paragraph. For less than full price, of course.

But perhaps that was too crass for the opening of my autobiography, I decided. Is that really what I wanted to emphasize about my life and my career? And would Priceline meet my price? So that opening too, was rejected.

And then it occurred to me: I don't need an opening. By the time you've reached this paragraph my autobiography has already started. Of course that was very similar to my career; I was already in the middle of it before I realized it had begun.

The first time I stood on a stage I made the audience cry.

Let me establish the rules for this book. I will tell all the jokes unless I specifically identify a straight line. In which case you will have the opportunity to make up the jokes.

I was six years old, attending Rabin's Camp, a summer camp for Jewish welfare cases run by my aunt in the mountains north of Montreal. I wanted to box at that camp — hitting people seemed like fun — but my aunt instead put me in a play named *Winterset*. My role was that of a young boy forced to leave his home because the Nazis were coming. In the climactic scene I had to say good-bye to my dog, knowing I probably would never see him again. My dog was played by another camper, costumed in painted newspaper. We performed the play on parents' weekend to an audience consisting primarily of people who had escaped the Nazis, many of whom still had family members trapped in Hitler's Europe. So many of them had left everything they knew or owned behind — and there I was, saying good-bye to my little doggie.

I cried, the audience cried, everybody cried. I remember taking my bow and seeing people wiping away their tears. I remember the warmth of my father holding me as people told him what a wonderful son he had. Just imagine the impact that had on a six-year-old child. I had the ability to move people to tears. And I could get approval.

Something in me always wanted to perform, always wanted the attention that came from pleasing an audience. Years before my camp debut my older sister remembers my mother taking the two of us downtown. Apparently I ran away and it took them several hectic minutes to find me — dancing happily in front of an organ-grinder.

Where did that come from? That need to please people? What part of me was born with the courage to stand in front of strangers and risk rejection? There was nothing at all like that in my family history. The Shatner family was Polish and Austrian and Hungarian, and apparently several of my forebears were rabbis and teachers. Like so many Jewish immigrants my father was in the schmatta business — he manufactured inexpensive men's suits for French-Canadian clothing stores. Admiration Clothes. They were basically suits for workingmen who owned only one suit. Joseph Shatner was a stern but loving man, a hard-working man. I can close my eyes and remember the smell of his cutting room. The unforgettable aroma of raw serge and tweed in rolled-up bales, mixed with the smell of my father's cigarettes. Saturday afternoon was the only time he would relax, lying on the couch and listening to New York's Metropolitan Opera on the radio. He came to Montreal from Eastern Europe when he was fourteen, and worked selling newspapers and in other labor-intensive jobs. He started in the clothing business packing boxes and eventually became a salesman and finally started his own small company. He was the first member of his family to come to North America, but eventually he helped all ten of his brothers and sisters leave Europe. My friend Leonard Nimoy likes to joke about the fact that I never stop working; he does an imitation of me in which he says, "It's quarter of four. What's scheduled for four-ten? If I'm done there by four-thirty can we get something for four-fifty?"

Perhaps there is some truth to that. Every actor has spent days . . . months staring at the telephone, willing it to ring. And living with the hollow fear that it might never ring again. Painting the walls over again while waiting for the next offer. After beginning my career I went more than twenty years without taking a real vacation, petrified I might miss a phone call. Having had that experience, having lived in the back of pickup trucks in the parking lots of summer theaters, indeed I am open to opportunities. But there is a general belief that I will accept almost anything that I'm offered and that certainly is not true. It was less than two years ago that I turned down an offer. Like any actor, I'm concerned about being overexposed, so I've been very careful to limit myself to acting on the stage and in dramatic television programs, hosting documentary-type programs and game shows, appearing in movies and commercials, endorsing products, doing voice-overs, charity appearances, radio programs, Webcasts, videos, *Star Trek* conventions, game shows, horse shows and dog shows, writing books and songs, making albums, creating, directing and producing television programs, performing at concerts, and appearing on talk shows, competitive reality-type shows, and award programs. But that's where I draw the line. For example, I rarely do bar mitzvahs and I've never worked in the Catskills.

My work ethic comes from my father. His dream was that I would eventually take over the business. So, as he had done, I worked in the factory packing suits. One of my skills is good packing. I know how to fold a suit with the shoulders touching inside-out, the

21

sleeves down, folded flat so it stays pressed. I know the correct way to fold pants and put them in a box. Had I not become an actor I could have had a fine career in folding.

But acting? What did my father know from acting? Acting smacting, that wasn't a thing real people did, it wasn't a job. It wasn't what people did to earn a living. It was playing.

From my father I learned the value of education, respect for others around me, and to be on time and prepared to work. Eleven-oh-five, he used to tell me, was not eleven o'clock. All my life I have been on time and prepared to work. I'll tell you how deeply that ethic is ingrained in me. In 2007 I was invited by ABC to participate in a show entitled *Fast Cars and Superstars,* actually a NASCAR celebrity race. This was an opportunity to drive as fast as possible in an oval without having to worry about speed traps. A racetrack is the one place in the world you can drive as fast as your skills and your courage allow. This was my kind of TV show. I said, "Of course, I'd love to do it." And then I began negotiating furiously for as much money as I could get.

As I was leaving the set of *Boston Legal* to fly to Charlotte, North Carolina, a producer gently put a comforting hand on my shoulder and explained, "Remember Bill, you've got to report for work Thursday at seven a.m. And if you're not here, if you've hit a wall and broken your arms and legs or turned the car over and are lying in a hospital somewhere covered from head to toe in bandages so you can't get back, this company can sue you." Then he paused and smiled broadly. "Other than that, have a great time."

I've loved fast cars all my life. I've long admired the great drivers. But I am aware of the danger. I know Dale Earnhardt Jr.'s fate. The reality is that race drivers die. They crash and burn, they roll over and catch fire. I've seen those pictures. Not me, of course, them. I have been in enough television shows and feature films to understand reality — the star never gets hurt.

There were twelve competitors divided into four groups. Each group of three people shared one car. For safety, there would be one driver on the track at a time. We were racing against time, not directly against each other. My group consisted of myself, former Pittsburgh Steelers head coach Bill Cowher, and volleyball player-model Gabrielle Reece. We drove for the first time in a morning practice round. I hit

160mph, and as I went around the turns I was convinced the car was going to slide out from under me and hit the wall. Well, it didn't, and 160mph put me way back in the pack.

I promised myself I would do better in the actual competition. I realized I had been holding back on the straightaways, anticipating the next turn. When we raced that night I intended to press down on the accelerator so I could remain in the race. The only question I had was who would be eliminated first from my group, Cowher or Reece?

My group was scheduled to race Tuesday night. Cowher went first. He spun out and hit the wall; the $500,000 car was badly damaged. We waited more than an hour for a replacement car; finally Cowher made his run and established his time. Gabrielle Reece had posted some very fast times in her practice runs, but during her run she also spun out and almost hit the wall. Now it was my turn.

I was wearing a completely fireproof jumpsuit and a large bulbous helmet with a face mask that covered my entire head. When they tried to strap me in I realized something was wrong. This car had been set up for Cowher and Reece, two very tall people. My feet didn't reach the pedals. And the seat wouldn't move. The only thing that did move was the telescoping steering wheel. But the wheel in the car was too large, so they replaced it with a much smaller wheel that was sticking into my gut, much smaller than any steering wheel I was used to. By then it was one o'clock in the morning, I was tired, and the lithium lights shining down on the filthy windshield made it difficult to see clearly.

In minutes I was going to be driving faster than 160mph with a steering wheel jammed into my belly and pillows stuffed behind me to push me forward so I could reach the pedals on a track I could not see clearly.

This was crazy and I knew it. I thought, what am I doing here? I could be killed.

I put my foot down on the accelerator and took off. I've learned in karate that your chi is below your belly button and as you do any physical activity you release it in explosive breaths. I've done that many times. My intention was to blow out my chi by yelling as I went around those turns.

Actually, I believe that my exact words as I raced around the corners were "Whooooooooooooooooooooooooo. Whoooooooooooooooooooooooo." I was not blowing out my chi, I was trying to contain my fear. I was seeing death. I knew I was going to die.

25

I could barely control the car, I couldn't see where I was going, and I was driving faster than 160mph. I never should have been in that situation. Drivers have told me about the feeling of Zen they've experienced in which they are one with the car. I didn't get that feeling, instead I felt like a foreign body that the car was trying to eject.

I finished my three official laps. I never learned my time; I was disqualified for a technical violation. But later I wondered why I had taken that risk. I risked my life for a television program? I did it, I realized, because the cameras were rolling. Believe me, if those TV cameras had not been there I wouldn't have risked my life. But the cameras were there; this was a show, a performance. This was my job. And as I had been taught by my father, I was there on time and ready to go to work.

It was my mother, Ann Shatner, who encouraged me to act. She sent me to acting school; she never missed a performance. She went with me to audition for radio roles and when I didn't get the part she would call the producer, Mr. Rupert Kaplan, to scream at him for not hiring me. Unlike some mothers she didn't follow me to college when I attended McGill — she didn't have to, we lived two miles from the campus.

My mother might accurately be described kindly as ditzy. Her own family had been relatively well off and she was somewhat spoiled; the contrast between this lovely young woman who had so much and a hard-working man struggling to bring his family over from Europe must have been extreme. My mother had a great dramatic flair. She wanted her life to be big and loud. When we went for dinner, for example, she would quite often inform the waiter that it was her birthday. I still get embarrassed thinking about it. She would sit there beaming while the rest of us were cringing as the waiters gathered around our table to loudly sing "Happy Birthday." I'm certain people would look at our table and wonder why this entire family was looking down and not singing "Happy Birthday" to that lovely woman. What a reputation we must have had: that Shatner family won't sing "Happy Birthday," imagine that. My mother had more birthdays than anyone in the world.

She always took great pleasure in my success, and even more pleasure in sharing it. I can still hear her saying those memorable words, "I'm William Shatner's mother." I can still hear it because she never stopped saying it. Everywhere she went. If she got on an elevator before the doors closed she would say, "Hello everybody, I'm William Shatner's mother." In department stores, in every restaurant, "I'm William Shatner's mother." On occasion I'd get on an airplane and the stewardess would tell me she'd had my mother on a flight. I didn't need to ask how she knew it was my mother. I would tell my mother over and over, please don't do that. It's embarrassing. I hate it. Don't do it. And she would look at me sadly and say, "Okay, I won't do it." And then she would turn around, "Hi, I'm William Shatner's mother."

My father used to remind me with tremendous emphasis, "She's *still* your mother." Meaning no matter what she's done, how much you don't understand her, you will treat her with respect. She's still your mother.

She was an elocution teacher. She was not, as she often corrected my father, an *execution* teacher, she was an *elocution* teacher. I want you to do something for me please, try to pronounce these words aloud as you read them: ten tin men, ten tin men. The difference between "ten" and "tin" is elocution. My mother was probably a frustrated actress; there really was no place for a middle-aged Jewish mother of three to perform in Montreal, so she would act out monologues at home. When I was seven or eight years old she enrolled me in the Dorothy Davis School for Actors, which was run by Miss Dorothy Davis and Miss Violet Walters in the basement of someone's home. It was in that basement that I learned the skills necessary to succeed in the difficult thespian world — specifically, get up on stage, say my words, get off the stage — skills that eventually allowed me to play such memorable roles as Prince Charming and Tom Sawyer at a theater in the local park. I am proud to say I am the most famous graduate of the Dorothy Davis School for Actors.

I don't remember being taught how to act, we just acted. And the school charged admission to watch us act. Actually, I don't believe acting can be taught, but what you can learn is the discipline of learning your words, having to appear, and having to say them.

I was a lonely kid. I'd walk to school by myself. In school, on Valentine's Day, I would send myself valentines. Those would be the only ones I would receive. One year I got six valentines from myself! Truthfully, I don't know why I didn't have many close friends. It might have had something to do with the neighborhood in which we lived. While all my relatives lived in the Jewish section of Montreal, my family lived in a comfortable house on Girouard Street, in the more affluent, mostly Catholic area NDG, Notre Dame de Grace.

There was always trouble between the Jewish kids and the Catholic kids, there was a lot of anti-Semitism. When I had to go to Hebrew school I'd walk on the opposite side of the street, actively pretending I didn't even realize the synagogue was there — until I got in front of it. Then I'd look both ways and run for the door. I actually planned my strategy for getting there safely. Not that I minded a fight, I wasn't a big kid but I never backed down from anybody. We had fights almost every day. My nickname was "Toughie," as in, Hey, watch out everybody, here comes Toughie Shatner! Actually, you might not want to mention that to little Lenny Nimoy, another Jewish kid growing up at exactly the same time in Boston. I'd hear stories about Jewish soldiers who had come back from the war; one or two men taking on a whole gang of anti-Semites and beating them into submission with an ax handle.

I played football and skied in high school and I loved both sports, but it was acting that made me feel complete. Acting made me special, and I was good at it. I never had difficulty pretending to be someone else. At camp, not only did I make the adults cry, I literally drove a camper crazy. I was working as a counselor with my friend Hilliard Jason — he required me to call him Hilliard. We ran a bunk filled with kids who had survived the Holocaust, kids who had seen their parents slaughtered, kids who just as easily could kill you with a pencil as become friends. I was able to control them because I was the camp storyteller. At night, in the dark, I would read Poe and Kafka with great elocution. One night I read "The Tell-tale Heart" — "You fancy me mad. Madmen know nothing. But you should have seen me" — and one child broke down in fear. He let free all of those emotions kept inside for so long and it was too much for him. He became hysterical. The next day he was sent home, wrapped in blankets in the backseat of a car.

What had I done? I felt terrible. Awful. That had not been my intention. But I was also astonished. Once again I had seen the extraordinary power of words to evoke great emotion. Look what I could do! Just by saying some words!

I acted throughout my childhood. When

Dorothy Davis established the Montreal's Children Theatre we put on our plays at the Victorian Theatre in the park and on local radio. For five years I saved damsels on *Saturday Morning Fairy Tales,* even if I wasn't quite certain what a damsel was. What eight-year-old doesn't want to be Prince Charming? Or Ali Baba? Or Huck Finn? I got to be them all. Acting was playing. I was being me being someone else. It came easily to me. I crashed my sister Joy's sweet sixteen party, for example, costumed as an old man. Joy had no idea it was me, no idea. She came over to me and said, politely, "Excuse me, but I don't think I know who you are." When she got close enough and looked into my eyes, she knew. But the concept that I could do this as a profession, that I could earn . . .

Oh, excuse me. I just have to go star in another movie with Sandra Bullock for a little while. Here, please hum along with a song I wrote with Ben Folds and I'll be back in a few sentences:

I know what she's gonna do; And I can't wait for her to do it. She knows me and I know her; what I hate and what I prefer. Dum de dum, dum de um. I know her scent, I know her touch; where to hold

32

her and just how much.

My lady belongs here and so . . .

Okay, I'm back. Where was I? Growing up, the concept that I could continue to do this playing as an adult was not something that occurred to me. It was just something that I loved doing. In high school I played football and acted in school plays and for the first time I allowed myself to dream. Under my photograph in my senior yearbook I finally admitted it out loud: I wanted to be an actor. Not *that* out loud of course, not loud enough for my father to hear me.

While still in high school I got my first real job in the theater — as a stage manager. I was fifteen years old and I had absolutely no experience. Looking back, I suspect I got the job because I was young and good-looking and oh so terribly naïve. A well-known French male singer was starring in a play at the Orpheum Theatre, which housed all the touring companies. It was thrilling for me. I was in the theater; backstage, but inside the theater. The actor was tall and good-looking and early in the run he asked me if I wanted to join him for dinner.

Well, I thought, I must be a great stage manager. The star of the show has asked me to have dinner with him. Naturally I accepted his invitation. As we left the theater that night he asked me if I had a jacket with me. "No," I admitted.

"That's fine," he said casually. "I've got a jacket that'll fit you in my hotel room."

Welcome to show business, Shatner. The strongest memory I have of that night is being chased around the bed. Football season had recently ended so I was in good shape and strong. I stayed out of his reach. Incredibly, I didn't even know what he wanted. I was unaware of homosexuality. I didn't know that men could be attracted to other men. It was not something spoken about in middle-class Jewish homes.

What happened that night changed my attitude toward women for the rest of my life. I understood the anger and frustration that a woman feels when she says no, and means no, and the man believes she is saying yes.

Acting had become my passion. I was hungry to stand before an audience and perform. I accepted every opportunity offered to me. When I was sixteen I got a part in a production of Clifford Odets's *Waiting for Lefty* being done at a Communist organization meeting hall in Montreal. Every serious young actor wanted to do meaningful theater, even if we didn't understand the meaning. I didn't know anything about Communism, but I knew the history of Clifford Odets and the Group Theatre. I remember being on stage, looking nobly to the ceiling, my fist raised, screaming, "Strike! Strike!" And the audience — my God, they went out of their minds! "Strike! Strike!" When the audience responded I could feel the power of my performance. Me, little Billy Shatner from the west end of Montreal, not quite Westmont, holding this audience in my hand. Strike! Strike! It was magnificent, beautiful. Strike! Strike!

I had absolutely no idea what I was doing. No understanding of political philosophy. I was acting, that's all. Giving life and emotion to words written on paper. The red-baiting movement started several years later, just as I was beginning my career in America. I was terrified that someone would ask me about my work for the Communist party.

At West Hill High School I was never a very good student, more because of a lack of interest than a lack of ability. In school, those things about the world that would one day intrigue and delight and fascinate me didn't even interest me. I wanted to act and play football, that was it. I barely graduated from high school and yet was accepted to the McGill University School of Commerce. The business school. I was admitted under a Jewish quota that existed at that time. With my grades they must have been marking on a very large curve. My family believed I was at McGill to learn how to bring modern economic practices into my father's clothing business, so I could turn it into the hugely successful corporation we all knew was just the completion of my college education away. But I knew I was there to perform in their shows.

I spent considerably more time in the drama department than going to class. I got by, I always managed to get by, but more important, I wrote and produced and appeared in several campus productions. I was also working part-time as a radio announcer at the Canadian Broadcasting Company. Here, remember these words: "Stay tuned for our next exciting program." That was me.

Growing up, I wanted to be like the kids who lived in Westmont, the moneyed part of the city. I wanted to be like the upper-class English kids who drove their MGs to college. I remember when I was five or six years old I found a five-dollar bill. That was all the money in the world to a child, but I wanted to share it with my only friend — so

I tore it in half.

I understood the importance of money — but acting was more important. I knew I would never make as much money acting as my father earned in the schmatta business, but I didn't care. I suspect every actor has a financial goal when they begin. Mine was a hundred dollars a week. I thought, if I could earn a hundred dollars a week as an actor I will be a very happy man. Leonard, whose father was a barber, wanted to earn ten thousand dollars a year, but Leonard always had extravagant dreams.

Telling this to my father was one of the most difficult things I have ever done. My father's dream was that we would work together one day. As a teenager I would go with him on sales calls. We'd put on our best suits and drive to these small French villages outside Montreal. He had friends in every village — this is my old friend Jake, my old friend Pierre, my old friend Robert — people he had sold to for years. To each of these men he would proudly introduce me, "This is my son," and they would comment on how tall I was, how much I looked like him. It was the salesman's dance. I was being brought into the family business.

I didn't know how I could tell him. One afternoon, during my third year in college, for some reason we were in my bedroom and he asked me casually if I'd thought about my future. Just as casually I told him I wanted to be an actor. And his heart just plummeted.

He sat down on my bed as the enormity of that hit him. He didn't understand the theater. Acting wasn't a job for a man. Actors were bums. For him, it was like being a minstrel. The chances of succeeding, of having any kind of meaningful life were very, very slim. I knew he was devastated, but the only thing he said to me was, "Well, you do what you want to do. There's always a place for you here. I don't have the money to support you, but I'll help you the best I can." The only thing he asked of me was that I not become a "hanger-on." By that he meant being dependent on other people, on unemployment insurance, a man who couldn't earn his own keep.

How brave he was to put aside his dreams so I might pursue my own. And how it must have hurt him. He was a man rooted deeply in the reality of a paycheck; the life of an artist was inconceivable to him. But rather than trying to talk me out of it, or offering advice, he gave me freedom.

And he always kept that place for me. Just in case.

I graduated from McGill University with my degree in commerce and I immediately put that degree to work. Mrs. Ruth Springford, a woman who had directed me in several college plays, was the director of a summer theater, the Mountain Playhouse. Having seen my work, she hired me as the assistant manager. The company was performing mostly one-set Broadway shows like *Roman Candle* and *The Seven Year Itch.* In those days playwrights were writing shows with minimal scenery and sets, knowing that if their play was successful on Broadway the number of companies that produced it in local theaters — and paid those royalties — would depend greatly on how many sets it had. Generally those plays were light comedies featuring a young guy — often a shy or bumbling young guy — with an innocent smile big enough to reach the back rows.

I was a terrible assistant manager. A disgrace to my commerce degree. I kept losing tickets and mixing up reservations, which were basically the only responsibilities I had. Actors were easily replaceable, but the survival of the theater depended on getting the ticket sales right. Most actors get hired; to save the theater I was fired into the cast. I began playing all those happy young man roles.

These were Broadway shows coming to Canada; the audience was ready to laugh. My talent was knowing my lines and waiting until the laughter stopped before speaking. I had no formal acting training, I never did. I would read about actors in New York City studying The Method. Well, I had my own method, I said my lines as if I were the character. I learned how to act from acting. The audience taught me how to act. If I did something and the audience responded, I did it again. So this experience of working every night, learning new roles, studying lines, experimenting with movements and expressions, that was my acting class.

A few years later, when I was a member of the company at the Stratford Shakespeare Festival, they held classes in technique and voice production and even swordplay for the young actors. The problem was that we were working much too hard as actors to find the time to take classes to learn how to act. By the time I had learned technique we had already opened our second show of the season and were in the middle of rehearsals for the third show. But at Stratford I did work with classically trained actors, among them James Mason and Anthony Quayle. We worked with experienced actors every day, we rehearsed with them, we played small roles, we understudied, and when we weren't onstage we watched them. I learned to act by watching other actors, reading about acting, and living with actors. I studied my craft, but I learned acting by acting.

I was a serious actor, I knew I must be a serious actor because I wasn't making any money at it. Those days prepared me very well for much later in my career when I would be a well-known television actor and wasn't making any money from it. I still dreamed of one day earning one hundred dollars a week, but that seemed far away. At least once a day, sometimes more, I spent twenty-seven cents for a plate of fruit salad at Kresge's lunch counter. I lived on fruit salad and grew to hate fruit salad. My one luxury was my forty-dollar car. That's what I paid for it, and it was worth that price. The driver's door was jammed shut, so to get in and out I'd have to climb through the window, and it burned so much oil that every forty or fifty miles I'd stop at a gas station and pour used oil into the crankcase. In those days you could buy oil that had been drained out of other cars very cheaply, which was my price. Generally I'd pour in oil once a day.

When that summer ended Mrs. Springford recommended me to the Canadian National Repertory Theatre in Ottawa — as their assistant manager. Again my uncanny ability to lose tickets and mix up reservations — although sometimes I would mix up tickets and lose reservations — ended up with me joining the cast — at a salary of thirty-one dollars a week!

During my second season in Ottawa a woman contacted me and told me very seriously that a company was being formed to perform Shakespeare in Stratford and invited me to join the company. I thought she was kidding. Give up a secure job that paid thirty-one dollars a week to go to some little town and become a member of some Shakespeare company I'd never heard of? What did they think I was, an actor?

"Thank you," I said, "but I have a regular job and I'm going to keep that one."

The Stratford Shakespeare Festival opened and within months had become celebrated throughout Canada and eventually around the world.

But I had my job. I worked at the Mountain Playhouse in the summer and at the Canadian Rep in the winter. We would do a different play every week, rehearsing and performing every day. They were almost exclusively laugh-a-second Broadway comedies. It wasn't just laughs, it was laughs within laughs. When you're doing a comedy silence is absolutely deafening; you not only can hear it, it cuts right through you. Oh no, what did I do wrong? That got a laugh last night, what did I do differently? When you're onstage and you don't get a laugh there is a clang in the mind of every performer on that stage; everybody immediately adjusts and tries to find the rhythm.

I did those comedies for almost three years. I thought I had experienced the worst possible clangs until I had this great idea many years later. This was long after James T. Kirk had become so well known. This was one of those epically bad ideas that seem so good at the time, and only later cause you to question the very existence of life: I was asked to perform at the Comedy Club in Los Angeles and I said, "I've got a great idea. I'm going to go in there like Shatner thinks he's Captain Kirk, and I'm going to go in there like Captain Kirk thinks he's funny."

The owner of the club looked at me seriously, "Bill, that's not funny," he said.

Now really, who's going to know what's funny? The actor who had spent several years performing light comedies in Canada or the owner of a comedy club that features stand-up performers every night? I said, "Let me explain this to you. It will be very funny because they will get that I'm Captain Kirk who thinks he's funny, but he's not funny, which is why he will be funny."

I remember that very strange look he had in his eyes. It was clear to me then that he did not understand the essence of comedy. I told all the usual Van Allen Belt jokes — you can probably imagine them: "Hey, a funny thing happened to me on the way to Zetar," "Take my Klingon, please." "A Romulan walked into the transporter room with a chicken on his head . . ."

That audience laughed like a roomful of Vulcans. Oh my, it was just awful. The problem, I discovered, was that the audience did not grasp the intricate sophistication of my act. Rather than understanding that I was playing Captain Kirk who thought he was funny, but wasn't funny, which was why he was funny, they watched me perform and instead decided, "Wow, Shatner's terrible."

That was the worst comedic night of my life. But I had started preparing for it in Ottawa. I struggled in Ottawa. My father's offer, there would always be a place for me, resonated in my head. It would be unfair to

44

say I was a starving actor; I wasn't making enough money to be starving. My father gave me a few thousand dollars, telling me, "I can't do any more." It was enough to help me survive but not enough to really live on. I know he must have been torn between wanting to help me but also wanting me to experience how incredibly difficult the life I'd chosen could be.

After my third year with the Canadian Rep I was once again invited to join the Stratford Festival to play the juvenile roles. This time I accepted the offer. The Stratford Festival had begun when a Canadian named Tom Patterson, who lived in the small town of Stratford, Ontario, had a very strange vision: he was going to create a theater in Stratford using Canadian players to perform all the classic plays. So he went to England and actually managed to convince Sir Tyrone Guthrie, then considered one of the greatest stage directors in the world, that he should come to Stratford to run this theater.

And so it happened, and Guthrie brought with him to Stratford some leading designers and actors in England. Alec Guinness starred in the first play, and the Stratford Festival almost immediately earned a reputation as the finest classical theater in North

America.

I packed my belonging — that's not an exaggeration — into the back of a used Morris Minor my father had bought me and headed for the bright lights of Toronto. A Morris Minor was a compromise between a very small car and nothing. While driving to Toronto in a fierce rainstorm I crossed over a bridge; as I did, a sixteen-wheeler, water spewing out of its front tire wells, raced passed me going in the opposite direction. The force of the truck and the water almost blew me over the side of the bridge into what must have been the Ottawa River. And I remember thinking that if this car went into the river there would be no marks on the earth that I had ever lived. There would be no residue of my presence other than the sorrow of my mother and father. Essentially I had no friends who cared about me, no girlfriends with whom I'd established any kind of bond, and no accomplishments. That was a devastating thought, and it summed up how little I was leaving behind in Montreal. It reminded me of a line from *Macbeth,* "A tale told by an idiot . . . signifying nothing."

At Stratford we presented three plays a season, from May through September. We rehearsed the first play and while it was running began rehearsing the second play. The same actors worked in all three plays. I was one of a half-dozen young actors in the company and we competed with each other for roles. Mostly we were supporting players, usually we were the chorus. Getting a few lines was an accomplishment. We all lived in awe of God, who took the human form in Stratford of Tyrone Guthrie. Guthrie was legendary in England. All of the great actors either worshipped or at least respected him. When he came to Canada the few people serious about acting felt the horizon was moving toward us. And so we trembled at the sight of him, this great man who had come to us to cloak us in his wisdom.

Guthrie was about six-foot-six with a huge potbelly and a hawk-like nose. The theater was little more than a large hole in the ground covered by a great tent. We would be on the raked stage at the bottom of this pit and the tent flap would part and the sunlight would burst in and from that great brilliance Tyrone Guthrie would emerge. It was quite an entrance. And he would stand there and pronounce his decisions, "And you will play the role . . ."

It was hypnotic, "Yes, I will play the role . . ."

Tyrone Guthrie wasn't much of a teacher. He didn't offer a lot of instruction; to read a line or interpret the meaning of that line, you had to work on and discover by yourself. But he was a master at the grand design, at producing extraordinary theater, at creating memorable events on stage. Once, I remember, he put his arm around my shoulders and said earnestly, "Bill, tell me about Method acting." Me, explaining Method acting to Sir Tyrone Guthrie? I began to explain what little I had read about it, how an actor can become the character and feel the emotion flowing through . . .

After I had explained what little I knew, he asked, "Why don't they think of a beautiful sunset?"

I understood that wasn't really a question, but rather a suggestion. He was reminding me that there is a greater scheme at play in a beautiful sunset than in simply trying to call up some emotion to service a character. And that an actor should not get so caught up in perfecting technique that he misses the lyricism and beauty of everything that is going on around him.

Within weeks of arriving in Stratford I was playing a small role in *Henry V,* starring Christopher Plummer. Chris Plummer and I are about the same age but rather than going to college he had started working in the theater and was probably the leading young actor in Canada. He was part of the very small community of successful actors in Montreal, very much part of the "in" crowd. He was prematurely mature and I had envied him. At Stratford he played all the young leading-man roles. In *Henry V* I was assigned the role of the Duke of Gloucester, for which I was onstage about five minutes, as well as understudying Chris Plummer.

King Henry V is one of the longest roles written by Shakespeare, so when we weren't rehearsing I studied those lines. Whenever I had a few extra moments, at night or in the bathroom, I memorized all of his speeches. Because we had opened the play after only a few weeks' rehearsal there had been no time for an understudy run-through. During the staging of the play the understudies kept an eye on the roles we were supposedly preparing to play, but none of us thought it was possible that we'd actually have to go on one day to replace a sick actor. The company consisted of young, healthy, ruddy-faced, beef-eating, apple-chomping Canadian actors; nobody ever got sick. Basically, the rule was that if you took more than two breaths a minute you were still alive and had to go on.

The play opened to excellent reviews. *The New York Times* called it a "stunning piece of work . . . penetrating and exuberant." Chris Plummer got rave reviews, the show was sold out for its entire run. This was by far the most successful work I'd done; I was a member of a prestigious company, working with some of the most respected actors in Canada. Darn right it was penetrating and exuberant. Mondays were my only day off, and one Monday morning about two weeks into our run I got a call from the production office. Chris Plummer was suffering from a kidney stone; could I go on that night?

Could I go on that night? Could I go on that night? Replace Plummer in one of the greatest roles ever written for the stage? Absolutely. Without doubt. Of course.

Clearly I was insane. I had never even said the lines out loud, but merely muttered them between flushes of the toilet. I hadn't done a single rehearsal in that role so I didn't know the staging. I hadn't even met some of the other actors. Any actor in their right mind would have said, sir, how dare you ask me to go there and risk my reputation. Or something like that.

And they would have responded, of course

we can't. It's impossible. We'll call off the performance and refund their money and . . .

Refund their money? Ah, there's the rub. The production office tried to schedule an emergency rehearsal but finding actors on a day off is even more difficult than getting a profit participation check from a movie studio. At about five o'clock someone suggested I try on the wardrobe to make sure it fit. Fortunately Chris and I were about the same size so it fit me well.

The odd thing was that the impossibility of what I was about to do hadn't hit me yet. I was completely calm and confident. It never occurred to me that I was risking my career — not that I actually had a career, of course — but if this turned out to be a debacle I was the one who was going to get the blame for it. And it had the kind of big debacle potential that inspires comedy writers.

Tyrone Guthrie wasn't even there. Moments before I was about to go on Michael Langham, the director, asked, "Are you all right?"

"Sure, I'm fine," I said, thinking I knew the play. There are few moments in the life of a stage actor as dramatic as this one. It is the actor's cliché: I was the unrehearsed understudy going out on that stage as a nobody and coming back as probably a bigger nobody. I don't know why I wasn't nervous. Certainly any rational person should have been close to panicking. Instead, I was excited.

Stratford had a thrust stage, meaning it was surrounded by the audience on three sides. There are no wings. All entrances and exits are made at the back of the stage. So when you're onstage you're almost in the audience. If you forget a line there's no way somebody can feed it to you — unless it's a member of the audience.

There were twenty-five hundred people in the audience, including most of the critics who had originally reviewed the play. Apparently they had learned that an unknown understudy was going on and didn't want to miss what promised to be a memorable night in the theater. Finally the lights went down and I walked out onto the stage to begin the most important performance of my life. Whatever happened in the next few hours, if someday I ended up in the Ottawa River, I would have had this one night.

I looked around the theater and . . .

This is where we should pause for a word from our sponsor. I've spent so much of my life on television that I'm used to building to a first-chapter climax and cutting to commercial. However, as this is a book we haven't sold commercial time. However, there will be space available in the soft-cover version.

. . . and felt exhilarated. I had been doing a play a week for three years. I had learned the lines of hundreds of characters. I had been a comedian, a charlatan, and a convicted con man. That night I was ready to be a king.

Perhaps the proper word to describe the way I was feeling is stupefied. I was completely calm, in the zone, Zenned out, at one with the stage and the audience. It came together in a way it never should have. A few years later I would be working for Rod Serling in *The Twilight Zone,* a place where unimaginable things happened for which there could be no explanation. Like my performance that night. I was "Once more into the breach, dear friends"-ing as if I had been playing this role for seasons. "Stiffen the sinews, summon up the blood." "We few, we happy few, we band of brothers."

A stage actor needs a minimum of ten performances in front of an audience to understand the timing, because the response of the audience has to be incorporated into that performance. Audiences react in unexpected places, and you learn where to leave room for the audience to respond. You don't want to walk into their reaction with your next line, which might be key to the plot. So the audience becomes a character in a play, but you don't see that character until you are in front of the audience.

Except for that night. I took from the audience an internal strength that made me capable of an inexplicable performance. Until near the very end, the last few lines, only seconds away from perfection.

The play changes character for the last few scenes. After all the grander and marshal speeches, Henry has some playful scenes with the French princess and the play is over. I got through all the breaches, all the blood of Englishmen, after the battle of Agincourt, all the way to the brilliant repartee with the princess. And then it hit me.

The French princess entered and I went totally blank. And I'm standing onstage with twenty-five hundred people looking at me with rapt expectation and there was nothing. A dead pause. The hopelessness of my situation began to hit me. I didn't have the slightest idea where to go, what to do, what to say. It was the equivalent of being at an important business party and starting to introduce your wife to your boss and suddenly realizing you can't remember your wife's name. Into that breach, dear friends, flowed the tidal wave of panic.

I looked across the stage, hopelessly. I have met so many thousands of people in my lifetime that sometimes it's difficult to recall the names of people I've known for years. Yet as long as I live I will never forget Don Cherry. Don Cherry, with blondish hair and the longest blond eyelashes I've ever seen. There stood salvation. Don Cherry had a photographic memory. He knew the entire play! Every line. During rehearsals if someone forgot their line he would give it to them. And he was only twelve feet away from me, playing my usual role. So Henry walked over to him and put his arm around his shoulder, an extraordinary piece of staging that had never occurred to anybody before or since. The exhausted king goes to his younger brother and leans on him for support. I leaned in closely and said, "What's the line?"

And Don Cherry with his photographic memory looked at me blankly. He had not the slightest idea. But in that instant I remembered the words I was supposed to say and continued on successfully to the end of the play. I received a standing ovation. Even the cast was applauding. The critics loved it, lauding my instinctive and original movements onstage and my halting interpretation of the part. It was one of the greatest moments of my life.

That was the night I knew I was an actor. Now if I could only find a way to make that hundred bucks a week.

At Stratford I rose from bit parts and walk-ons to become a leading player in *Julius Caesar, The Taming of the Shrew,* and *The Merchant of Venice.* In our third season Guthrie resurrected a play he'd had great success with in England, his own version of Christopher Marlowe's *Tamburlaine the Great.* Anthony Quayle was the lead and Guthrie told me, "When we do this, you will play Usumcasane, the second lead." As it turned out the second lead consisted mainly of carrying Anthony Quayle around the stage in a sedan chair. But obviously I did it well because Guthrie named me the Festival's Most Promising Actor that year. The Stratford production received such good notices that the legendary Broadway producers Roger Stevens and Robert White-head decided to bring us to New York.

I still thought of myself as this little Jewish kid from Montreal, Billy Shatner, who was just trying to figure it all out — but I was going to Broadway, to New York City, to the mecca of serious actors.

This was my second time in New York and this time I was going in theater style. My first trip had been very different — I'd paddled there in an Indian canoe.

Two

Like paramotoring down the Ohio River into the largest paintball fight in the world or hunting a brown bear in Alaska with a bow and arrow or singing "Rocket Man" on national TV, this was one of those grand ideas that falls into the seemed-like-a-good-idea-at-the-time category. At the end of a summer during which I'd worked as a counselor at a B'nai B'rith camp, the head of the camp announced he was going to paddle an Indian war canoe up the St. Lawrence to Lake Champlain, across Lake George, then down the Hudson River all the way to New York, and invited six of us to go with him. I have always loved history and the concept of traveling this ancient waterway to America — just as the Indians must have done hundreds of years ago — enthralled me.

I have always had a love affair with America. I believed completely in the

American myth, that the president of the United States was a great and noble man and the Chief Justice of the Supreme Court rose to that position because of his experience and equanimity and wisdom and that J. Edgar Hoover, the head of the FBI, was watching out for us all. Hoover wearing a dress? How could anybody believe something so preposterous?

I remember being frightened by Senator Joseph McCarthy's warning that Communists were hidden in the State Department and then realizing that Americans had seen many crises yet somehow the Constitution survived and actually grew stronger. I thought of America as this place of promise, where dreams were possible. I had always wanted to go to America.

So seven of us climbed into this wooden war canoe and our journey began. It was a romantic vision, we were paddling a thousand miles to America. And within a few strokes I remember realizing: we're paddling a thousand miles to America?

It certainly didn't take long for that romance to end. Within a day we were exhausted and cold and there was nothing we could do but keep paddling. I remember standing up in the canoe in the middle of Lake Champlain on a gray day and trying to pee into the lake. Six guys turned to look at me and I got so self-conscious I couldn't do it, so I sat down. The media loved the story, seven kids paddling from Canada to New York. We were scheduled to stop in Kingston, New York, for a big celebration the Jewish community had prepared for us, but just before we got there a sailboat threw us a rope and began towing us — right past Kingston. The welcoming committee was standing on a dock waving happily to us. We waved right back to them and just kept going.

We camped out at night, under the mosquitoes. To keep the meat we'd brought with us fresh we trailed it behind us in the water — and it got just as rotten as it would have if left in the sun. Within a couple of days the only thought in our minds was, we gotta get out of this damn canoe. It might have been about that time that I understood that I wasn't an Indian, I was a Jewish kid with blisters on his hands from all that paddling. But finally we made it to America, to New York City, tying up at the 79th Street marina.

This was my first time in New York City and I was truly naïve, an innocent in the big city. I had heard all the stories of this city and I knew I had to be very careful. But the people were so nice. I was walking past Radio City Music Hall and a nice man asked me, "Would you like to go to the show?"

Wow, who knew New Yorkers were so friendly? He bought me a ticket and we sat down and the lights went down and the Rockettes came onstage and he put his hand on my knee . . . I stood up and literally ran right out of the theater.

I remember walking through Times Square and seeing the Broadway theaters for the first time and being totally enchanted by the bright lights and the overwhelming sense of life going on all around me. I wanted so much to be part of it. On another day I met someone else and we started talking and I told him I wanted to be an actor and finally he said, "I've got some people you'd like to meet." I went with him into a club and into a back room. There was a large rectangular table with probably ten people sitting around it. When we walked in he looked at me and smiled warmly, then said, "We were expecting you."

I ran right out of that room, too. This was some city, this New York.

A couple of years later I spent a summer hitchhiking across the United States. Following my freshman year at McGill, a friend and I had decided to explore America. We had no money, so we made signs reading TWO MCGILL FRESHMEN SEEING THE U.S. and hit the road. We spent three months living in cars and sleeping on the grass and on the beach. We made it from Montreal to Washington to San Francisco, then Vancouver and home. We had no fear and no problems at all. We got rides easily. We made it to Santa Barbara and we were sleeping on the beach, near train tracks. Very early one morning a train stopping at the local station woke me. As I looked at a Pullman car somebody raised the blinds in a compartment and I saw, just as it might happen in the movies, it was a beautiful, naked woman. Well, in my memory she was beautiful, but I am sure she was naked. She saw me looking at her and closed the blinds and minutes later the train pulled out. California certainly is an amazing place, I thought. I'm sleeping on the beach and I look up to see a beautiful, naked woman. One thing became certain at that moment: I definitely was going to Hollywood!

But my dream was to live in New York, to work in the theater with the greatest actors in the world. From the time I had started working at Stratford I'd been saving my money so one day I could move there. After a couple of seasons I'd managed to save five hundred dollars. That was all the money I had in the world. One of the good acquaintances I had made in Toronto was Lorne Greene, then a famous Canadian radio announcer who had been hired by Guthrie because of his stentorian voice to play a Roman senator, and who eventually became the star of *Bonanza*. Lorne wasn't much of an actor, but he was a wonderful man. And almost every day he and this other actor used to go to the office of the local stockbroker to day-trade. They invited me to come with them one day and I'd never seen anything like it. It was a very small office with a moving ticker running across the wall showing the movement up and down of various stocks. It was the most amazing thing I'd ever seen: Lorne and this other actor would go into the trading room with a small amount of money and within a few hours they would come out of the room with more money. Every day! Well, this certainly was an amazing discovery. And neither of them had their degree in commerce from a prestigious university. I wondered why they hadn't taught me about this miracle at McGill.

They were speculating in options, commodities. In commodities trading you buy a contract on a commodity, anything from gold to pigs, with the hope or expectation that the value of that contract is going to increase. To purchase the contract you're required to put down only a small percentage of the total value. If the value goes up you can sell the contract for a profit. If it goes down . . . I didn't know, that didn't seem to happen to Lorne Greene. All the two of them did was make money.

I had my very hard-earned five hundred dollars. I had been guarding it with my life. I thought, I want to go to New York to look for work as an actor after this season. I'll bet if I follow these guys, I can turn my five hundred dollars into a thousand. The way I lived I could survive in New York for quite a long time on one thousand dollars.

In the summer of 1955 the hot commodity was uranium. Apparently it was the necessary material for atomic power, so naturally it was very valuable. So on a Thursday I went with my friend Lorne and this other actor to the stockbroker's office and spent my entire life savings buying uranium futures. And I heard the voice of God, Lorne Greene, tell me, "You're going to make a lot of money, Bill."

I thought, wow, I'm going to make a lot of money. I went to the office Friday morning to check out my contract and uranium was doing very well. But when I arrived at the theater Friday night Lorne came over to me and said, "I've got some news for you, Bill. It's not good."

Not good? What about my savings?

"The prime minister of Canada's giving a speech tonight. Canada is going to stop buying uranium because they've stockpiled enough. I don't want to think about what's going to happen to the market Monday morning."

We did three performances that weekend. And all I could think about was my five hundred dollars. On Monday morning uranium plummeted. I'd blown my entire life savings on uranium. And somewhere in the back of my mind was the feeling that the prime minister had heard about my investment and decided to get out of that market.

So when Guthrie told us we were going to New York in *Tamburlaine the Great,* to the largest theater on Broadway, I was elated. I knew this was fate: even the collapse of the uranium market couldn't keep me out of New York. We opened at the Winter Garden Theater in January 1956. It was a limited run, originally scheduled for twelve weeks. It was even more limited than that; we closed after eight weeks.

This was one of the greatest seasons in Broadway history. Among the shows playing on Broadway in 1956 were *My Fair Lady, The Most Happy Fella,* Leonard Bernstein's *Candide,* Rosalind Russell in *Auntie Mame,* Paul Muni in *Inherit the Wind,* and *Cat on a Hot Tin Roof.* Of all those shows, we were the only one that featured beautifully choreographed violent battles, murder, mayhem, and torture. So in retrospect, it was probably not the right play for the theater groups from Long Island. But it was great fun to do, a truly primal stage production. Obviously unlike anything else on Broadway that season. We received excellent reviews: according to Louis Kronenberger it was "an evening full of stunning theater, of slashing rhetoric, of glorious spectacle, with scene after scene suggesting a kind of richly lighted Delacroix canvas."

And even in a supporting role I attracted attention. For the first time agents began calling me. I'd heard about agents, I knew what they did, but I'd never had an agent of my own. Suddenly agents wanted to represent me! And I had offers from the great movie studios, asking me to sign long-term multi-movie contracts, telling me I could be a movie star. M-G-M offered me a five-year contract at exactly seven hundred dollars a week. Or maybe it was a seven-year contract at five hundred dollars a week. I was living rent check to rent check and they were offering tremendous security. It was every actor's fantasy.

The night before I was going to sign that contract I went to a New York party. An actor I didn't know, and who I don't believe I've ever seen again, advised me not to sign it. Somehow that made sense to me. The next morning I told the agent I had decided not to sign the contract. That was the moment I learned the definition of "apoplexy." When the wind's blowing right I think I can still hear him screaming. I really couldn't explain to him why I'd changed my mind because I didn't know the answer. I still don't. Maybe I wasn't the toast of Broadway, but I certainly was a shot glass of whisky of Broadway. An extraordinary world was opening up for me, I had made it to Broadway, the New York columnists were writing stories about me, agents were calling. I just didn't want to give up control of my career even before it had really started. The mystical dreams of the actor had conquered the prosaic needs of the commerce student from McGill.

Anything seemed possible. Although I do

have to admit that anything probably didn't include the fact that one day I would be starring on a television show making love to a blow-up doll and costumed as a pink flamingo.

My ambition was to be a serious actor. I turned down all those offers and returned to Toronto with the Stratford Festival. In the winters of those years I was managing to eke out a living performing in radio dramas on the Canadian Broadcasting Company on Jarvis Street, getting occasional small parts on early Canadian television, even writing half-hour plays for the local TV stations. There were about thirty professional actors in all of Canada, meaning these were men and women who did nothing else to earn a living. I was one of perhaps twenty professional actors living in Toronto. We got up in the morning, searched for work, or were actually working that day.

Each job lasted the length of the show and then we started all over again. I'd get a job Tuesday, work Wednesday, and begin looking for the next job Thursday. Then I'd have to wait two weeks for my thirty-five-dollar check. For the first time I lived every day with the feeling that this job might be the last job I'd ever get; that after this job my career might be over. Fortunately that feeling has lasted only sixty years.

I lived in a tiny studio apartment on the top floor of a rooming house a few blocks away from the CBC. The bed actually had a rope mattress. For most of my first year in Toronto I was desperately homesick, it was only when I was working that I could forget how lonely I was. I was younger and less experienced than most of the people I was working with, so I wasn't part of that group. I had some acquaintances but no real friends.

I was living in a garret and I was starving. I was always cold, I was frightened of being alone in my room; afraid of the present, afraid of the future, afraid of being knifed in the back when I walked down the dark streets. I was living a fearful life. I told myself that this was the life of an artist. I didn't dare believe I was paying my dues — I couldn't have afforded that.

There was a hotel with an all-you-can-eat buffet for $2.50 (Canadian) a few blocks from my rooming house. To save money I ate there most nights. Early in the evening it was a family restaurant; workingmen could come in with their wives and children and eat well, and then go back in line and eat again. It was a festive family place, ringing with loud voices, chattering mothers and fathers, and yelling children. It was alive with life, and I would sit there by myself, every night, usually reading a book. I sat there for several hours, until they closed the cafeteria. I had no place else to go.

By eight o'clock the families would leave. And across the lobby in this flea-bitten hotel was a seedy bar that opened when the cafeteria closed. I would move from the cafeteria to the bar and a whole other life began. It was like the second movie on a double bill. The first feature was a family movie, then after the intermission they showed the adult films. Once the families left the prostitutes moved in. It actually took me some time before I realized this was a hot-sheets motel, a brothel; the girls would pick up their johns in the bar and take them upstairs. And I would sit there watching the whole thing just as I'd watched the families.

After awhile the girls became accustomed to seeing me there and they would sit with me and talk. Then they'd get up and go upstairs and eventually come back. I don't know what we talked about, but I know I was much too shy to talk about what was going on upstairs. For me, it was conversation; interacting with another person. There was no sex, the concept of paying for sex never occurred to me. That would be the worst of all the traits of a hanger-on; a hanger-on pays for sex.

Many years later I'd make a movie for television entitled *Secrets of a Married Man* in which I played a husband so straitlaced I wore a tie and jacket when having dinner with my family. Michelle Phillips played my wife and Cybill Shepherd played a call girl with a heart of cash. In one scene I was sitting at a bar with a cowboy-type who looked at a prostitute and said admiringly, "Whoa. Now, that's somebody that'll teach a man how to yodel. For a price."

But for me it wasn't like that at all. I was sitting in a bar and these were my friends. How I could not be curious about their lives I don't know, but it was something we never discussed. So I sat there with them week after week, month after month, searching for jobs in the day, passing the nights, waiting for the Stratford Festival to reopen so I could regain some prestige.

One night one of the girls took me home with her. She wasn't really much older than me, but she seemed so worldly. And she took me into her life and became my teacher. We slept in her bedroom while the other girls with whom she shared that apartment were talking in the living room. That began a relationship that lasted several months. It wasn't a love affair, we weren't in love with each other, but it was warm and soothing and nurturing. She cared about me and offered me her being. It was lovely.

Some months later I'd written a play, *Dreams,* for the CBC and cast a beautiful young woman to play the female lead opposite me. Her name was Gloria Rosenberg and I fell in love with her. Both figuratively and literally, she was the woman of my *Dreams.* That wonderful summer I called her every night from Stratford. We were on the phone so often that the operator from the Canadian Exchange felt sorry for me and allowed me to call for free. I didn't fit into any of the groups that had formed at Stratford and I was very lonely there without Gloria. Finally I told her, "I love you, please come up." She raced to be with me in Stratford, it was so romantic. It seemed like there was only one thing to do: I asked her to marry me.

Marry me? I'd known her for only four months. After she'd gone home to make preparations for our wedding I began wondering if this was the right thing to do. One night, I remember so well, I was caught outdoors in a thunderstorm and as the rain fell and the wind raged and the thunder burst above me I thought, I'm living an experience from a Shakespearean play. It was an incredibly dramatic moment and I had no one there to share it with; I was so lonely and I was in love and so we were married.

At the end of the season we returned to Toronto. I remember one cold fall night coming out of a theater with Gloria and her parents. As we stood there I saw my prostitute walking down the sidewalk. Working in the night. I can close my eyes and see her now: a low-cut dress, red hair, black pumps. But when I saw her that night I turned my back on her. I was ashamed, I was embarrassed, I was terrified she would recognize me as she walked by.

She was so wise; as she walked by she did nothing to indicate she knew me, but she subtly acknowledged my presence. As she passed I looked at her, and she looked back over her shoulder. I know she saw me but she kept walking and the moment was gone and I never saw her again.

This was a woman who had taken a naïve, middle-class, untutored boy, an alien really, and gave me the comfort I so desperately needed. And then, when it became convenient for me, I turned my back on her. In the end, that was the true source of my shame — I had turned my back on someone who had been good to me. It was a moment I've never forgotten and I still feel shamed by it.

As if it's any excuse, I was in love for the first time in my life. Of course I had absolutely no idea what love was, but she was a beautiful young woman and she was attracted to me and when I was with her I felt something very special. That feeling had to be love, I figured. She was an actress, professionally known as Gloria Rand. Oh, that was perfect, I thought, we shared a passion for the theater. We shared the same dream.

As I discovered, there is only one problem when two actors marry: they're both actors! Actors tend to be extremely focused, of necessity narcissistic and often highly competitive. One dream isn't big enough for the two of them. If both careers are progressing even roughly equally it can be wonderful. But when one is having success while the other is staying home with kids, it can be less than wonderful. Difficult. Of course, Gloria and I didn't know any of that. We were both young and . . .

Oh, I just found out that the *New York Post,* in an article listing the 100 best cover songs of all time, named my version of

Frank Sinatra's "It Was a Very Good Year" number 60 — ahead of Elton John's cover of "Lucy in the Sky with Diamonds" (72) and Joe Cocker's "With a Little Help from My Friends" (86). Note to self: Do cover versions of every song ever written.

So, Gloria and I were both young and . . . and young. That really explains it.

We both wanted to work in America, so we took the $750 I'd won as Stratford's Most Promising Actor and moved to New York City. We got a small apartment in Jackson Heights, in Queens, four subway stops from Broadway.

It was during this time that I'd made my American television debut. I suspect because of my considerable experience as a featured player at the prestigious Stratford Festival I was offered a role that utilized all of my many talents. I was given the opportunity to create the role of Ranger Bob on the *Howdy Doody Show,* co-starring with several puppets and a live clown named Clarabelle who rather than speaking honked her answers on a bicycle horn. "And how are you this morning, Clarabelle?"

Honk, honk.

Admittedly that cut down on the dialogue between us. And made it unusually easy for Clarabelle to remember her honks. But there are a limited number of things an actor can do when playing opposite a clown who honks. A good actor responds to whatever emotion is presented to him or her by another actor, although, admittedly, on this show there were times when I wasn't always certain how best to respond to the bevy of honks.

I had a little more success on Canadian television. My first major TV role in Canada was the lead in Herman Melville's tragedy *Billy Budd,* co-starring with Basil Rathbone. Basil Rathbone! I'd grown up watching him playing Sherlock Holmes in the movies. He was a very well-respected stage and movie actor, but this was one of his first, if not his very first, live television appearances. Some people wondered how he'd respond — a lot of veteran actors had difficulty making the transition to TV — but during rehearsals he didn't seem to be the slightest bit anxious. "Do you know why I'm not nervous?" he asked me.

I could hear the confidence of many years' experience resonating in his voice. I shook my head.

"Because, you see, in the United States there's thirty to fifty million people watching a television program, but in Canada it's only five to ten million."

Oh. Only ten million? That rationale seemed absurd to me, but if it worked for him, hey, that's all that mattered. The night of the broadcast he really was perfectly calm. This was just another acting job for him. We went on the air and the first act was progressing very well, right until the moment he walked onboard the ship and stepped into a bucket. His foot got caught in the bucket and he couldn't get it off. The camera shot only his upper body so none of the viewers could see him madly shaking his leg, trying to get his foot out of that bucket. He was working so hard to get his foot free that he forgot his lines. And when he forgot his lines he began to sweat. The rest of us tried to feed him his lines, but that was hard to do because we were too busy laughing. It was like acting in a cartoon: Basil Rathbone had caught his foot in a bucket and was hobbling through the scene. It was a disaster. But fortunately it was seen by only ten million Canadians.

Gloria and I moved to New York, right into the Golden Age of Television. Of course at that time nobody realized it was the Golden Age, a lot of people still considered TV a gimmick that would eventually fade away. But immediately I started working regularly. I was exactly the type of actor television producers were desperately searching for: I worked cheap and was always available. And I had substantial stage experience. TV was considered a very long step down from motion pictures, the theory being that if the audience could see you for free they wouldn't buy tickets for your movies. So established movie actors wouldn't risk their careers by working for a small salary on the tiny black-and-white screen. New York's theater community disdained the medium but loved the work; actors could work on a TV show during the day and earn enough money to survive, and still be able to perform on the stage that evening.

My experience onstage had taught me theatricality. I knew what to do with my voice. I knew how to stand and how to walk and how to memorize lines. And I knew how to respond without panicking when Basil Rathbone got his foot caught in a bucket. I was dependable.

I began by appearing regularly on the Sunday morning religious shows like *Lamp Unto My Feet.* There was sort of a perfect symmetry: these shows were the answer to a young actor's prayers. They paid about seventy-five dollars and needed six to ten actors every week. These were Biblical dramas and they required all the actors to speak in hushed tones: St. John never yelled, St. Peter didn't have a Brooklyn accent, and St. Matthew didn't forget his lines.

My first starring role on TV was in a play called *All Summer Long* on the *Goodyear Television Playhouse* in 1956, one of the many dramatic anthology series then on the air. Every major corporation seemed to be sponsoring its own series. These shows did an original drama, live, every week. The great television director Daniel Petrie had seen me on Broadway and offered me the role. After that I began working regularly. In the next decade I would play leading roles in more than hundred different TV dramas. I played every type of character imaginable, including blind U.S. Senator Thomas Gore, foppish Englishman Sir Percy Blakeney (who in reality is the swashbuckling Scarlet Pimpernel), a town marshal and a town bully, a priest and a physician, a killer and an attorney, an explorer and a terrified plane passenger. I played married men and single men, I even played a Burmese seaman. Very quickly I became one of the busiest actors in the city. It seemed like I was always working. Just about every morning I'd take the subway from Queens to the East Village, to Sixth Street and Second Avenue, to a famous rehearsal hall directly above

Ratner's Kosher Delicatessen. We'd rehearse all day and then I'd get back on the train and go home to Gloria. On air dates I'd do the show — and then get on the subway and go home. One show ran into the next; from week to week I didn't know if I was doing a *Kaiser Aluminum Hour,* a *U.S. Steel Hour, Studio One,* or a *Kraft Television Theatre.* I suspect I'm one of the few actors to have starred in quirky dramas on *Alfred Hitchcock Presents, Suspense, The Twilight Zone, One Step Beyond,* and Boris Karloff's *Thriller.* I did a scene from *Henry V* on Ed Sullivan's Sunday night variety show, I co-starred with Christopher Plummer in *Oedipus the King* on Sunday afternoon's *Omnibus,* and I played Marc Antony in *Play of the Week*'s *Julius Caesar.* It was all the same to me: show up, know my lines, do the show, and start looking for the next job the next day. Occasionally programs would overlap, but generally producers were very good about arranging rehearsal times around other jobs.

For the first time people began to recognize me on the street. They didn't know exactly where they had seen me, but they knew my face was familiar. I can't begin to tell how often people stopped me and said,

"I know you from somewhere. Aren't you a teacher at the high school?"

I often found myself working with legendary movie stars, but generally they were older actors whose film careers had pretty much ended but whose name recognition made them valuable to TV producers. Many of them had difficulties adapting to the demands of live TV, including the short rehearsal schedules, the small budgets, the fact that they had to memorize their lines, and the unique technical demands. Movie sets were large and the cameras moved freely, often on cranes; TV studios were very small and the cameras were attached to long cables. Directors had to choreograph the movement of the cameras to ensure that the cables never crossed, so the actors were restricted in their movements. There was no room to improvise, you had to do a scene exactly as it had been done in rehearsal.

I remember doing a show with Lon Chaney Jr., who had a drinking problem. In the first act we had a big fight scene in which we completely broke up a room. The furniture was all props, breakaway tables and chairs made of balsa, the vase was made of some kind of hard sugar, but because we had such a small budget we couldn't afford to actually rehearse the action. If we broke it we couldn't replace it. So instead we walked through the scene, each of us describing our actions. Chaney had memorized his movements: "Right here I pick up the chair and hit you over the shoulders with it and you roll backward. Then you fall over the table, which will break and I'll pick up the leg and hit you over the head. You go down right on that mark and the cameras'll pick you up." We went through it every day, being very careful not to break any of the breakaway furniture. Chaney was great. He showed up on time, sober, and had his lines down cold.

I guess he began to get nervous during the dress rehearsal in the afternoon. But we went through the scene and everything seemed okay. ". . . I pick up the chair and hit you over the shoulders . . ."

At the end of the dress rehearsal the director gathered the cast around him and gave us his final notes. "We're going on in exactly forty-seven minutes. Good luck, everybody, it's been a pleasure working with you. I know we're going to have a wonderful show. Now you have a little time to eat because we're going on in exactly forty-three minutes . . ."

So we all went back to our dressing areas and got ready to do the show. Apparently

Chaney started getting very nervous and to calm himself down had a few drinks. Forty-two minutes' worth of drinks. He managed to get through the first part of the show until we reached the fight scene. As the scene started he looked at me angrily and said, "Right here I pick up the chair and hit you over the shoulders with it and you roll backward. Then you fall over the table . . ."

With that the stage manager lifted his head and screamed, "We're on the air, you son of a bitch!"

That was the problem — and the excitement of live TV — it was live. Fortunately, my stage training had taught me how to deal with unexpected events. Once, for example, I was in a play in which the whole plot hinged on my shooting another actor, but when I reached for the prop gun it wasn't there. The stage manager had forgotten to put it back after the previous performance. But the guy had to die or the play was over, so I picked up a corkscrew and screwed him to death.

That presence of mind was perfect for live television. On one show I was involved in a shoot-out. The actor who had to shoot me got much too close, and when he shot me, the blank shell — which was made of wax — hit me right under my eye. It was painful as hell, but I just kept going. Keep going, that's what actors do. Except the blank had caused a huge blood blister to form, a big red blot right under my eye. And it just kept growing, it kept getting bigger and bigger. It was like the blimp of blood blisters. It was like a clown's red nose stuck to my face, growing and becoming a deeper shade of red. Of course I didn't know that, I couldn't see my face, but it was the only thing every other actor could look at. And they looked at it with great wonder, this mammoth red golf ball growing on my face. This was a murder mystery but they couldn't say two lines without breaking into complete hysterics. And naturally because the other actors were looking at something on my face and couldn't stop laughing I became very self-conscious. I was trying to look down, which of course is impossible, but worse, it forces the viewers at home to look down too. The red pustule had become the focus of the entire show. And somehow we got through it. We always got through it, although there were some difficult times.

For aging movie stars just trying to keep their careers alive by working on TV the hardest thing to do was memorize their lines. In the movies they'd only had to remember a few lines at a time and if they forgot them the cameras stopped and they reshot the scene. But this was live television, there was no going back. Paul Muni had to be fitted with an earpiece because he just couldn't remember three sentences. I co-starred with Bert Lahr in a play called *The School for Wives,* Walter Kerr's adaptation of a Molière comedy, on *Omnibus.* Bert Lahr! The Cowardly Lion himself, the great burlesque comedian. Sidney Lumet was directing. It was thrilling for me, for the whole cast. We were all nervous for him, we didn't want to see him struggle with this new medium. When he came in to rehearsal the very first day we all sort of held our breath, all of us ready to help him. But he didn't even glance at his script. He had memorized every single word. So while we were stumbling through the first reading he had already mastered the nuances. Well, this was great. The next day we came in and we'd all learned a little more and Bert Lahr forgot a couple of words. As we got closer to the airdate most of us knew large sections of the play and he was forgetting full pages. The more nervous he got, the more he forgot. By the time we went on the air he'd forgotten almost the entire play and we ended up ad-libbing large sections of the Molière comedy. I know there had to be people watching that play and wondering why they'd never heard those lines before.

One reason I was in demand was that I learned my lines very quickly. Those years doing a play a week in Canada were paying off. Only once did I have a problem. I was doing a two-parter called *No Deadly Medicine* for *Studio One,* in which I played a young doctor trying to save the reputation of an aging doctor no longer capable of practicing safe medicine. Lee J. Cobb played the older physician. At that time Cobb was probably the most respected actor in America. He had starred in the original production of *Waiting for Lefty,* the play I'd done at the Communist meeting hall; he'd created the role of Willy Loman in the Broadway production of *Death of a Salesman.* And he'd been nominated for an Oscar for his supporting role in *On the Waterfront.* Every serious actor was in awe of him. And I was co-starring with him. It was the most important role of my career. And the fact that Lee J. Cobb was starring in a two-part show on television made it a major event, so we knew we were going to have a huge viewing audience. In one scene all I had to do was walk across the set. I took three steps and suddenly I remembered Basil Rathbone's words, "There's thirty to fifty million people watching . . ." And it hit me, thirty to fifty million people were watching me walk.

More people were watching me walk across that set than had seen Julius Caesar in his entire lifetime. More people were watching me walk than the entire population of most of the countries in the world. And I became conscious of the way I was walking. Was I walking too fast? Were my strides too long? Did it look natural, was I walking like I really walked? Was I acting like I was walking or walking like I was acting? I felt my legs begin to tighten up. I couldn't believe it, I was getting stage fright. Walking may well be the most natural of all movements — and I couldn't remember how to walk naturally. It probably took me eight steps to get across the set, the longest eight steps of my entire life.

Many years later I was narrating a documentary series entitled *Voice of the Planet,* for which I traveled around the world. For one amazing shot a helicopter dropped me off on top of a twenty-thousand-foot-high glacier and left me there alone. "Don't move," the producer warned me. "There could be a fault line here somewhere covered by snow. You might step into a crevasse and no one would ever know it."

"Don't worry," I assured him. "I'm not going to move." Move? I wasn't so confident about breathing too deeply. The concept was that the chopper would rise slowly to the top of the glacier and suddenly see one man standing there, the only living thing in this vast sea of snow. It was a great idea — until the helicopter took off and left me there more alone than I had ever been in my life. That feeling of loneliness was absolutely incomprehensible. I kept reminding myself that soon the helicopter would be coming back to get me off and I'll be with my friends and we'll go down to the village and eat and drink and laugh and talk about what a great shot we did. But then I looked down and realized the helicopter's landing pads had left two deep impressions in the snow, which would spoil the shot. I've got to move just a few feet, I decided.

I moved several inches at a time, small, tentative steps, testing the snow before I put my weight down. It took me at least ten minutes to move about twenty feet.

And that's exactly how I felt walking across the set on *Studio One.*

It was an extraordinary time, we were creating television on a weekly basis. The only rule was that there were no rules, you could do anything you could get away with.

Most of the TV studios were converted live theaters, and we also did a lot of filming on city streets. It was all very seat-of-the-pants. We didn't have trailers, we changed our costumes in restaurant bathrooms or even telephone booths. We froze in the winter and sweated in the summer. We dealt with whatever problems occurred. For example, I was shooting a *Studio One* on a midtown street and the script required me to bump into someone, which led to a fight in which the other actor fell and hit his head and was killed. There were no such things as permits and shutting down streets; you got a camera and went outside and you shot the scene using available light. It was important to film only the backs of pedestrians so the producers didn't have to ask them to sign a release, so most of the time we had to walk against the flow. So I bumped into the other actor and started the fight and suddenly I felt people grabbing me and trying to break it up. What could I tell them, we're not actually fighting but please let me kill him?

On a weekly basis I was working with legendary movie figures like Alfred Hitchcock, Lee J. Cobb, Raymond Massey, Ralph Bellamy, and even Billy Barty, as well as talented young actors just beginning their careers, such as Lee Marvin and Jack Klugman, Paul Newman, and Steve McQueen. I worked with Steve McQueen in a classic legal drama titled "The Defenders" on *Studio One*. Ralph Bellamy and I played father-and-son lawyers defending McQueen on murder charges. At the conclusion I used a courtroom trick, fooling the only eyewitness by planting a McQueen look-alike in the spectator section, to get him off — at the cost of my father's respect. I remember watching McQueen work and thinking, wow, he doesn't do anything. He was inarticulate, he mumbled, and only later did I understand how beautifully he did nothing. It was so internalized that the camera picked it up as would a pair of inquisitive eyes. Out of seemingly nothing he was creating a unique form of reality.

The show was so well received that CBS decided to develop it as a series, offering the leading roles to Bellamy and myself. We both turned it down. I was too smart to get caught in that trap. Serious actors didn't do a TV series. Instead E. G. Marshall and Robert Reed starred in the show, which has been recognized as one of the great courtroom dramas in TV history. Among the young actors who worked on the show were Robert Redford, Dustin Hoffman, Gene Hackman, James Earl Jones, Martin Sheen, and Ossie Davis.

I also turned down several commercials for the same reason: serious actors did not do commercials. I couldn't imagine the audience accepting an actor in a dramatic role after they'd seen him selling cigarettes or laundry detergent. A serious actor has to draw the line. I was adamant, I would not sell laundry detergent!

I had become one of the leading men of television. There were few roles that I wanted and didn't get. It was magical. I learned to love doing live television. There was an indescribable excitement and energy that came from knowing you had only one opportunity to get it perfect. No cover shots, no second chances. The cameras we used were very large and contained a lot of very hot tubes, and so they also had small fans in them. The fan made a low wooooooooooooooosssssssssssssssssssshhhhhhhhh-hhhhhhing sound as it cooled the innards of the camera. If you listened closely, it almost sounded like they were purring. Behind the camera was the cameraman, but often he was mostly hidden by it, so it looked like it was moving on its own. One time I saw two cameras on electrical dollies get loose. They came toward each other, hit, and fell over, like massive prehistoric animals.

And when the red light came on it was as if they were alive. Watching you, moving after you. If I had to make an entrance in the middle of a scene I would stand right next to the camera, feeling its warmth, hearing it purr. I loved that camera, you could pet it, savor it, but it never frightened me.

I was getting the kind of notices every actor dreams about. On *Studio One, Variety* raved: "Both Lee J. Cobb and William Shatner were magnificent." After I played a bigot and the leader of a lynch mob on *Playhouse 90,* the *New York Times* wrote: ". . . the embodiment of hate and blind physical passion, Mr. Shatner's attention to detail in putting together the picture of ignorant and evil social forces was remarkable . . . Two of the season's superlative performances by Rod Steiger and William Shatner." *Variety* described my performance on *The U.S. Steel Hour* as "moving . . . [Shatner] is unforgettable as the young priest."

The only problem I was having in my life was with Gloria. I was becoming a star; she was remaining my wife. And for an actor, the role of a star's wife is not a very pleasant one to play. She was working, but not as often as I was and in smaller parts. But finally she was invited to audition for a role for which she was absolutely perfect. It was as if it had been written specifically for her. This was going to be the role that established her — and she didn't get it. It was devastating, the worst possible thing that could happen to a person with such a fragile personality. It was the ugliest side of an actor's life: from the euphoria of the possible to the despair of reality. It was very difficult for me to enjoy my career when every success I had was a painful reminder of her lack of success. This beautiful girl who had a great deal of talent just wasn't getting the opportunity to work. She was terribly frustrated. Every success I had seemed to magnify her lack of success. There was always this underlying feeling that I'd better not talk too much about what happened in rehearsal that day or mention I was offered this part. So I acted all day and then went back to Queens and played another role.

As it turned out movie producer Pandro S. Berman was producing an epic version of Dostoyevsky's *The Brothers Karamazov,* and had already signed Yul Brynner, Lee J. Cobb, and Claire Bloom. The director was Richard Brooks, who was well known for films like *Blackboard Jungle, The Catered Af-*

fair, and *Something of Value.* Berman happened to see me in "The Defenders" on *Studio One,* and was impressed with my work and my cheekbones, which apparently resembled Brynner's. The cheekbones, I mean. I was asked to do a screen test, an audition really, and in preparation I read the novel. I know it's an extraordinary piece of literature but . . .

Oh, this *is* good news. The Biography Channel just called to tell me they've decided to produce an interview show I've created entitled *Shatner's Raw Nerve.* Basically, I'm going to interview actors and politicians and ask them about subjects they generally don't discuss. That's great. In the same press release the Biography Channel also announced another new show, *Small Medium at Large,* about "a four-foot-tall psychic medium who uses Chinese meditation to commune with the dead." That's great, maybe I'll do a short interview with him. I can just imagine the response from some people when they read this release: "Shatner has an interview show?"

. . . so, I read *The Brothers Karamazov* and I couldn't make sense of it. It's very difficult reading. It's the classic story of a nineteenth-century Russian family ripped apart by money, passion, some patricide, love, and snow. A lot of snow. Eventually I was offered the role of Alexei, the youngest of the four Karamazov brothers. Yul Brynner was my oldest brother, Dmitri, who was scheming to get our father's fortune. Lee J. Cobb was our lecherous father, whose character was described in his line, "Each man should die on his own chosen field of battle — mine is bed."

This was my big break, this role was going to make me a star! While it wasn't going to make me rich, it would make me financially secure for the first time in my career. Even working as often as I did, I still had not managed to save more than eighteen hundred bucks. That was my goal, to have more than eighteen hundred dollars in the bank, and this role would enable me to do that.

Gloria and I had bought a little sports car, a convertible. We packed all our belongings, put down the top, and drove across America. When we got closer to Los Angeles I put up the top and in that sudden quiet I realized I hadn't spoken with my wife in four days. That trip put a distance between us that I'm not sure we ever really closed.

We rented an apartment in a complex in Westwood that was popular with people in the entertainment industry. Among them was a beautiful young woman who would sit around the pool all day wearing large sunglasses, always by herself and never talking to anyone. She was so wonderfully mysterious. What was the secret behind this beautiful young woman who never left the building and refused to speak to anyone? Only later did I find out she had been stashed there by Howard Hughes, who never showed up. That was her job, waiting for a man who was never going to arrive. But seeing her there, day after day, fit so perfectly with my image of Hollywood.

This was my initiation to the movie business: as I drove to the M-G-M lot on the morning we were to begin work I thought about my father's plea that I not become a hanger-on. Five years he'd given me, and here I was literally on my way to becoming a movie star. It was an extraordinary feeling. I pulled up to the front gate and the guard asked for my pass. His name was Ken Hollywood, and I will never forget it. I didn't have a pass. I was in a major motion picture, I explained, I didn't need a pass. He looked at his clipboard and shook his head, "You're not on the list," he said.

"I'm William Shatner," I said, and for the dramatic purposes of this book I'll assume beads of sweat began forming on my forehead. "You see, I've got to be on the set at nine o'clock . . ."

"You're not on the list," he repeated firmly, directing me to make a U-turn and leave M-G-M. I drove all the way back to Westwood and sat in my apartment all morning until the confusion was cleared up. Apparently someone had forgotten to put me on the list. Perhaps that should have given me some idea of my importance in this production.

The Brothers Karamazov was my first experience on a big-budget film. Most of the television shows I'd done had taken less than a week to complete and the budgets were so small we had to wear our own clothes; the shooting schedule for this movie was several months. From the very beginning what surprised me was the ease with which vast sums of money were spent on things other than the actual production. Lunch cost more than an entire *Playhouse 90* production. The meals, the cars, the perks, the amount of money that was spent on everything but the movie was astonishing. And nobody seemed to even notice.

The process of making this movie had absolutely no relation to any acting experience in my career. It seemed to me that most of the other actors would learn their lines on the set. I was working as I had learned to work: I knew the entire script before I got to Hollywood. To me, that's the work of acting. Acting is memorizing, absorbing the words and knowing what they mean to the character and how you want to say them. Once you've done that, it's sandbox time. Playtime. What we're doing is pretending, so let's go ahead and pretend with the tools we have, the shovel and the pail, or in the actor's case your lines and your knowledge of the character. But several actors literally would be learning their lines as we were shooting.

Director Richard Brooks was a bit of a perfectionist. I was actually witness to nineteen takes for the word no. It wasn't me, it was someone else, and it took nineteen takes to get it exactly the way he wanted it. Until that day, I didn't know there were nineteen different ways to say no. Is that how you want me to say it? No. No? No. You mean no? Yes.

After the first dozen attempts all the pretend has disappeared. By the time you say any word fifteen times you no longer even understand the meaning of the word. It's just a sound. Do you understand the meaning of the word no? No. Yeah, that's good.

I played a minor role in the film; mostly

my job was to stand in the background looking saintly. The problem with being saintly is that Yul Brynner kept kicking me in the pants. Being new to the movie business I didn't know exactly what that meant. That's the entertainment industry, when someone kicks you in the pants it's not just someone kicking you in the pants. It requires analysis: it might be a show of affection. I like you, therefore I can kick you in the pants to show it; or it might just as easily be a display of anger. I don't like you at all, so I'm going to kick you in your pants. Or it might even be a demonstration of power. I'm so important that I can kick another actor in the pants and no one will stop me. Or it might even simply be intended as a joke. We're all so serious and self-important here and what could be sillier than kicking someone in the pants?

I didn't know what to do. I remember knowing how demeaning it was but not how to respond. He was the star of the movie and I wanted to be successful and I believed he could make or break me. So I didn't know whether to say, "Mr. Brynner, would you mind not kicking me in the pants?" Or ask him, "Would you like to kick me in the pants again?" I was torn between those two responses and a third, which is really what I wanted to do. I wanted to punch him out.

Well, he was in pretty good shape too. So for the rest of the film I did my best to keep my pants out of the way of his foot. And I learned a very important lesson that I have followed throughout my career: don't kick other actors in the pants.

Later in life, when Yul Brynner had cancer and was making his final tour in *The King and I,* I went to see him. He was very affectionate in his emotional memory. He remembered a wonderful shoot. All I remember is getting kicked in the pants. The film received very nice notices. *Variety* wrote: "Shatner has the difficult task of portraying youthful male goodness, and he does it with such gentle candor it is effective." In other words, I was very good at portraying being very good.

At the same time I was learning how to be married. Supposedly it was Sir Donald Wolfit who said on his deathbed, "Dying is easy, comedy is hard." Well, compared to being married, comedy was easy. I had no experience in the great art of living with another person. The great surprise of marriage is that the other person is always there, and has needs and desires that are often in conflict with your own — and sometimes, may actually be right. Everything I knew about marriage came from my mother and my father, and they never raised their voices to each other. Gloria knew how to have an argument; I didn't. Instead of raising my voice and flailing my arms I remember feeling that her actions were unjustified. I didn't understand how someone could love you and still yell at you. So from time to time I was set right back on my heels.

What I didn't know how to do was put myself in somebody else's shoes. Or more specifically, someone else's high heels. I always thought of myself as being sympathetic and loving and kind. But I didn't think of myself as wrong. It has taken me four marriages to understand the part I have to play in a marriage and to learn how to do it.

The challenge to me with Gloria was to not scream back. But finally, I let myself go just a little and I found myself yelling. Well, listen to me. I can do that, I can yell just as loudly as she can. Isn't that a surprise. I hadn't known that part of me existed. One thing didn't change, though: I still believed that if you really loved another person you couldn't shout at them — like I was doing. Which led directly to the inevitable and dangerous thought: well, maybe there's no love here.

Even after my first starring role in a movie I still considered myself a stage actor. Movies and television were the things a stage actor did between great parts. So when I was to audition for the male lead in a new play written by Paul Osborn, being produced by David Merrick and directed by Joshua Logan, I desperately wanted the part. I don't remember too many auditions, but this one I will never forget. By the time I got back to New York I had memorized the entire script, I knew all my lines. As I started to say the words, I dramatically threw down the script and continued.

Josh Logan told me later, "That's what got you the part. That you had the panache to do that, the arrogance, the bravado. It was perfect for the character."

The World of Suzie Wong was the show that was going to make me a star! Merrick, Osborn, Logan, and Shatner, that was it. My problem was that I was under contract to M-G-M. Before giving me the part in *The Brothers Karamazov* the studio had insisted I sign a multipicture deal. If that picture made me a star, they wanted to own me. I didn't know how I was going to get out of that deal.

Fortunately, the first of many projects that were going to make me a star had not made me a star. A year earlier, for the first time in its history, M-G-M had lost money and was actually trying to get rid of its contract players. If they were letting actors like Paul Newman go, they certainly weren't going to fight to keep William Shatner. I suspect that when I officially requested to be released from my contract executives must have leaped in the air and started cheering.

Ken Hollywood didn't even wave goodbye. I didn't mind, I was going to New York again to be a star.

THREE

I've faced death several times in my life. I hunted a brown bear, one of the most ferocious of all animals, armed with only a bow and arrow. I had become an archer while making the movie *Alexander the Great.* I loved archery; I reveled in the beauty of the recurved bow and the perfectly balanced arrow. Hitting a target with a handmade bow is truly an art. I had practiced and became proficient at it. I had hunted deer and a pig, so when the TV show *American Sportsman* asked me to hunt a brown bear in Alaska with a bow and arrow it seemed like an exciting adventure.

I had no concept of what I was getting into. Somewhere in my mind was the thought that I don't get hurt, only the stuntmen get hurt. I think I began realizing that wasn't precisely true as we got off the airplane in Anchorage, Alaska, and watched as two men on stretchers were carried out of a small plane and rushed into an ambulance which immediately raced off with sirens wailing. What was that all about, I asked a guard, and he explained grimly, "They got mauled by grizzlies." Someone else told me about a large World War II Quonset hut whose entire rear wall was covered by the skin of a giant grizzly. And I heard stories about an Indian village that had been ripped apart by a maddened grizzly that had killed twelve people. The grizzly bear is an astonishingly powerful animal. Over a short span it is faster than a racehorse, it can break a caribou's back with a single swipe of its paw, and when threatened it attacks.

The brown bear is larger and more savage than the grizzly bear. The brown bear can be nine feet tall and weigh as much as a thousand pounds. I had my bow and arrow.

We flew up to the Aleutian Islands. This was actually more complicated and dangerous than an ordinary hunt — and I'd just seen the results of an ordinary hunt carried off an airplane. This was a hunt for television. Meaning that the camera crew had to be standing directly behind me and get the entire sequence in a single shot. The "kill shot" it was called. If the audience didn't see my arrow hitting the bear, we believed, then people might suspect it had been edited. In addition to myself, our team consisted of two two-man camera crews and a professional guide armed with a high-powered rifle.

We lived in a shack on the riverbank for ten days, which was more than long enough for me to begin to question my sanity for doing this. Is there anything more horrific than the thought of this mammoth creature eating you alive? Not knocking you unconscious, not starting at your throat, but ripping at your entrails with his huge claws while you're conscious. Bears kill by scooping out your insides; you don't die right away. I started having nightmares about how I was going to react at the moment this animal reared up and looked at me and I had to shoot. One shot, that's all I was going to get. There was no stuntman, no retakes, just me armed with a bow and a single arrow. This was crazy. That bear did not know that I was only an actor.

What am I doing here? I wondered every day. Finally, after ten days we were radioed that a bear was coming in our direction. It had been spotted from an airplane, which was against the law, but this was American television. We waited along the riverbed. The far side of the riverbed was covered with a

106

line of trees and bushes, and beyond that was limitless tundra. We didn't talk very much, I think the other members of the crew were just as nervous as I was.

It was late fall. I was dressed in a bulky parka. I'd never shot an arrow dressed like that and it was awkward. As we waited the guide indicated a copse of low trees with very thick brambles. The bear was moving through the root system, staying in the cover. I looked, but I couldn't see it. There was a break in the tree line and there he was. "Here's what he's going to do," the guide whispered. "He'll come close to the middle of the tree line and stand up on two legs at the edge and look around. If he doesn't spot us or sense us, he'll get down on all fours and come toward us. If he knows we're here, he'll run for the tundra, the open."

I was shaking. One shot. I'm an actor, I'm an actor. Finally he moved into the open and stood up. This was the most magnificent and terrifying creature I had ever seen, it was almost prehistoric. He was forty yards from us and only at that moment did I truly appreciate the hell I'd put myself into. Only then did I have to face my fears.

He lowered himself onto all fours and began coming toward us. But instead of coming across the river he dropped into the bed, which was about two feet below the level of the land. I could see his back moving diagonally across the horizon in front of me. Totally instinctively — I certainly couldn't have been thinking — I moved out into the open and ran toward the bear. The cameramen were running right behind me. My arrow was cocked. The bear turned away from me at a right angle, giving me a very small target, but while on the run I lifted my bow and launched my arrow. I watched it fly as if it were on a towline. It seemed to drive right into the bear. But the bear continued running; he turned and ran right back into the woods.

It took me only a few seconds to realize that we were only twenty or thirty yards from a wounded bear. We didn't know what he was doing. The guide raised his rifle and swept the area, waiting for him to spring out of the tree line at us. We heard him crashing through the thick foliage, but then that sound stopped. The guide said softly, as if we were in a movie rather than on a TV show, "We got ourselves a bad bear." Nobody moved; we believed we were being stalked by a desperate animal.

We sat where we were, waiting in complete silence. Well, silence except for the deafening sound of my heart beating. Unlike a bullet, which kills on impact, an arrow is essentially three or four razor blades and it kills by cutting, so a shot animal lies down and bleeds to death.

A wounded animal waits to attack. We waited in place for about a half hour and then the guide walked into the woods to search for that bear. The camera crews were behind him. They found the dead bear in the bushes. In the sunlight, with the shadows of the branches moving across this giant animal's back, it looked as if it were still alive and that alone was terrifying. We poked at it to make certain it was dead.

At that moment I changed from being a hunter to someone who will catch a fly and let it loose out a window. I have never shot at any living creature again. Looking at that magnificent animal, the amazing stupidity of what I'd done just humbled me. I realized that to destroy life was to destroy part of myself. The vanity of it, the idiocy of it, but until I faced that bear it had nothing at all to do with courage.

Which brings us to being onstage with the very beautiful France Nuyen in *The World of Suzie Wong*. Gloria and I moved back to New York and we bought a little house in Hastings-on-Hudson for nineteen thousand dollars. This was an amazing step for me, this was roots. For an actor, that kind of commitment can be terrifying. But I was confident I could afford it, I was going to be paid $750 a week to star in a Broadway show. That was a tremendous amount of money in 1958. My name was going to be above the title, WILLIAM SHATNER IN . . . It was in lights, WILLIAM SHATNER IN . . . I remember when the titles first went up on the marquee. I walked up and down West 44th Street just looking at it, and then I went back at night to see it all lit up.

Of course I knew the risks. A Broadway show can open and close in one night. If you get enough bad reviews you clean out your dressing room the next morning. If that happened I would be paid one-seventh of my weekly salary, so I'd get a hundred dollars for my performance and a hearty handshake. And the mortgage would still be due at the end of the month.

But I wasn't worried about that. I was working with Broadway royalty: Merrick, Osborn, and Josh Logan. Logan had directed shows like *Mister Roberts* and *South Pacific* and *Fanny* and *Annie Get Your Gun;* he'd won a Pulitzer Prize and a year earlier had been nominated for an Oscar for directing *Sayonara*. Merrick had produced *Fanny* and *The Matchmaker.* Paul Osborn had written the Broadway classic *Morning's at Seven* as well as the screenplays for *East of Eden* and *South Pacfiic.* Their names on the marquee had been enough to generate the first million-plus-dollar advance ticket sale for a drama in Broadway history. A lot of that money had come from a new Broadway phenomenon: suburban theater groups, large groups of people who purchased blocks of tickets before a show opened based on word of mouth. In our case I suspect some of them mistakenly believed they were buying tickets for Rodgers and Hammerstein's new musical, *Flower Drum Song,* which was opening across the street. But I couldn't have been more confident. Hello, Broadway, here I come. I was Mr. Broadway, I got the town by the tail.

I don't remember precisely when I knew *The World of Suzie Wong* was a complete disaster. It might have been during rehearsals, when my co-star, France Nuyen, stopped speaking to Josh Logan so he stopped coming to rehearsals. Or it might have been early in our run, when I had that unfortunate fistfight onstage with a member of the cast who swung at me and missed, accidentally coldcocking an eighty-six-year-old prop man. Or it might have been that night early in the run when I heard a member of the audience whisper loudly, "Will you still love me after this?"

Merrick and Logan must have known, they were too smart and experienced not to have known; my guess is that by the time they realized that they were about to launch the *Titanic* of Broadway shows there was too much advance money in the box office to close it. The problems began with France Nuyen, who only three years earlier had been working in France as a seamstress when she was discovered on a beach by *Life* photographer Philippe Halsman. Almost immediately after arriving in America Josh Logan cast her in the movie version of *South Pacific,* which was great because the character she played spoke only pidgin English. Based on her success, he offered her the lead role of a Chinese prostitute in *Suzie Wong.*

France Nuyen was absolutely gorgeous, I mean people were just thunderstruck by her beauty. She would have been a great star in still pictures or in a wax museum, but on Broadway actors have to move and talk and express emotion — all of which is very difficult for an actress who doesn't speak English. She had learned all her lines phonetically. Much of the time she didn't understand the emotional meaning of the words she was speaking. She knew absolutely nothing about being onstage. As far as I knew, she had never even seen a Broadway show.

The World of Suzie Wong was a love story set in Hong Kong. I played a Canadian artist who falls in love with a Chinese prostitute and tries to reform her. We opened to universally tepid reviews. If theater groups hadn't been invented we would have closed the next morning, but we were sold out for three months so Merrick kept the show open. The audience just hated the show. There is an old joke that applied to this show: the audience was moved by our performance — entire rows would literally stand up in the middle of the show and walk out. These people had decided that standing on a Manhattan corner in the winter, waiting for the bus that was to take them back to suburbia, was preferable to watching our show.

I felt like I was watching my career walk out the door. I was desperate. But just when it seemed like the situation could not possibly get any worse, the bear stood up on its hind legs! It was monstrous. France Nuyen was the most remarkably naïve young woman — who at the same time was tremendously arrogant. It was a street arrogance, a defense mechanism that expressed itself as anger. I'd never seen anything quite like it. If she was crossed in any way she would become furious. It's the kind of emotion an experienced actor might have used in her performance, but she just got angry. I don't quite remember how Josh Logan had crossed her, but after that she refused to speak to him. Not only wouldn't she talk to him, she said if Logan even came into the theater and stood in the rear she would stop talking. The audacity of that — this little girl had ordered the king of Broadway out of the theater! Although truthfully, I suspect Logan was thrilled. Saving this show was beyond even his prodigious talent. I, however, had a two-year contract. I had to be onstage with her every night.

One night shortly after we opened I spoke my line and waited for her response. There is a very old tradition in the theater: when the playwright has gone to all the trouble of writing a line, the actor is supposed to say it. It's not optional. She was sitting in a chair, staring at the audience — absolutely silent. She wouldn't speak. Apparently, in the dimly lit theater she thought she saw Logan standing in the back. After a few seconds I ad-libbed something, well, what I really meant to say was . . . and again I waited. Once again, she didn't say a word. I made up something else. For an actor this was considerably worse than forgetting your own lines, at least in that situation there's hope that someone will feed them to you. But this . . . In that situation you do whatever you have to do to survive. You take a deep breath and start talking. At one point I wandered offstage and asked the stage manager what to do. The stage manager, who was supervising the play in Josh Logan's absence, shrugged his shoulders. I wandered back onstage and kept talking. Finally, mercifully, the curtain came down, ending the act.

"Are you out of your mind?" is what I should have said. Instead I asked her what was wrong.

The bear looked at me and said in a broken, nasty French accent, "I saw Logan."

It got worse every night. Meanwhile, she had fallen desperately in love with Marlon Brando and wanted to get out of the show. The producers refused to release her from her contract, so she decided that she would catch pneumonia. At intermission one performance she went outside and stood in the rain, then came back onstage absolutely soaking wet, as if she had been in the shower.

From performance to performance I never knew what she was going to do. Sometimes she would simply walk off the stage and not return. Other times she would refuse to speak. I didn't know which way the bear was going to turn. I was onstage for the entire play, so I began to prepare monologues for myself in case she decided not to come back onstage.

Something happened between us. Perhaps it was that cigar that I inhaled deeply and exhaled in her face, but she stopped talking to me too. Most of the cast was young and Asian and as inexperienced as she was and they all stopped talking to me too. So I was the lead in a Broadway show, my name above the title, Mr. Broadway, my town, and nobody in the cast was speaking to me except for a couple of white-skinned actors. Thank goodness, I thought, at least I have someone to talk to; of course that was before the brawl.

One of these actors was an Australian who had been an Olympic swimming champion, and unfortunately he felt he should receive better billing. Merrick refused to give it to him, so he was angry too. He had one big scene in the show with me in which he was supposed to get a big laugh. Now, normally, at the end of the final dress rehearsal a show is frozen, meaning that's the way it is supposed to be performed every night. What generally happens is a show slips, the timing changes slightly, and over a period of time that slight variance in timing has become gigantic. Every play slips and usually the director comes in every few weeks and redirects it. But Logan wasn't permitted in the theater so he never came back. Instead the stage manager redirected the play and it began to go lopsided. It fell apart.

After this Australian actor said his laugh line he put his hand on my shoulder. After a few weeks I noticed that if he got his laugh he laid a nice firm hand on my shoulder — but if he didn't get that laugh this Olympic swimmer who was built like an Australian Olympic swimmer pounded on my shoulder. Finally I appealed to the stage manager, "I'm living in dread of this moment. If he doesn't get his laugh he whacks me on the shoulder. Could you ask him nicely, 'Please don't hit Bill on his shoulder'?"

Well, that just made him angrier, and he began to clap me harder and harder. I went to Josh Logan, I went to the union. I tried everything to stop this guy from slamming me on the shoulder. But nobody could help me because the play had become chaotic. It was completely out of control.

Before a performance I went to his dressing room. "I've asked you nicely," I explained. "Now I'm telling you. You hit me on the shoulder one more time, I'm going to hit you back right on the stage."

Rather than a warning, he took that as a challenge. In our next performance he clapped me on the shoulder. I turned around and punched him. He was stunned, though somehow he got off the stage. The moment the first act ended and the curtain came down he raced across the stage and reared back to throw a punch at me that might have put me into Shubert Alley. I ducked, and instead he hit our eighty-six-year-old prop man. He knocked him out cold on the stage. That's when the Act 2 curtain started to go up.

I was desperate. I had a wife and a child and a mortgage. So in my desperation I began to speed up my lines. I changed the intonation and the emotion. Just by speaking faster and putting emphasis on different words I shortened the play by fifteen minutes — and people began to laugh. I *love* you, had become, I love *you?* We were making fun of this turgid melodrama. We turned it into a lighthearted comedy.

The show became a hit. A comedy. We ran for fourteen months and I won several acting awards from major theater organizations. And when the movie version of it was made, I was invited to buy a ticket to watch William Holden playing my part. I was quite surprised by Holden's performance. Apparently he didn't understand the play — he thought it was a serious love story.

Several years later I was doing *Star Trek* and there was a part for an Asian girl. They asked me how I felt about casting France Nuyen. It was all these years later, and I was curious what she would be like. Hire her, I said, she'll be great. When she came on the set she was delightful. That defensiveness I remembered so well seemed to have disappeared, and I found myself wondering what could have possibly gone so wrong. And then she needed some makeup and she said, "Makeup. Come here." And it all came back. It was the arrogance, I remembered every bit of it.

Obviously France and I both grew older and wiser and smarter and better looking and . . . and well, we've worked together on several more projects. Although we've never discussed those old days.

Before we continue with the narrative of my life, just let me pause here for a few seconds to check out the latest new additions to ShatnerVision.com, the Web site run by my daughter Lisbeth, who has not yet been born. In this book, I mean. ShatnerVision is a compilation of short videos. Oh, look at that, that's clever. Good, I see they've added the little piece I did especially for you. Take a look at it, it's easy to find, it has your name on it.

But please, don't mistake ShatnerVision for WilliamShatner.com, which is my official Web site. That's an easy mistake to make, but they're very different. For example, the wonderful store from which you can order anything from a DVD of a movie in which I starred named *Incubus* — the only feature film ever made in the artificial language of Esperanto — to an exclusive *Wrath of Khan* twenty-fifth-anniversary bloodied Kirk action figure, is at WilliamShatner.com, but the video of me explaining why I don't like to take off my pants on *Boston Legal* can be found on ShatnerVision. What surprised me most were the incredibly low prices on an array of remarkable items. I could buy my own autograph for considerably less than I would have expected to have to pay for it. And if I sent a check, I would have to sign it, putting me in the somewhat unique position of using my autograph to sign a check to buy my autograph. Of course, you wouldn't have that problem. So, that should clear things up.

Now back to my life. Somehow I managed to escape *Suzie Wong* with my reputation intact. In fact, once the show had settled in I began working on television programs during the day, then rushing to the theater at night. By day I was a respected television actor, playing the blind senator in a show written by Gore Vidal, appearing on *Hallmark Hall of Fame* with Ellen Burstyn, Carol Channing, and Maurice Evans, and starring in one of the first nationwide broadcasts on PBS, *The Night of the Auk.* This was a play that had flopped on Broadway several years earlier, starring, naturally, Chris Plummer and Claude Rains. It took place on a spaceship returning to Earth from the first successful manned landing on the moon. I played the wealthy young man who had financed the entire expedition. This was my first voyage on a television spaceship and it established one of the enduring truths of drama: if Shatner is aboard a spaceship, it is guaranteed that something is going to go wrong. In this story it's atomic war on Earth and a lack of oxygen in the ship. There are five passengers, but only enough oxygen left to enable two of them to survive long enough to get back to Earth in time to die in the war. I don't want to ruin the ending for you, so let us just say I don't die in the atomic war.

I've never had great fortune planning my career. That is a luxury enjoyed by very few actors. Insecurity is part of the job description. I would describe my career plan pretty much as answering the telephone. My problem was that I never had anyone I felt comfortable soliciting advice from; no one whom I trusted to direct my career. So I made my own decisions based almost entirely on my gut feeling. Acting is one of the few professions in which you feel good about turning down work. Later in my career, after my three children were born, I found myself accepting jobs only for the money and feeling bad about it — and conversely feeling very good when I felt secure enough to turn down a job I knew I shouldn't accept. I've subscribed to the notion that work makes more work — the more producers and directors see you work the more chance there is they will offer you more work. There were many times in my career that I'd taken roles I shouldn't have in terms of creating a long-term career — but it was a paying job and hanging over me always was my father's plea that I not become a hanger-on.

When you do accept a role, you never, ever have any concept of what the end result will be. Did I know when John Lithgow offered me the prestigious role of the Big Giant Head on his sitcom *3rd Rock from the Sun* that I would be nominated for my first Emmy Award? Did it occur to me that people might recognize the subtle skills it took to properly convey the emotional life of Head? What I knew was that I was going to show up and say all my lines and they would pay me. That's acting.

Sometimes, though, it is about the role. About the opportunity to use the talent I had been given to make an important statement. Obviously actors have to survive, but occasionally you do get offered a role that you just savor, that you really want to do.

The great C-movie producer-director Roger Corman offered me such a role. Seriously. That Roger Corman, who was already becoming well-known for films like *Attack of the Crab Monsters, Creature from the Haunted Sea,* and *Little Shop of Horrors,* cheap, get-em-made exploitation horror, T&A, and shoot-em-ups with low budgets and lower production values. But for some reason he wanted to do this film. By this time he had made seventeen films, all of them profitable, but every studio he approached with this script turned him down. Apparently making this film meant so much to him that he and his brother Gene mortgaged their homes to pay for it. Now, it's possible I made that up, but I remember Roger and Gene did something very courageous to raise the money they needed to make this movie. Roger had seen me in *Tamburlaine the Great* and sent me the script. As soon as I read it I knew I wanted to play this role. This film changed my life.

The movie was called *The Intruder.* It was from a novel by a very respected writer named Charles Beaumont. *The Intruder* took place in the Deep South just after the 1954 Supreme Court decision that ordered schools to integrate. It was based on the true story of a white supremacist from New York, a neo-Nazi who traveled throughout the South organizing Ku Klux Klan–type citizen groups and fomenting riots. This was easily the most despicable character I'd ever played. But it was a wonderfully written portrait of the worst kind of bigot. I had grown up in Canada, I didn't know this kind of institutionalized racism existed in the United States. I was stunned when I found out it was all true.

We shot it in black-and-white in three

weeks, and the entire budget was about eighty thousand dollars; that was probably just a little more than lunch on *Karamazov.* In order to help the Cormans make this film I took a percentage of the gross rather than a salary. There were times I was an embarrassment to my economics degree. In the end I earned about two hundred dollars more than it cost me in expenses.

What made this project unusually exciting is that for some inexplicable reason Roger Corman decided that we would shoot this movie in the South. This was 1961, when schools throughout the South were still being forcefully integrated. This was less than five years after President Eisenhower had to call out the National Guard to escort black teenagers into Little Rock High School. And we went to Charleston, Missouri, which was in Mississippi County, a few miles from the borders with Kentucky, Arkansas, and Tennessee, to film it.

The entire cast and crew was housed in a small motel just outside of town. The day we arrived we were briefed by a policeman, who advised us, "Now, if I were you, I'd just take a few minutes and plan my escape route." Escape route? As he explained, the town had found out what this movie was about and they were not happy about it.

Really not happy. The only integrated group in the whole town was a prison gang and supposedly this gang had been hired to kill us in the motel. "We've got all this spotted," the policeman said, "but we can't hold back the waters."

Kill me? But I'm an actor! And I was only being paid a percentage of the gross.

There had been some unpleasant moments in my career, but this was the first time I actually had to make an escape plan. I had a pretty good one. There was a window in the bathroom that looked out on a cornfield. If it became necessary I was going to climb up on the toilet, wiggle out that window, and start running into the cornfield. I figured I could hide in the cornfield.

I think there were only five professional actors in the cast. To save money the Corman brothers hired local people to play the minor roles. But just to be on the safe side, they gave them a different script than the one we were actually shooting, a script that didn't include some of the more inflammatory language and scenes. One of the professional actors was Leo Gordon, who had made a nice career out of playing tough-guy roles, but in this film he was cast as a hard-working, kind of average Joe. In fact, Gordon had been a boxing champion in the military and knew how to protect himself. We were talking one day near his car and he casually opened the trunk — and there was practically an arsenal in there. The trunk was filled with guns. He took whatever he wanted out of the trunk and slammed it shut, never even mentioning the trunk was filled with guns.

Okay, he's an actor too. But he's a well-armed actor. I began rethinking my escape plan.

Naturally I tried to make friends with as many people in the town as possible. There was one man in particular who showed up almost every day to watch us shoot . . . filming. He was a big guy, a huge guy, and the word was that he was one of the really bad people in the town. But obviously he was intrigued by the making of a movie and continually volunteered to help. Let me move this lamp for you. You can't, it's a union job. But I want to help. He was one of those few people whose offers to help sound suspiciously like threats.

Somehow I befriended him. Maybe I thought I could manage him by including him in the process. But eventually he actually became a member of our crew, and he was so big that when other grips were carrying one light, he would take two. He did a

127

fine job, but even if he hadn't it wouldn't have mattered. Believe me, nobody was going to fire him.

Eventually he found out that I loved fast cars and horses. "You know, we have a lot in common," he told me. "I got the fastest car in the whole four-state area. I got a Daytona racer." He brought it to the set to show me. It truly was a beautiful car, immaculate on both the outside and the inside. He had customized the engine to increase its power by who knows how much. "This is the one I win all the time with," he explained in the true manner of Southern generosity. "I got my soul in this car, but if you wanna borrow it to take it into town, you just go right ahead."

Well, that was extremely gracious of him.

"Tell you what," he continued. "I also got me a quarter horse. That boy is faster than lightning. But you can ride him anytime you want." He opened up the trunk. "This here's where I keep the chaps I wear when I ride him. These are my lucky chaps — long as they're in the car this car's gonna win every race. I love these chaps. But any time you want you put on these chaps and take my horse for a ride."

One day I needed to drive to Cairo, Illinois, and I asked to borrow his car. He was thrilled to lend it to me, because I was his friend and that's what friends do for each other. "One more thing," he told me. "See the backseat over here? Down there's where I keep the fire extinguisher. You got to know where that is, 'cause sometimes, not too often, but sometimes the raw gasoline going into the air cleaner catches fire. It's no big deal, but if you smell fire you just got to open the hood and hit the fire with the extinguisher, just blows it right out."

This was a beautiful, finely tuned race car, and on those back roads I could let it out. I had a fine drive into town and on my way back I stopped at a light. Purely coincidently somebody from our company pulled up next to me and shouted, "Your car's on fire!" What? "There's flames coming out the bottom of your car."

I leaped out of the car. Smoke was coming out from underneath. I knew what to do: raise the hood, get the fire extinguisher, and blow out the fire. Unfortunately, I immediately discovered I didn't know how to raise the hood. I looked around desperately for the hook or something, a lever, anything to pop it open, and I couldn't figure out how to do it. The smoke was starting to get a little thicker. I was beating on the hood with my fists, trying to get it to pop, but it was locked shut.

Okay, I figured, I'll get the fire extinguisher and crawl under the car. I can blow it out from there. I opened the door and grabbed for the fire extinguisher, and then grabbed for it again. The fire extinguisher had fallen beneath the seat. I couldn't reach it. By now the smoke was starting to get very thick.

I opened the trunk and grabbed the first thing I could find. As I started to shut it I saw a crowbar. Great, that's what I needed. I took the crowbar and literally pried open the hood. Then I started beating out the fire with that thing I'd grabbed out of the trunk. I beat that fire again and again but it was much too late, the engine just melted. Eventually I stopped and just stood there, leaving that smoking rag I'd used to beat down the fire sitting on top of the melted engine.

Oh man, I thought, now what am I going to do? And it was just about that time that I realized I had tried to snuff out the fire with this guy's lucky chaps. I'd melted his car and destroyed his lucky chaps, it was just awful. Incredibly, this man accepted my apology because I was his friend, and because I had enabled him to become part of the movie company. Apparently that was one of the great thrills of his life. In fact, just to show me that he truly wasn't angry, a few weeks later he invited me to take his horse for a ride.

And he didn't even complain when his horse came up lame.

The script included some incredibly powerful and potentially volatile scenes. In a key scene I had to stand on the courthouse steps and inflame the townspeople. I had to make them rise up, I had to put the fear of the devil in them, I had to implore them: Take to the streets! Stop the integration of the high school! Save the South!

Dressed in my white suit, I told them, "They kept the facts away from you! . . . What I'm gonna tell you is gonna make your blood boil. I'm gonna show you that the way this country's gonna go depends entirely, and wholly, on you! . . . Now, you all know that there was peace and quiet in the South before the N-double-A-C-P started stirring up trouble. But what you don't know is this so-called advancement of colored people is now, and has always been, nothing but a Communist front headed by a Jew who hates America . . .

"[T]hey knew that the quickest way to weaken a country is to mongolize it . . . So they poured all the millions of dollars the

Jews could get for them into this one thing . . . desegregation. [The judge] belongs to a society which receives its funds directly from Moscow! Your mayor and the governor could have stopped it — but they didn't have the guts . . . The Negroes will literally, and I do mean literally, control the South! . . . [If you want to stop it] right here, today, I'm with you. Because I'm an American and I love my country, and I'm willing to give my life if necessary to see that my country stays free! White! And American!"

It was an extraordinary speech for anyone to dare give on the steps of the courthouse in a Southern town in 1961. Luckily, as it turned out, two days before we were scheduled to film this scene I came up with a case of laryngitis. This is absolutely true. The doctor told me if I didn't speak for an entire day my voice might make it through the scene. I didn't say one word for more than twenty-four hours. If I wanted something I wrote it down. By the next night my throat felt just a little better.

At dusk that night about three hundred people, mostly farmers, gathered in front of the courthouse. It was a lovely town, the courthouse was on the town square with a beautiful old tree right in front of it. Roger decided that he would begin by shooting

132

the crowd-reaction shots over my shoulder, and to save my voice I shouldn't say my lines. Instead he read some absolutely innocuous lines to get reaction. Let's go, Missouri Tigers! We love the St. Louis Cardinals! Let's hear it for the red, white, and blue! Who wants apple pie! How about that big sale at Sears! When he needed anger he asked those people how they felt about the University of Alabama football team. Roger got that crowd screaming, cheering, pumping their fists, whatever reactions he needed. By midnight most of the crowd had gone home. Being an extra in a movie is fun for about a minute. After the first few hours it gets really boring. So they went home.

That's when he shot me doing the real lines. My voice was there and I shouted for them to rage and pillage and burn. The following morning Roger and I were walking down the main street and the publisher of the local newspaper stopped us. He'd stayed the whole night because he was working on a story. "You guys are unbelievable," he said. "You really did a smart thing."

We did?

"Darn right. See that tree right there," he said, pointing to the tree in front of the courthouse. "That's where they lynched a Negro about fifteen years ago. A lot of people in that crowd were there. That tree is the symbol of white supremacy 'round here. Had those people heard what you were saying . . ." He shook his head. "Your picture might've had a real different ending."

We believed we were in danger every day. We were prevented from shooting certain scenes in the town, Roger received a series of death threats, and the local police and one night even the state militia had to come in to stand guard. We saved the most harrowing scene for the last day. In this scene a long parade of Ku Klux Klansmen in their white hoods drive slowly through the black section of town. The scene takes place at night. We all checked out of the motel and packed our belongings. We shot that scene and just kept driving — all the way to St. Louis.

The Intruder was a powerful movie, so powerful in fact that Roger had an extremely difficult time finding a distributor. We got great reviews, the *Herald-Tribune* called it "A major credit to the entire motion picture industry." The *Los Angeles Times* wrote that it was "the boldest, most realistic depiction of racial injustice ever shown in American films." I won several Best Actor awards at film festivals, but the subject was so controversial theater owners were afraid to screen it. It showed in only two theaters in New York City, for example. That was unbelievably frustrating for me. I believe this was the only film Roger Corman ever made that lost money. His next film was *The Premature Burial.*

A few years after its initial failure it was re-released under several different exploitation titles, including *I Hate Your Guts* and *Shame.* Finally it got some distribution. In England it was released as *The Stranger.*

One of the things that made *The Intruder* considerably different from most of the projects I was doing was that Roger Corman did not promise that this film was going to make me a star. He didn't even guarantee that I would get paid. At that point in my career it seemed like every phone call I got from a movie director or TV producer or an agent began with the statement, "Bill, honestly, this [fill in the blank] is the one that's going to make you a star." Okay, I admit it, I was ready. To me, being a star meant having more than eighteen hundred dollars in the bank. It meant security. Gloria had given birth to our second beautiful daughter and security had become extremely important to me. I could see it, it was within reach, it was right there, at the end of the next project.

When I was offered a featured role as a young prosecutor in Stanley Kramer's new movie, *Judgment at Nuremberg,* my agent told me that this was the one, this was the film that was finally going to make me a star. He may have even called me "kid," as in, "This is the one, kid." Truthfully that did seem possible; this was going to be a big-budget star-studded film about an unbelievably serious subject directed by Stanley Kramer. Abby Mann's screenplay was based on the true story of the trial of four Nazi judges after World War II, but really the German people were on trial. I had worked with Abby Mann on several television shows and I suspect he supported me for the role. I do remember my agent telling me, "This is a great part. You have no idea who wanted it."

That was the other thing I was often told: you have no idea who wanted this role. I didn't. But why wouldn't they want this role, if it was going to make them a star?

Looking back, I sometimes wonder how I spent so many years in Canada knowing so little about what was going on in the world. Until I was offered this role, for example, I knew very little about the full extent of the unspeakable horrors that had taken place in

Nazi Germany. But then, almost no one did.

I remember the day I became aware of it.

There were films. When the U.S. army liberated the concentration camps they had filmed the survivors, as well as the results of Hitler's final solution. Abby Mann and Stanley Kramer required the entire cast and crew to watch these films. Hundreds of people. They wanted us to understand what this film was about. They set up two screens on either side of a stage and turned on the projectors. These films had not yet been released to the public; very few people had seen them. We didn't know what to expect. I vaguely remember a little stirring, some people whispering — and then the silence. The absolute silence. We watched scenes of bulldozers shoving piles of bodies into mass graves. We saw the survivors, their eyes bulging, their bones practically protruding from their bodies. We saw the crematoriums and the piles of shoes. People gasped in shock, others started crying. If I close my eyes I can rerun these films in my mind, and I remember exactly where I was sitting and what the room looked like. Certainly it was the most horrifying thing I had ever seen in my life, but that doesn't even begin to describe the impact.

When the lights finally went on the room

stayed silent. It stayed silent as we all walked out. But from that night on we understood the importance of the film we were making. A lot of the cast and some of the crew were Jewish, so this picture had an even deeper impact on us. Every day I went to work feeling like I was doing something important. Stanley Kramer continued to emphasize that we were recording history, and the story we were telling should never be forgotten. And Abby Mann carries himself with a sense of importance, anything he does is important — he went to the bathroom, it was important. Although probably not historic.

The movie starred Spencer Tracy, Marlene Dietrich, Burt Lancaster, Richard Widmark, Maximilian Schell, and Montgomery Clift — most of them working on it for one day. I've co-starred in many movies with actors I've never met. We had no scenes together, we probably were scheduled to work at different times, we may not have even been on the same location. That happens all the time. But I had never seen anything like when a few years earlier the biggest movie stars had begun making cameo appearances — basically one scene or even a one-shot walk-on — in big-budget movies. The studios hired a star for a small role, a part that could be shot in a day or two, paid that star substantially less than their usual salary, and still got the value of that star's name in all the advertising. *Judgment at Nuremberg* was the perfect example of that. Most of the stars had only one or two scenes; usually they were testifying in the courtroom. My role consisted primarily of sitting at a long table watching this parade of fabulous stars whose luminosity was fading — but who were still stellar — put to use all of their experiences, all of their abilities, to create memorable performances. I had a few scenes with some of them. Early in the picture I showed Spencer Tracy to his large office and told him, "I trust you'll be comfortable in this room, sir."

To which he responded, "Captain, I have no doubt that the entire state of Maine would be comfortable in this room!"

Working with a great star like Spencer Tracy, an actor I'd watched with awe while growing up in Montreal, was absolutely thrilling for me. I loved Spencer Tracy. However, acting with me was obviously less thrilling for him. After Spencer Tracy had flawlessly delivered a stirring ten-minute summation I asked him, with all the arrogance of youth and the confidence of a stage actor, "Did you memorize all of that?"

I did not know that Spencer Tracy had started his career on the stage. He just looked at me, that's all, just looked at me and never spoke to me again. I'm sure he thought, who the hell is this young punk thinking I came to the set unprepared? Or that I didn't think he could memorize his lines.

Burt Lancaster played a proud former Nazi judge who accepted responsibility for his actions, giving it the full teeth-gritted Burt Lancaster. We shot his scene in one day. But when we came to work the next morning we were told that Mr. Lancaster wasn't satisfied with his performance, he wanted to do a retake. He knew he could do better. And then he gave exactly the same teeth-gritted Burt Lancaster performance he'd done the day before. That's better, he said, and went home happy.

I remember Richard Widmark's intensity and Judy Garland's fragility and Montgomery Clift. Montgomery Clift played a mentally incompetent German civilian who had been sterilized. He fidgeted and stammered and continually shifted in the witness chair. I thought he was brilliant, not knowing then that he had been addicted to pain-killing drugs and had become an alcoholic after being disfigured in a terrible car accident about five years earlier. What I thought was his performance was his pain. Of course I knew nothing about any of that at the time.

Some of the concentration camp footage that we had been shown privately was included in the film. By this time Americans knew about the concentration camps, but nothing could have prepared them for seeing these atrocities. Distributors wouldn't touch *The Intruder* because of its provocative story, but *Judgment at Nuremberg* was considered one of the most important films Hollywood had ever made. It was showered with awards. It won two Academy Awards and was nominated for nine more — including Best Picture, which was won by *West Side Story.* Maximilian Schell won for Best Actor; Judy Garland, Spencer Tracy, and Montgomery Clift were nominated and I . . . and I . . . this film did not make me a star. It made me a paid actor and when it was done I started looking for work again.

There is one advantage to not being a star. Every young actor gets warned about the dangers of being typecast. The reality of the profession is that once you're perceived to be a specific type or character it's very difficult to play other roles. Burt Lancaster played Burt Lancaster. John Wayne, John

Wayne. It's very good advice, although it has little to do with the reality of life for most actors, which is, basically, work. I was very lucky early in my career. I was able to move easily between the stage, television, and movies. I could play comedy and drama, I could be the leading man or a supporting player, and I was offered a broad variety of parts. Part of the reason I was becoming better known was what people perceived to be an unusual. Speech. Pattern. Apparently I was becoming known for. Pausing, between words, in. Unusual places. People have commented that it calls attention to the. Words, I'm saying. It provides a different kind of emphasis on a line. I have no idea where that. Came from. Possibly it came from the fact I was working so often in so many different types of plays and television program and movies that at times I did need to hesitate to remember my next words. Possibly, that's just an assumption, but the reality is that I don't even hear it. I can mock the idea. I understand people hear me speaking. That way. They've even put a name to it, calling it Shatnerian. As in, ah yes, the character spoke with true Shatnerian eloquence.

But it's certainly nothing I'm doing intentionally, nor do I do it in real life. I have seen several William Shatner impersonators speak in that. Clipped. Punctuated manner. Okay, if people recognize the impersonation as me, then it must be me. When an impressionist did Jimmy Stewart or Edward G. Robinson or Jimmy Cagney or Cary Grant, I knew exactly who they were doing. I always wondered, if Jimmy Cagney and James Stewart were having dinner at home, did Cagney say, "Pass the salt, you dirty rat?" And did James Stewart reply, "Um, ah, ah, ah, I . . . I . . . here . . . here it is." But when I watch them doing me, speaking that. Way. The audience laughs. So it must be what. I'm doing. But I don't recognize it in myself.

One thing that often does happen to an actor is that elements of the character they're playing seep over into their real life. It's quite different from speech patterns. You can't go to work every day playing a monstrous man and then go home at night and enjoy a party. The intensity of the work is too strong. You have to inhabit the character's body, and the transition back and forth between the character's life and real life is often a difficult one to make. When we were making *Star Trek,* for example, Leonard Nimoy remained true to Spock the whole day. He couldn't easily go in and out of a taciturn, cerebral, emotionless character like that and as a result remained distant from the rest of us. Sometimes when a role is completed it's very difficult to shed your character and move into a completely different life. In the early days of television it was easier because the whole job lasted less than a week. There wasn't time to get deeply invested in a character. But now I had spent months trying to understand and portray the worst kind of racist, and then an assistant prosecutor of the people who had provided legal cover for unimaginable atrocities to take place. It was time for comedy.

The wonderful actress Julie Harris was going to star on Broadway in *A Shot in the Dark,* an English version of the French farce *L'Idiot,* and she decided she wanted me to co-star with her. I don't know why, I'd never met her, but apparently she'd seen me on television and wanted me. I remember what my agent said when he called to tell me about this: "Trust me, Bill. This play is going to make you a star."

More than anything else, I love being on the stage. At times during my career I've been able to connect emotionally with an entire audience, and during those rare moments it literally feels as if a relationship exists between us. We're in this experience together. And this was an opportunity to do a farce and work with the legendary director Harold Clurman. Clurman had been a founding member of the Group Theatre, he was involved in the original Broadway production of *Waiting for Lefty,* and except for the fact that he did not want me in his play and did everything possible to make my life miserable — except kick me in the pants — we got along very . . . badly.

He seemed to get some sort of perverse joy out of insulting me: Just what do you think you're doing? What are you, trying to be charming? No, no, no, that's not the way to play it. And just how long have you been acting?

In addition to Julie Harris, the play co-starred Walter Matthau and Gene Saks. I played French Examining Magistrate Paul Sevigne, who is investigating his first case, a murder in which the beautiful parlor maid was found unconscious, naked, and holding a gun next to the body of the dead chauffeur. Naturally, as this was a farce, I didn't believe she had committed the crime.

Matthau played the fabulously wealthy Benjamin Beaurevers, who may have been having an affair with the maid. The play got nice reviews and ran for eighteen months.

But there was one moment during the entire run that I will never forget. Walter and I were playing a scene across a table; basically I was accusing him of committing the murder and he was accusing me of being an idiot. Something happened, truthfully I don't remember what it was. I could make something up but . . .

In fact, I will make something up. It makes for a better story. And honestly, I do make things up. It's part of the actor's craft. For example, and I'm not making this up, I used to love to ride motorcycles with stuntmen I'd met while making *Star Trek* in the desert. We'd race through Antelope Valley, in Palmdale, and in those years there were a lot of stories about Unidentified Flying Objects, UFOs, being seen in that area. There was a photograph of one hovering directly above a power line. So when I rode in the desert I'd look into the sky. I figured if the aliens could read my thoughts they'd know that the actor who played Captain Kirk on *Star Trek* was out there. If they wanted publicity, what could be better than contacting Captain Kirk? I'm not making any of this up.

I was riding with five guys and we were using the buddy system — keep the man behind you in your rearview mirror so if anything happened you could help. I was last in line because they were all faster than me, looking up into the sky. Unfortunately, about a century ago miners would dig gravelike holes in the ground, maybe three or four feet wide, six feet long and six feet deep, to see what types of minerals might be found. If they found nothing of interest they'd abandon the hole and dig another one a half mile away. So the desert floor is pocked with these holes. So I was looking into the air, last in line, and I drive into one of these holes. Boom! I was going 30 miles an hour and I went straight into the hole and flying over the bike. I was wearing protective leather clothing so I got bruised a little, but not hurt. Unfortunately, the stuntmen forgot all about the buddy system and disappeared. All true.

I'm alone in the broiling desert, I'm covered head to toe in a helmet and leathers, and the bike is in this hole. I had a big decision to make: I didn't know whether I should take off the helmet and leathers and die of sunstroke or keep them on and die of heat prostration.

I managed to get the bike out of the hole but it wouldn't start. This was a beautiful Bultaco and I didn't want to leave it there because I was afraid someone might steal it. So I started pushing the bike and falling down. I actually managed to find a road and pushed the bike until I found a gas station. It wasn't that far. The mechanic found a wire that had been disconnected, reattached it where it belonged, the bike started, and I drove home. Truth.

Not too long afterward I was being interviewed for a television program and the interviewer said, "I heard you love riding motorcycles."

"Oh, I certainly do," I said. I told him the whole story, driving with head in the air, big potholes, flying through the air, live or die, lost, where to go, start pushing the bike and then . . . and then this is the part I made up: "And then I saw somebody standing on a ridge, dressed in a silver suit. He was sort of gleaming in the sunlight, this man from out of nowhere standing atop a ridge in the desert. I didn't know what to do. And he motioned to me, follow me. And I follow him, and I follow him and I don't know whether I blanked out from heat prostration or sunstroke, but suddenly he was gone and I was in a place where I could be saved. He had led me to civilization. I was able to fix my bike and I know now that an alien saved my life."

It's a wonderful story and every bit of it is not true. But the tabloids picked it up and ran it: "Shatner Saved by Alien." I loved it. I'd put one over on the gossip rags. Several years later a man named John Newland called me. John had produced and directed the series *One Step Beyond,* which purportedly investigated and dramatized paranormal phenomena. Newland had taken LSD on camera before anybody knew what it was. The show was off the air but he was doing a special *One Step Beyond* with celebrities, hoping to bring back the show. Because I was Captain Kirk he thought I'd be the perfect guest. "Has anything sort of strange ever happened to you?" he asked.

"No, not really," I said.

"Well, here's a letter that somebody wrote about witnessing an airplane crash on the Simi Valley Highway that never happened. Could this have happened to you?"

Obviously he wanted me to say something happened. "No, I don't . . ." and then I remembered. "That never happened — but I'll tell you what did happen." Looking up, hole, push, silver suit, saved.

"Perfect. You can be the star of the special." I wrote the script, an alien saved my life. We filmed it at Moses Lake in Washington. Rather than holes dug in the ground, there were large sandbanks. A Canadian stuntman was hired to play me. I drove the motorcycle to the top of the sandbank and stopped; they moved the cameras to the far side of the rise and the stuntman went flying over the top and took a terrible spill. That was the dramatization of the fall I took with my bike.

Unfortunately, the stuntman hit it wrong and broke his back. He was lying there in the sand unable to move. It was awful. I went rushing over to him. The stuntman's girlfriend was kneeling over him, but as I approached she stood up and sand trickled down onto his face. This girl looks at me, tears in her eyes, and says to me, "Mr. Shatner, could I have your autograph?"

Several months after we'd finished shooting the segment Newland invited me to meet astronaut Edgar Mitchell, who had become known for conducting paranormal experiments from space, and was going to host the program. That was very exciting for me; obviously I had tremendous admiration for the astronauts. When we met he shook my hand firmly and looked me directly in the eyes and said, "Bill Shatner, I've admired you for a long time, Captain Kirk, it's great to meet you. Boy, that is some amazing story about what happened to you in the desert."

He thought it was true. I had made up

this whole story, and he believed it. How could I tell an astronaut that he was being fooled? That this never happened? "It certainly was amazing," I agreed.

The show never went beyond that special episode — but for more than three decades the tabloids have been telling and retelling the story of the day William Shatner's life was saved by an alien.

I truly love making up reality. I did a movie entitled *Free Enterprise* in which I played myself, but a me whose dream it is to do a musical version of *Julius Caesar* in which I play all the parts — except Brutus, of course, but only because of the technical difficulty involved in stabbing myself in the back. *Free Enterprise* was a low-budget movie being made by young filmmakers, so we were asked to provide our own wardrobe. In an army-navy surplus store in Westwood I found a beautiful leather bomber jacket, a white scarf, and a World War II captain's hat. I bought them for about fifty bucks and wore everything in a scene.

The producers entered the film in the Cannes Film Festival and invited me to come to France to assist in promotion. The producers had decided to donate my bomber jacket, scarf, and cap to the Hard Rock Café. They held a press conference

151

there. Reporters asked me about the clothing and I told the truth as quickly as I could make it up. "I found this jacket," I said. "It's Eddie Rickenbacker's jacket." Eddie Rickenbacker was one of America's first aces in World War I, winning the Congressional Medal of Honor for shooting down twenty-six enemy aircraft. "This was his original jacket," I continued. "It was in a glass case in a museum, I believe, and it was stolen. I found it in a used-clothing store and I've treasured it ever since. His jacket, scarf, and this is his hat. I would like to donate it to . . ." The Hard Rock Café in Cannes, France, where it occupies a case of honor.

That's the true story of how I made up a story. So, I'm onstage with Walter Matthau in *A Shot in the Dark* at the Booth Theatre and there is a scene in which I'm about to reveal the result of my investigation — the murderer is the gay butler, who had been carrying on a secret affair with the married chauffeur! As the audience knew, Julie Harris's character, Josefa Lantenay, and I had literally cooked up a plan — we had baked the victim's wedding ring into a bread pudding and at the climax of my brilliant explanation I was to exclaim, "The proof is in the pudding!" And we would produce the wedding ring.

This being a farce the plot couldn't be that obvious. The actual murderer was Walter Matthau, who was in love with Julie Harris and believed she was having an affair with the chauffeur, who really was just using her to cover up his secret affair with the butler, so Matthau's wife, who was in love with the chauffeur, would leave him alone, which is why Matthau had to kill the chauffeur. That's farce. So in the middle of my dramatic discourse in which I explained precisely how I had maneuvered through the twisted turns of the labyrinthine murder plot to reach the inevitable conclusion that the butler did it — all the time being chided by Matthau who believed I was an incompetent idiot — just as I reached the moment at which I was to whirl around and point an accusing finger at the gay butler, unbeknownst to me the gay butler took a sip of poisoned wine and fell face forward into the pudding.

"And so," I exclaimed, whirling around and pointing my finger at the butler now lying dead facedown in the bread pudding, "I can now reveal that . . . the poof is in the pudding!"

Matthau and I just locked eyes. The audience knew that I had blown my line and was waiting to see if either one of us would break up in laughter. But for farce to work it has to be played earnestly. If the characters are in on the joke, if we were to start laughing, the entire suspension of disbelief would disappear, ruining the show. It's an unforgiving moment, the audience had paid their hard-earned dollars to see a farce, the last thing they wanted was laughter.

Walter and I understood that. We were both experienced stage actors. So we froze and we looked at each other. Someone in the audience had giggled at my faux pas. Then someone else tittered. We held it. Someone else laughed, and then another person laughed. Laughter is infectious and it was spreading. And Walter and I didn't move; I barely breathed for fear I would start laughing. Gradually, the audience understood that we were trying desperately not to laugh, which of course is hysterical. The more obvious it became that we were fighting it, the funnier it was to the audience. The titters had become hysterics.

Because I had more water in my cells than Walter, I began to sweat. At first I glistened. I merely shone. But the audience could see the change from the flat pancake makeup to the glisten. Then as I strained to hold it, almost like holding your bowels, the sweat began to come down my face in rivulets.

The twenty-five hundred people in the audience and the actors on the stage were totally aware of what was happening. The challenge was not to laugh. Whatever Walter and I did, we could not laugh. The audience could laugh, Julie Harris turned away from the audience and was laughing, but we must not under any circumstances laugh.

The longer the laughter continued the louder it got. The audience was laughing at the sound of its own laughing. I was meditating on the sound of my own breathing. I was focusing on the sound of my breath going in and out of my lungs, breathing into the knowledge that I could not break up. I was drenched in perspiration, sweat was rolling down my brow and my cheeks. The laughter would begin to die down, and then it would catch hold again. Walter and I did not move. And finally, after at least five minutes, the audience got laugh fatigue, it literally got tired from laughing — and we were able to proceed with the play.

I need to pause here. I've just had a very interesting idea. One of the projects I've been working on for quite some time is called *Gonzo Ballet*. In February 2007, the Milwaukee Ballet created an original ballet set to the music from my CD, *Has Been*, although they named the ballet *Common*

People. Gonzo Ballet is a documentary about the making of the ballet *Common People.* But getting it done has been a long, laborious process that had numerous and unexpected complications. So while there have been numerous documentaries made about the making of a movie or an album or, in this case, a ballet, I don't believe anyone has done a documentary about the making of a documentary about the making of something. And why not?

Think about that while I go put on my makeup for the next chapter.

KVAR

Saluton, a amik, câpitr/o kvar. Ni babilu. Vi? Vi odoras kiel krokodilo. Which in Esperanto means either: Welcome, my friend, to chapter four. I would like to express my gratitude for your support for so many years. Or: Welcome, my friend, to chapter four. Let's chat. You? You smell like a crocodile.

This is a true story. Even I could not make this one up: on a TV show called *The Outer Limits* I'd played an astronaut who returned from Venus having contracted a strange disease which made it impossible for me to get warm. The executive producer of that show was Leslie Stevens, a well-respected writer known primarily for his very strange imagination. Shortly after we'd done that show he called and told me he had a script he wanted me to read. It was called *Incubus* and it was very interesting. The story was compelling in its simplicity and starkness; it was an almost legendary tale of good confronting evil. It was going to be made with a small budget, but it was very powerful; it was so intriguing that after reading it I told him I would do it.

Unfortunately, there was one piece of information I did not have at that time. Perhaps it was my mistake, but the script was written in English so I just assumed the movie would be made in English. When I met with Leslie Stevens he told me he had some very exciting news for me. "Guess what," he said. "We're going to do it in Esperanto!"

Rather than realizing that this idea was *frenezla,* crazy, I thought it sounded interesting. Perhaps I was *frenezla.* I had a vague awareness of Esperanto; the universal language invented in 1887 by Dr. Ludvic Lazarus Zamenhof, using the pseudonym Doktoro Esperanto. It was supposed to be a second language in which the various cultures of the world could come together and truly communicate with each other to reach worldwide peace. Supposedly, Leslie Stevens told me, "There are seven million people around the world who speak Esperanto, and there has never been a picture made in Esperanto."

Never been a film made in this language?

Seven million people speak it? Wow, it did seem like a very good idea. Seven million people would want to see it, that's great box office. Of course, at that point it did not occur to me that of those seven million people who spoke this language, eight of them lived in Cleveland, five were in Cedar Rapids, and there was one guy in Syracuse. There was apparently a large contingent in Liberia but we couldn't reach them because there were no telephones. So it would probably have been less expensive to make individual copies of this film and send them to the Esperanto speakers than show it in a theater. But nobody had thought about that; instead we were all very excited, we were making history!

Obviously no one in the cast actually spoke Esperanto. So we were taken to Esperanto camp, deep in California's redwood forest. We camped outside and in the evening Leslie would lean against a giant redwood, smoke his pipe, and tell us about this movie. We had tutors in Latin and Greek who taught us the proper pronunciation of the words. I was given a script in which the Esperanto was written phonetically on one page and the English translation was on the facing page, so I would have some idea of the emotional context.

During the making of this film Leslie Stevens insisted that everyone, the crew as well as the cast, speak only Esperanto. And naturally that created some difficulties. For example, if Leslie said to a grip, *"A la lumeina puse a sar,"* put the light up there, the grip was like to reply, *"Mi fluido cãcar poop-poop,"* thank you but my car doesn't need carburetor fluid.

This was the only film shoot in history in which no one making the film actually spoke the language in which the film was being made. Leslie directed in Esperanto. Nobody understood anyone else, which accounted for the marvelously strange tone of the film; the somewhat desperate looks on the actors' faces in the meaningful scenes which invoked Fellini or Bergman or Kurosawa, scenes in which the actors looked as if they were attempting to comprehend fate or understand the magnificent works of God — but it wasn't that at all. We were simply trying to figure out what the hell Leslie Stevens was trying to tell us.

The cinematographer was Conrad Hall, who was nominated for eight Academy Awards and won for *Butch Cassidy. Incubus,* as he described it, was "A metaphysical witchcraft picture. Lots of mists and people with horns."

Perhaps the one area in which we did not have any trouble was that no one forgot his lines; although that may have been due to the fact that no one knew their lines, no one understood their lines, and no one knew if anybody else was saying their lines correctly.

My co-star was a truly beautiful young woman named Allyson Ames, who played the role of Kia — the demon, not the car company. She was living with Leslie Stevens, which made my love scenes with her a bit awkward. During those scenes I was never quite certain if Stevens was urging me, "Show more passion, hold her tightly," or warning me, "Keep your hands off her if you know what's good for you." But I will never forget the day Allyson stopped me as I was walking back to the set and said softly, "Bill, *kie estas la necesejo.*"

She was speaking our language. So I directed her to the Port-O-Johns.

The story takes place in a wooded land known as Nomen Tuum. I played a good man who is confronted by a gorgeous succubus who seduces men and then kills them, thus claiming their souls for the devil. But when she truly falls in love with my character, all hell breaks loose. Actually, in this film, literally. That's when they called in the horrible incubus.

Generally, when principal photography on a film is completed it takes a minimum of six months to a year for it to be edited into its final form. But Leslie Stevens decided to screen *Incubus* at the Venice Film Festival, hoping that would create a buzz about the film. In preparation for the festival Italian subtitles were added. When the film was finished I was invited to a screening. More than six months had passed since we'd shot the film, during which I'd done numerous projects, so I'd forgotten every word I'd learned in Esperanto, and I understood no Italian. So I sat there watching this film in which I'd starred, having not the slightest idea what it was about. I didn't understand one word of the dialogue and I couldn't read the Italian subtitles.

Only one other time in my career was I involved in a situation even remotely similar. In the animated film *Over the Hedge* I played Ozzie the Opossum, whose primary survival technique is playing dead, but truly dramatically playing dead. Shatnerian playing dead. Jeffrey Katzenberg, the head of DreamWorks, sent the cast, including Bruce Willis and myself, to the Cannes Film Festival for the premiere of the film. As we were walking up the red carpet, surrounded by photographers, we were introduced to the French actors who had played our characters in the French version. Wait a second, I wondered, we're the stars of this film, right? I knew we were stars, our names were in big letters on the lobby cards and in the credits. But as this is an animated film our faces weren't on the screen, and now our voices were being replaced by French actors. So we were the stars of a film in which we didn't even appear. What were we doing there?

Incubus finally premiered at the San Francisco Film Festival. It received a lot of attention and very little distribution. There is a famous French director and film critic, Henri Chapier, who loved this film and arranged for it to be shown in Paris. The French were quite enthusiastic about it, apparently because they didn't understand a word of it. As it was explained to me, true French film connoisseurs find great meaning in those things they don't understand.

This was certainly the most unusual film in which I've ever been involved. After its release a terrible mistake made in a lab destroyed the negative and all of the prints. Many years later one print was found in the permanent collection of Cinémathèque Française in Paris and digitally remastered for video. I'm very pleased to be able to announce that the DVD is currently available at the online store at WilliamShatner.com for the remarkable price of only $9.95 plus shipping — that's two dollars less than Amazon! And not only that, my friends, if you act now, and you spend more than fifty dollars (not including shipping) it would be my pleasure to include a free — that's right, absolutely free — "Trelane: The Squire of Gothos" nine-inch action figure while supplies last.

When they were preparing the DVD they asked me to provide a narrative about the making of the film. Doing so brought back many memories, including a few words of this language, which unfortunately after the original release of the film seems to have lost its cachet. But as I finished the voice-over and looked at the film, I do remember wondering, as we used to say, ewhat ethe ehell eare ewe edoing ein ethis emeshugana efilm/o?

When I made this film I had been working regularly for almost fifteen years and still didn't have more than eighteen hundred bucks in the bank. I did have three — count 'em — absolutely beautiful daughters, a small house in Los Angeles, and a marriage that was not going very well. It was terribly frustrating, several of the young actors with whom I'd started in television were becoming major movie stars, fine actors like Paul Newman and Steve McQueen, while I was still doing one-shots on TV series and making primarily low-budget movies.

For a time I may have been the hardest-working actor on television. For example, on *The Outlaws* I played a man on the run for a murder I had not committed. In *Robert Herridge Theatre* I was a gunfighter hired to kill the honest sheriff in a one-horse town. I did several *Thrillers*; in one I became obsessed with the reflection of a woman in a mirror found in an old house, which caused me to accidentally kill my wife. In another one I was a desperate man trying to kill my rich aunt and her husband to inherit their fortune. On *Alfred Hitchcock Presents* I pushed my wife off a cliff instead of my mother-in-law. In "The Defenders" on *Studio One,* I accidentally killed a man in a street fight. On *Arrest and Trial* I was an ambitious TV executive planning to kill my way to the top. In *The Virginian* I was a gold miner driven by greed into trying to kill my rivals and in *The Fugitive* I was a psychotic killer.

When I wasn't killing people I was saving them. On *Alcoa Theatre* I was a doctor with serious emotional problems, on *The Nurses* I was a doctor who had to deal with euthanasia, on *Ben Casey* I was an unconventional children's doctor, and on *Dr. Kildare* I was, finally, a patient.

If I wasn't killing them or saving them I was catching them or defending them on *The Defenders* and *Checkmate* and *Burke's Law* and *For the People.* I never stopped working; if it's Tuesday it must be *Naked City.* And I treated each of those parts as if they were equally significant; my work ethic is such that I never made a distinction between an important job and an unimportant job. And one show almost always led to something else.

And the reality is that if you throw enough programming against the wall, some of it is going to get framed and be called art. Certainly one of the most memorable programs I did during that time was a *Twilight Zone* episode entitled "Nightmare at 20,000 Feet." Memorable now in television history, but truthfully I probably wouldn't have remembered too much about it a month and three or four other shows later. The story concerned a . . . Here, let *Twilight Zone* creator Rod Serling describe it: "Portrait of a frightened man. Mr. Robert Wilson, thirty-seven, husband, father, and salesman on sick leave. Mr. Wilson has just been released from a sanitarium where he spent the last six months recovering from a nervous breakdown . . . Tonight, he's traveling all the way to his appointed destination which, contrary to Mr. Wilson's plan, happens to be in the darkest corner of the Twilight Zone."

Basically, as I'm flying home with my wife I look out the window into a raging storm and see a hairy creature at play on the edge of the wing, tearing away at the metal. But when anyone else looks, the creature hides. I know the creature is not a figment of my imagination; I know it, do you hear me, I know it! "Gremlins!" I scream, "Gremlins! I'm not imagining it. He's out there. Don't look, he's not out there now. He jumps away whenever anyone might see him. Except me."

If I persist in screaming that there's a creature playing on the wing at twenty thousand feet my wife will believe I'm having another nervous breakdown and send me back to the crazy house — yet if I don't the plane will be destroyed and all aboard will die. Finally I grab a revolver from a sleeping police officer and kill the creature. The flight ends as I'm taken off the plane in a straitjacket — but as viewers can see I will soon be vindicated, because a portion of the wing has been ripped apart. Or, as Serling explains it so beautifully, "[T]angible manifestation is very often left as evidence of trespass, even from so intangible a quarter as . . . the Twilight Zone." **Do**-do-do-do, **do**-do-do-do, doooooooooooo — ba da da daaaa.

That half-hour has been parodied numerous times, including an episode of *The Simpsons* entitled "Terror at 5 1/2 Feet" in which Bart sees a gremlin tearing apart his school bus, and a music video made by the metal band Anthrax. And when a full-length *Twilight Zone* movie was made in 1983 this episode was one of the three chosen to be remade, with John Lithgow playing my role. They had actually asked me to appear in the film, but I was doing *T.J. Hooker* and couldn't get a release.

Believe me, at the time nobody realized we were making a classic television episode. This was the fifth season of *Twilight Zone* and they were just churning them out. I met Rod Serling, but I certainly didn't get to know him. He always seemed so busy to me, so removed from the actual production, but perhaps he didn't consider working with an actor worth the time it would take.

This was a series in which they spared

every expense. But the writing was so good, as was this script by the great Richard Matheson, that the story overwhelmed the cheap production values. The gremlin was portrayed by an acrobat named Nick Cravat in a ridiculous furry costume; it looked sort of like a distant relative of Chewbacca, and by distant I mean several light-years away. This was such a cheap costume, it looked like the actor was molting. That animal would have been uncomfortable in a tree, much less on the wing of an airplane in flight. It was just unbelievable, everyone knows that a real creature playing on an airplane wing at twenty thousand feet would be considerably more aerodynamically shaped.

But viewers didn't care what the creature looked like, that was the brilliance of the story. They could have put someone out there with a lamp shade on his head and people would have been scared. One reviewer commented that this show "Did for the fear of flying what *Psycho* did for showers."

However, as tribute to this program, you can buy a twelve-inch action figure of the gremlin holding a piece of the wing — in fact, there are two different gremlin action figures, both of them dressed in that same cheesy costume. Not from my store at Will iamShatner.com, of course, but elsewhere.

While I had been offered the lead role in several different TV series, I'd turned them all down. I had been trained in the old school, although that was in the formative years of television so it actually was the new school: a real actor did not sign to do a series because then he couldn't accept the starring role in the Broadway play or Hollywood film that was going to make him a real star. Or, worse, you would become typecast, locked into a specific category of roles which could mean the end of a career. So I had turned down several offers to star in a series — and watched as Richard Chamberlain became a major TV star playing the role I'd turned down as *Dr. Kildare* and Robert Reed became a star playing the role I'd created in "The Defenders." Maybe they had stardom and security and more than eighteen hundred dollars in the bank, but I still had my actor's integrity!

Unfortunately, I was also starting to get typecast — as an actor who starred in meaningful movies that didn't make a lot of money and every TV series from *The Nurses* to *The Man from U.N.C.L.E.* But truthfully, a guaranteed weekly paycheck was beginning to look very enticing. And I was practically a regular on *The Defenders;* I made five appearances on that show and six on *Dr. Kildare.* For someone who didn't want to be tied to a series, I was tied to just about every series — without the publicity or the paycheck. Based on the success of his show featuring father-and-son defense attorneys, *The Defenders* producer Herb Brodkin created another show that told legal stories from the points of view of an older and a younger prosecutor. He asked me to co-star with a fine veteran actor named Howard Da Silva.

This is it, he told me, this is really truly cross-my-heart no kidding honest-to-goodness the show that is going to make you a star. It's your turn, Bill.

Finally. Once again. Of course, this was long before we'd learned the hard reality of life that just before Charlie Brown kicks the football, Lucy is always going to pull it away from him. So I accepted the role of Assistant District Attorney David Koster in Herb Brodkin's *For the People.* It wasn't *The Defenders,* it was better than *The Defenders.* This wasn't a repeat of something that had been done before, at that time this was a new and exciting idea. The trials of a passionate prosecutor, a dedicated man with a single-minded zeal to defend the criminal justice system of the United States of America. And it was perfect for me: I mean, maybe I'd never been inside a real courtroom in my life, but I'd often played a lawyer or a criminal on TV. So I knew the TV legal system inside and out.

Howard Da Silva, who played my understanding boss, had been blacklisted by McCarthy, but somehow managed to retain his idealism. He was a terrific actor and while making this series we became good friends. I loved him. Jessica Walter played my beautiful wife, a free-spirited musician who performed in a classical string quartet. While the scripts focused on my work, they also included plot lines about our family life, which was a very innovative concept at that time. That was as close to a real family life as I was living. We shot thirteen episodes in New York so I had to leave Gloria and our three girls in Los Angeles while I stayed in the city. Working.

For the People was a very good show about meaningful legal issues. *TV Guide* wrote that it was "more compelling" and "probing" than *The Defenders,* and that it put me in the "big leagues" of TV actors. The character I played, as I told a New York reporter, was the kind of dedicated prosecutor who did "a regular Spanish Flamenco heel dance on the toes of anybody who crosses my way."

This was it, for real, this was the show that was going to make me a star. Herb Brodkin was producing it. Not only was Brodkin the most successful producer in live television — he also did the most meaningful programs. We had the finest New York actors and writers and directors. We were considered the companion show to *The Defenders*, a top-rated program. Critics loved the show. Many people were rooting for Howard Da Silva, whose career had been destroyed by the blacklist, and this was his comeback. Justice was going to triumph in real life as well as on the show. The show went on the air in January 1965.

Let me explain what happened this way: They will never be making a twelve-inch action figure of passionate Assistant District Attorney David Koster.

In its great wisdom, CBS decided the perfect time slot for our show was Sunday night at 9 p.m. Now, what other program would every man in America be watching at that time? How about the most popular television program in America? The number-one ranked western, *Bonanza.* Now, sometimes you really do wonder if all the top CBS executives happened to be sitting around after work one day and one of them said, I got a great idea, let's play a big joke on Bill Shatner. We'll spend all this money to make a TV series, we'll make him think that this is reallllllllllly the show that's going to make him a star, and then we'll put it on the air opposite the top-rated show on television. And they all laughed. I never understood why CBS would bother going through all the trouble and expense of hiring talented writers and actors and technicians and then dropping a very good program into the worst time slot in television. *Lamp Unto My Feet* had a better time slot — which I know for certain because I played a Roman soldier who picked up the cape worn by Christ, after which I converted to Christianity, while *For the People* was being run. Test patterns had better time slots.

But I was still optimistic. I figured, maybe people are tired of well-made westerns. *Bonanza* starred my old friend Lorne Greene, whose investment advice years earlier had cost me my five-hundred-dollar life savings. This was my chance to get even with him for uranium.

Got me again. As philosophers like to ask, if a TV show broadcast opposite the number-one program on the air is canceled, does anyone know it? *For the People* never had a chance. After thirteen weeks it was canceled.

Almost every actor goes through periods of great frustration, when you wonder seriously why you're pursuing this often-impossible profession. Usually it happens when you know you've done very good work, when you're proud of what you've accomplished, and no one sees it; it disappears. And when that has happened several times you begin to wonder, what am I doing this for? Am I wasting my life? I was born in 1931, right into the Great Depression. While I don't remember details, I can remember the sense of desperation that seemed to pervade our lives. My father gladly accepted responsibility for many members of his family and it was the money he gladly shared that helped keep many of them alive. I had the same sense of responsibility, and there were many nights I lay thrashing in bed wondering how I was going to support my wife and our children, how I was going to make the mortgage payment. The reality of my situation was pretty cold: I was constantly struggling to support my family, I was living from job to job with no security, and talent didn't seem to make any difference between success and failure. Believe me, there were times when I thought about giving it up, when I never dreamed that someday I might achieve the kind of success that would lead to Howard Stern inviting me to join him in his famous homo room.

Actually, *For the People* was not the first series in which I starred, just the first one that got on the air in America. In 1963 I had been hired by producer Selig J. Seligman to star in a weekly series as Alexander the Great. Seligman, who had actually been an attorney at the Nuremberg Trials, was then producing the successful World War II series *Combat!* And although I didn't realize it, *Alexander the Great* was intended to be *Combat!* in drag. It was going to be a big costume drama in which the men wore little loincloths and the women carried trays of grapes and wine and wore as little as permissible.

We filmed the two-hour pilot in Utah — for six months. Adam West and John Cassavetes were also featured in the cast. I rarely do any research beyond reading the script, but in this case I saturated myself in the lore of Alexander the Great. And I was enthralled by him. What an extraordinary human being. What a truly inspiring life he led. How can this show miss, I thought? It's got action and adventure and beautiful women and guys fighting on horseback —

and it's based on fact. Perhaps it wasn't as exciting as a hillbilly family moving to Beverly Hills or a Martian sorting out life on Earth, premises for two of the most popular shows then on the air, but nothing like it had ever been done before on television.

I had yet to figure out that by this time when something hadn't been done on television, there probably was a good reason it hadn't been done on television.

Alexander was a soldier and a philosopher, taught by Aristotle, who marched his army over twenty thousand miles in eleven years, conquering most of the known world. He never lost a battle and introduced a common language — no, not Esperanto — and currency to a great part of that region, before dying at thirty-two years old. Coincidentally, I was precisely the same age he was when he died.

I spent more than a year preparing to play this role. This time I believed this role could make me a star. I worked out with weights and got myself in the best physical shape of my life. This is when I learned how to shoot a bow and arrow. I learned the elements of sword fighting and I learned how to ride a horse at a gallop bareback because Alexander had disdained a saddle as being too weak for his manliness! I learned how to do a flying mount, swinging up onto a horse from the side while it's moving. And I worked with an expert horse trainer, for example, to learn how to mount a horse from the rear, which is very difficult and can be dangerous and unusually painful. Let me give you a little bit of advice here: horses do not like to be mounted from the rear. They do not come equipped with a rearview mirror and, like any animal, they don't like to be surprised from behind where they are defenseless. But I learned how to do it.

Seligman wanted this show to be as historically accurate as possible. I had been outfitted in the hardened leather armor Alexander would have worn. During a pause on the second day of shooting, as I walked along holding the reins of a beautiful saddle-bred five-gaited champion, the director approached me with a worried look on his face and told me we had to reshoot a scene we'd done the day before. "We lost the sound when you were leaning over the dying soldier and saying kind words," he explained. "All that leather you're wearing is creaking and we can't hear the dialogue."

I looked out over all that I could survey of the hardened plains of Utah, dressed as

Alexander had been dressed, holding a horse that could have been his legendary horse Bucephalus, and I thought, I'm talking about a problem that Alexander had to have dealt with because they rode at night. They would ride great distances at a great pace, binding their horses' hooves in rags, and make silent forays into the camp of the enemy. In a flash I knew that Alexander had told his aides, "The noise we're making with our leather armor is warning our enemy. We've got to do something about it."

At that moment history came alive for me, it all sort of mystically came together.

Of course, Alexander didn't have to deal with sensitive microphones and studio executives. There wasn't too much we could do about the problem — they made some technical adjustments.

The pilot episode opened with a sonorous voice-over, proclaiming, "Persia, 2,297 years ago. A land of rock . . ." Unfortunately, Seligman couldn't sell the pilot of a show taking place in a land of rock to the networks and eventually recut it to movie length. Released as a theatrical film in Europe, it was very successful. But by the time it was finally shown on American television, to be accurate the voice-over should have begun, "Persia, 3,001 years ago . . ." With so much wonderful historic material to work with, the scripts were just riddled with clichés. Now, perhaps if we had put Alexander in a time machine and had him transported to Beverly Hills where we could see his wacky adventures, that show might have worked, but this show did not.

I took a lot of pride in the fact that I did all of my own stunts. Except for those truly dangerous stunts that require a stuntman with experience, that's something I've done throughout most of my career. Over the years I've done a lot of fighting, tumbling, running, jumping, car stunts, and unique tricks. I've always believed that doing the physical work, the stunts, is part of the actor's job — but it has to be done safely. The safety of the star is always foremost in everyone's mind. Not because they love you, but if you hurt your left pinky and can't make the next shot, it's going to cost the producers a lot of money. So generally they don't let the star do anything unsafe.

The reality is that even the most basic stunts can be very dangerous. On *Gunsmoke* I played a bad guy involved in a shoot-out with a deputy sheriff. According to the script, just before the shooting started one of my fellow bad guys was supposed to grab me around the neck and use me as a shield.

In the story I was shot and my life was saved by a Quaker family; I convinced the family that I was the good-guy victim — until their beautiful daughter fell in love with the deputy.

In this instance no one promised this story was going to make me a star.

The actor playing the other bad guy was a big man, who looked crazy. That's why they hired him, because he looked crazy. As it turned out, he looked that way because he was crazy. When we started shooting he grabbed me around the neck and actually started strangling me. I couldn't breathe. This was truly the serious actor's nightmare: I was going to die — on *Gunsmoke.* I grabbed him by the thumb and yanked him around. I was literally fighting for my life.

A similar thing happened many years later — when I saved Oddjob's life. Harold Sakata, who had created the memorable James Bond villain Oddjob in *Goldfinger,* was working with me in a low-budget film entitled *Impulse,* a title that had been changed from *Want a Ride, Little Girl?* I played your basic homicidal maniac, who is forced to try to kill a young girl after she sees me killing an old prison buddy. Harold was a huge man with no neck, he was just shoulders and a head. In this particular scene he chased me through a car wash and I managed to escape by climbing up onto a roof; when he walked by below me I threw a lasso over him and yanked him up. As he's being strangled I jump off the roof, hit him several times, then escape.

The stunt coordinator rigged Harold with a harness under his shirt which was connected to a steel cable. To the camera it appeared that I was pulling him up by the rope, but in fact he was being lifted by the cable. We practiced it several times, rope, pull, up, looks good. Then we rolled cameras.

I dropped the loop over his head and yanked him up. I jumped down to the ground and looked at him dangling three feet in the air, struggling to get loose. He was making terrible choking sounds. Boy, I thought, I hadn't realized he was such a good actor. He sounds like he's really choking. I punched him rat-tat-tat in the gut a few times and took off. And as I started running a thought struck me: Wait a second, he's actually choking. In real life one would probably have screamed, "Help!" but as this was on a movie set I yelled, "Cut! Cut!" and ran back to help him. Harold weighed about three hundred pounds but somehow I managed to lift his body enough to reduce the pressure on his trachea, enabling him to breathe, and then held him up until they cut him loose. I don't know where I got the strength, but I broke my finger holding him. Because we were filming on a tight schedule I didn't want to stop to see a doctor, so my finger never healed correctly.

The most serious injury I've ever suffered doing a stunt took place when we were filming an episode of my series *T.J. Hooker* in Hawaii. We were shooting a fight scene on the top of a hill overlooking, I believe, the North Shore and the Pacific Ocean. It was about a thousand-foot drop off the edge straight down into the ocean. Now, I admit it, I'm afraid of heights. It's a very odd sensation; I can fly an ultralight or pilot an acrobatic airplane or a glider, I've parachuted and I've been skydiving, I've stood alone on a plateau — but if I'm standing on the third floor of a hotel looking down I can lose it. I'm terrified I'm going to fall.

This scene had been carefully choreographed by the stunt coordinator. We'd rehearsed it several times: the villain and I are fighting on the top of this hill, he knocks me down, and I roll to the precipice, right to the edge, then he takes a sword — a sword! — and slashes at my head. His sword comes down just to the right of my head, I move my head to the left, then he slashes to my left and I move my head to the right. Right-left, right-left. Got it? Got it.

Finally it was time to shoot. My problem was that I had to be at the very edge of this cliff. So I laid down on my back about eight feet from the edge and crawled backward so I could get to the edge without looking down. I was truly frightened. I could have been attached to a cable, but I didn't want to do that; instead another stuntman was holding my leg. We went through the action in slow motion, "You're going to my right, I'll go to my left. Raise the sword. You're going to my left, I'll go to my right. Okay, let's do it, and please, let's get it right the first time because I don't want to be here any longer than I have to."

All right, ready, roll film, action. Now, I have never been certain whether I was to blame or if it was the stuntman's fault. I went one way, he went the same way and he slashed me right in the forehead. I started bleeding. I mean, really bleeding. The stuntman was mortified. "Oh jeez," he said. "We gotta get you to a hospital."

"I'm not going anywhere. I'm never going to be able to get this close to the edge again. Just patch me up and let's get this done."

"But there's a flap of skin . . ."

"I'm not moving. Push it back, tape it down, and put my hair over it." They stopped the bleeding and wiped off the blood. The second stuntman was still holding my leg. I hadn't moved.

And then I noticed the first stuntman glaring at me. Now that I was okay he was free to get angry at me for messing up the stunt; I'd made him look bad, he'd hurt the star. And then he picked up the sword again . . .

When we finally finished shooting the scene I said, "Drag me out of here." Because I was still too terrified to move.

I couldn't possibly even guess the number of stunt fights I've had in my career. I was actually pretty good at it. The key, I learned early, was knowing how to fall. And I'd learned that taking judo lessons. The proper way to fall is to expand your arms so that your entire body hits the ground at the same time. That spreads the energy of the fall. That's what professional wrestlers do. It makes a great thumping sound too. If you want to roll when you hit the ground you've got to hit the ground with a curved arm so you're actually a hub. You roll on your arms and there's no pain whatsoever.

Stunt falling requires a lot of training because you have to be able to sense where your body is in space, which enables you to anticipate the impact and properly distribute your energy. And when done correctly it looks painfully real. In the movie *Showtime* with Eddie Murphy and Robert De Niro, I played myself as T.J. Hooker teaching real cops standard TV cop procedures. In one scene I was supposed to show Eddie Murphy how to leap over the hood of a car — but I decided to make it look as if I hurt my back showing him how to do it without getting hurt. The first time I did it I rolled across the hood and fell behind the car. As I got up crew members were running over to me — it had looked so real they thought I was hurt and had stopped shooting.

People do get hurt in stunt fights. Actors get excited and lose their sense of space and have hit stuntmen. A lot of stuntmen are afraid of actors because they get crazed. Even I've gotten hit by other actors in fights. I always keep my punches short. As long as the camera is behind you the punches only have to travel six inches to look real. Once I became a leading man I don't remember ever losing a fight. While making *Star Trek* I was fighting all the time; I'd fight two men, three men at a time, and I would beat all of them. I was a very tough stunt fighter, as long as I had morality and the script on my side.

I was such a good stunt fighter I've even fought with myself on several different programs and movies. On *Star Trek,* for example, we occasionally ended up with two Kirks battling it out. In a movie called *White Comanche* I played half-breed Indian twin brothers who had to fight to the death. In those instances one of me was a stuntman whose body vaguely resembled mine and we shot over his shoulder. So perhaps I could have played both Caesar and Brutus in the Julius Caesar musical I wanted to make in *Free Enterprise.*

In fact, I was such a good stunt fighter that I almost got myself badly hurt. When my daughters were teenagers the four of us went to a go-cart track. They were very pretty young women and naturally they attracted teenage boys. As my girls rode along these boys were zipping back and forth, trying to cut them off, doing anything to get their attention. I was riding behind my daughters, trying to protect them. I was being the old bull, protective of the herd, trying to keep these young bucks from cutting in.

Finally I herded my daughters off the track and these three teenaged boys came over to us and started acting like young adolescents. Now I know that eighteen years old is an interesting age for boys, emotionally they're still kids, but they've got the physical presence of men. Of course, having teenaged girls I didn't quite understand that. So I stood up to those kids, demanding, "What do you think you were doing with my daughters? You keep that up you're going to kill somebody."

"Yeah? Who's gonna stop us?" Obviously they were real wiseguys.

I wasn't going to take that from these . . . kids. I took a bold step forward. And suddenly I thought, I can take all three of these guys. I'd been fighting stuntmen for decades. Just a week or so earlier Leonard Nimoy and I had taken six stuntmen. Just the two of us. We'd beaten six tough men. In my mind I began to plan my strategy, so when I went into action I wouldn't make any missteps. As Kirk I'd often done a fighting stunt in which I leaped into the air with a double-scissor kick and pushed off against a stuntman's chest. He would reel backward into a wall which knocked him out cold, while I hit the ground and rolled, then hit the second bad guy with an elbow and then . . .

Wait a second, I realized. That's pretend. Then I remembered Newton's third law: For every action there's an equal and opposite reaction. If I actually leaped into the air and pushed off against someone's chest, absolutely nothing is going to happen to him but I'm going to fall onto the floor. So if I tried to do that to these kids, they were not going to go reeling backward and be knocked unconscious. I was going to end up on the ground and they were going to kick me. And I would get hurt.

That certainly wasn't a good idea. So instead I began thinking about employing diplomacy. Kirk had often been called upon to use diplomacy to prevent one world from . . .

I do remember the most truly dangerous stunt I ever did. For real. What I don't remember is why I did it. We were making an ABC Sunday Night Movie called *Disaster on the Coastliner.* The *Coastliner* was a train set on a collision course by a deranged engineer attempting to avenge the accidental deaths of his wife and daughter — and among the passengers were the vice president's wife and daughter. We were filming on a deserted stretch of track in Connecticut. I played a con man with a heart of gold plating. In a key scene I had to stand on top of a speeding diesel locomotive and fight a stuntman while a helicopter was trying to swoop down and rescue me. When I

189

read the script I thought it was an impressive stunt, but I didn't know how they intended to do it.

When we started filming I asked the director, "How are we going to do this? Are we going back to the studio to do a green screen?" When he admitted he hadn't figured it out yet, I suggested, "Well, why don't we do it in real life?"

It was let's-put-on-a-play-in-the-barn, boys and girls, time. I have no idea what I was thinking when I said that.

His face lit up. "Really?"

"Yeah. Sure, why not?" Why not? Because I could have gotten killed, that's why not. But listening to myself talk I started getting excited. "Here's what we'll do. The train'll go five miles an hour and I'll get up on top and you can get some close-ups, then you can speed up the film and it'll look like a real fight."

"Really?" I think he was as stunned as I should have been. But there was a difference between the two of us. I was the one climbing up on top of the train. He was the sane one. "Okay," he said enthusiastically. "Let's do it. You go ahead and climb up there."

The problem, I quickly discovered, was that this was a diesel engine, meaning there was no smokestack, nothing to which we could attach safety cables. It's aerodynamic, flat. The only way I could be attached to a safety cable was to run the cable down the side of the engine through the window. But then we realized if we did that and I fell the cable would just drag me alongside the train. A bad second choice. So we couldn't use safety cables. I decided to do it anyway.

Really? The director was thrilled I was willing to do this stunt.

Finally I got up on top of the train. Admittedly, I was scared. As it rolled along at five miles an hour the director was in a car driving alongside with three cameras in it. We shot the whole fight scene. I took a deep breath when I got down to the ground. "How was it?" I asked the director.

He frowned. "Well, it looks like we're going five miles an hour."

Then I heard myself thinking, Hey, I'm the star. Stars don't get hurt. And then I heard myself saying to him, "Okay, let's try it again. We can go a little faster."

Now why would I say that? Why would I risk my life for a Sunday Night Movie? What could I have been thinking? Directors had been shooting similar scenes since the early days of film without it being necessary for an actor to stand on top of a moving train.

There were many ways of getting that shot. "Really?" the director said enthusiastically.

I climbed back up on top. Seven miles an hour became ten, became twenty . . . suddenly I was standing on top of a diesel locomotive going almost forty miles an hour and we were approaching a sharp curve in the track and beyond that was a low bridge. Wait a second, I'm an actor. What am I doing standing on top of a diesel locomotive racing forty miles an hour toward a trestle? At that speed the wind was so strong I had to bend forward into it just to remain upright. The wind was coming right up my pants legs, trying to lift me. The helicopter was starting to swoop down on me. In my role I was supposed to be frightened. Believe me, in that situation it did not require a lot of acting ability to look scared.

When we finished the scene the director told me proudly, "I got it." Reviewers wrote that the scene "looked real." Looked real? It *looked* real?

But when it comes to real stunts, absolutely nothing I've ever done was more realistic than co-starring with actress Tiffany Bolling and five thousand live tarantulas in the classic horror film *Kingdom of the Spiders.* Oh, the things I've done for my art.

It was a typical horror film plot; thousands of angry and hungry tarantulas attack an isolated town. I played veterinarian Rack Hansen, who desperately tries to warn the mayor that we needed to bring in the tarantulas' worst enemy, rats and birds, and lots of them, to save the town. Unfortunately, the mayor protests that letting loose legions of rats to attack thousands of tarantulas might affect business at the forthcoming country fair. As it turned out, that was a fair to remember.

We filmed in the small town of Cape Verde, Arizona. Just imagine the reaction of the townspeople when they found out a motion picture was being made there: Wow! That's incredible, a film being made in our small town. It'll be great for business . . .

. . . and they're bringing thousands of *what* with them? Often when making a movie on location the crew has difficulty keeping interested spectators out of the background. This, however, was not a problem on this particular shoot. Lock up your families, five thousand tarantulas are coming to town.

Before being given this role I had to sign an agreement that I would work with spiders. I didn't mind that — tarantulas don't kick you in the pants, bang you on the shoulder, or refuse to speak their lines.

Besides, as I learned, tarantulas have had very bad PR. They're actually not very dangerous, a tarantula sting is a little less painful than a bee sting — although they do make you itch. But I had a good concept for a stunt, I wanted to fall into the shot with a tarantula on my face — and then have it walk off so the audience would know that it was alive. The problem was how to keep the tarantula on my face as I fell. I began experimenting with glue, trying to determine precisely how much glue it required to keep the tarantula on my face as I fell, but still allow it to walk off my face.

It's an interesting question for an actor: Which is worse, standing on top of a speeding locomotive without any kind of safety cable or gluing tarantulas to your face?

It took me six tries to figure out how much glue I needed to make it work. And when we shot the scene it worked perfectly. Actually, once I got used to working with the spiders it didn't bother me at all; what did bother me was the fact that a lot of these spiders died making this film — you could actually hear them being squished when cars ran over them. And I didn't like working with the rat. This was a trained rat that had an invisible monofilament leash on it so it couldn't get loose — until it did get loose and jumped on me.

But perhaps the most difficult stunt I've ever done was a nude scene with gorgeous Angie Dickinson in Roger Corman's film *Big Bad Mama.* As the posters promised, the essence of this film was Hot Lead! Hot Cars! Hot Dames! Hot Damn! It was Roger Corman's "tribute" to *Bonnie and Clyde,* with a little more violence and a lot more skin, and it proved forever that Angie Dickinson is not a natural blonde.

Angie Dickinson played a gun-totin' mama who robbed banks with her two sexy young daughters; I was a con man who went along for the ride. And Angie Dickinson. Oh, she was a magnificent woman. Smart and beautiful. As a total package she was delicious. We did this film just before she became a TV star on *Police Woman.* They had already been filming for about two weeks before I arrived on the set. The only person I knew on the set was Roger Corman. The very first scene Angie Dickinson and I were going to shoot together was a love scene which required both of us to be totally naked. I wasn't overly concerned about working nude; let's be honest, I was working with Angie Dickinson, who was going to be looking at my body? Most people weren't even going to notice I was in the scene.

Before we shot we had a table reading with Roger Corman. Angie was very reluctant to do this scene. "I don't know about this nudity," she said. "You know, I've never been naked in front of a camera before. I'm very apprehensive."

Roger calmed her down. "Okay, Angie, here's what we'll do. We'll just close the set. We'll just do it with the minimum crew. We'll eliminate anybody who really doesn't have to be there."

"All right," she agreed. "But Roger, please, I don't want anybody else there. I don't want to look up in the rafters and see people looking at me."

Corman gave his word. "It'll just be you, Bill, me, and the cinematographers."

She smiled. "That's okay, then."

Roger turned to me. "How 'bout you, Bill? Are you okay with it?"

"If she's all right with it, it's fine with me. My only worry is that I'm going to get an erection."

Everybody laughed, assuming I was kidding. I wasn't. I was going to be in bed with a gorgeous naked woman. Not getting an erection was going to be very . . . hard. Normally when I was going to do a scene or a stunt I knew how to prepare for it. But in this situation I really didn't know what not to do.

We shot the scene that afternoon. Angie and I walked onto the set wearing bathrobes. "I'm so nervous," she told me.

"Don't be," I said, meanwhile trying to think about anything except the fact that this beautiful woman was completely naked beneath that robe.

"Okay, everybody," Roger said loudly. "Let's clear the set, please. Everybody off the set, and I mean everybody. I don't want to see anybody except Paul behind the camera. Come on, let's move it. Close the doors behind you, please."

Angie focused on my eyes, and then shyly let her bathrobe drop onto the floor. I stood there in awe. I was looking at the perfection of the female body. This was an ode to the beauty of woman. Her silken skin flowed mellifluously over her hips into the rising swells of her ripened breasts, her long blond hair just barely covering her . . .

But let me pause here for just one moment to tell you about something particularly meaningful to me. More than twenty years ago I attended a charity horse show at the Los Angeles Equestrian Center. It was a wonderful evening. The funds raised that night were contributed to a hospital at USC. Afterward I learned that the women running this show had decided that this would be its final year. I thought, if these women can run a horse show, why can't I? I'll get some people to help me and do this. In 1990 I renamed it the Hollywood Charity Horse Show. But then I needed to find a primary charity to be the recipient of the money we raised.

Fate intervened. One afternoon I was standing on the balcony of the equestrian center and when I looked into the ring I saw a demonstration that changed my life. An obviously severely handicapped child was sitting on a horse; a handler was leading the horse around the ring as spotters walked on either side of this child. This was the first time I had ever seen riding therapy. This was my introduction to a program called Ahead with Horses.

As I learned, when a physically or emotionally handicapped child sits astride a horse something magical transpires. Kids who can't walk get motion. Kids who can't talk garble something to the horse. Kids who have difficulty relating to the world somehow communicate with these horses. I saw children who literally could not hold up their heads lead horses through intricate exercises. Watching these children interact with horses will move people beyond tears. You see these children who have been afflicted with terrible handicaps just blossom, you see them smile and laugh.

I'd found my charity. So since 1990 the Hollywood Charity Horse Show has raised funds to support Ahead with Horses. A few years later we began adding other charities, among them Camp Max Straus, a summer camp especially for inner-city kids with physical, emotional, behavioral, or social interaction problems that would make it almost impossible for them to attend traditional camps.

The Wells Fargo — they have become the primary sponsor — Hollywood Charity Horse Show usually takes place in late April. In addition to a silent auction, top-notch entertainment, and an arena show, we serve a wonderful dinner. Tickets are expensive, in 2007 they were $250, but every dollar — not *almost* every dollar — *every single dollar* goes directly to our charities.

So if you'd like to make a difference in a child's life, please visit www.Horseshow.org for details. Now let us return to Angie Dickinson's naked body.

The set had been almost completely

cleared. I pulled back the covers of the bed and slid into it. "Wait a second," Angie said loudly. "You know what, Roger, I think we need the makeup people."

Roger yelled, "Get George back in here. Tell him he can stay."

"And the lighting director. We definitely need him."

"Fred, come on back in too."

"And the grips, maybe they should stay here too. Oh, and you know what? Sound, we've got to have the sound men here, don't we?"

I propped myself up on my elbow. Eventually she named just about everyone on the entire crew — you can stay, let him stay, you'd better stay. The only person she didn't name was a craft services guy — someone who served lunch — and he wandered off the set but snuck back on later.

Finally we shot the scene. It wasn't nearly as . . . hard as I had feared. Everything was so technical. Move your nose jusssst a little to the left, please, that's good. Now put your arm down. Now just move back and forth, wait wait wait, your arm's in the wrong place. Makeup! Please touch up Angie's eye shadow, thank you.

By the mid-1960s I was no longer even being offered parts that were going to make me a star. Gloria and I were living in a comfortable home — with the requisite pool — in Sherman Oaks with our three girls, Leslie, Melanie, and Lisbeth. Truthfully, I was struggling. It seemed like the more I worked the further behind I got. My parents would come down from Montreal to see their grandchildren and I can vividly remember my father sitting by the pool and asking me, "So? How are you doing?"

I told him the truth. "It's tough, Dad. I got the mortgage, I got all the things the girls need . . ."

"Can I help you?" he asked.

I probably smiled at that offer. "Dad," I told him, "you don't have enough money to help me."

I really didn't know what I was going to do. I felt trapped: I was doing what I had dreamed of doing, working as an actor. I'd appeared on Broadway and in important movies and on every respected television show. I'd worked with the best producers and writers and directors. I'd gotten many superb reviews and even won awards — but I wasn't earning enough money to support my family. Had I been single, with few responsibilities, I would have been fine. So I began to wonder if this was the time to find another career.

If there was something else I could have done, this was the time I would have done it. What I could not possibly know then was I was ending one chapter of my life, but another vitally important chapter was about to begin. That was chapter five.

FIVE

After the pilot for the *Alexander the Great* series failed to get picked up and the very well-reviewed *For the People* was canceled after thirteen episodes, I did a third series pilot for which I had little hope. I was much more excited about starring in a beautiful play entitled *The Hyphen,* which had been written especially for me by Norman Corwin. I so admired Corwin, who was regarded as the greatest playwright in radio; at McGill I'd performed in all of his plays.

A few years earlier he'd written the film *Lust for Life,* for which he'd been nominated for an Academy Award for Best Screenplay, Kirk Douglas had been nominated as Best Actor, and Anthony Quinn had won the Oscar for Best Supporting Actor. Norman just called me out of the blue and asked me to play the lead role in this play. My role was that of a scientist who was visited by a fairy, who had come to show me that the world is much more than a collection of scientific facts. We opened at the University of Utah, in Salt Lake City, and received tremendous reviews, and we were planning to take it to New York.

While we were getting the play ready to move to New York my agent called to tell me that NBC had decided to pick up the pilot. My first series was actually going on the air. Perhaps you've heard of it. It's called . . . *Star Trek*?

Well, if you haven't heard of it apparently you've been living in a cave on a remote atoll somewhere in the South Pacific or have been participating in some bizarre experiment. *Star Trek* is arguably the best known, most enduring, and influential television series ever produced. If you haven't actually seen an episode of this show, perhaps you might have run across some of the merchandise? Some of the estimated two *billion* dollars' worth of *Star Trek* merchandise that has been sold. Maybe you've seen one of the many dozens of collectible models of the Starship *Enterprise,* including the *Wrath of Khan* battle-damaged *Enterprise,* some models which light up or play recordings of my character, Captain James Tiberius Kirk; or the series of dozens of collectible plates including twentieth-anniversary editions of

"Amok Time," "Journey to Babel," "Piece of the Action," "The Trouble with Tribbles," or the twenty-fifth-anniversary Mr. Spock, Captain Kirk, Chekov, Mr. Sulu (with or without a certificate), a 3D McCoy plate and a 3D Scotty plate as well as Classic Kirk, Classic Uhura, and Classic Spock plates; or the Starfleet Academy T-shirt, DJ Spock T-shirt, Captain Kirk "Risk Is Our Business" T-shirt and the infant/toddler T-shirt; the Starfleet Academy mug, disappearing image transporter mug, the "I Slept with Kirk" mug and "I Slept with Kirk" large mug, the *Enterprise* stein, the tankard, collection of glasses, Icee cups, and glow-in-the-dark cups; the complete DVD sets of the original series, *Star Trek: The Next Generation, Star Trek: Deep Space Nine, Star Trek: Voyager, Star Trek: The Animated Series,* or videos of the ten *Star Trek* feature films; numerous recordings of the music; the literally thousands of different action figures, among them nine- and twelve-inch clothed figures, the twelve-inch classic edition Chekov, twelve-inch Dr. McCoy, and twelve-inch Engineer Scott, the nine-inch Kirk Casual Attire and the nine-inch Command Edition Captain Kirk, the five-inch fuzzy Tribbles, six-inch Mirror Scotty Ltd. Edition, seven-inch Commander Kirk and

Command Chair, the Dr. McCoy Action Figure European Special Edition, fourteen-inch porcelain Dolls from Hamilton Collectibles and Acrylic Sculptures; the United Federation of Planets blanket; Limited Edition Hand Phaser Prop replica kit, limited edition fortieth-anniversary bronze Phaser and the Danbury Mint Gold-Plated Laser; "Her Name is *Enterprise*" Journal; over one hundred novels including *Ashes of Eden,* hundreds of comic books and magazines and guides; *Star Trek* trading card sets from more than a dozen different manufacturers, including cards with glossy finishes, 3D cards, moving-picture cards, holographic picture cards, autographed cards, and even gold-plated cards, as well as playing card sets and trading card tins and card holders; visible Klingon postcards; *Star Trek* scripts; annual Christmas tree ornaments; the "Trek Chicks Rock" trucker's hat; Franklin Mint chess set, checkers set, 3D chess set in pewter, 3D chess set in wood; dozens of different watches, including the twenty-fifth-anniversary watch and video game watch, wall clock, desk clock, alarm clock, and traveling clock; the Evil Spock "Screw York Logic" women's cap and T-shirt and Evil Spock T-shirt; snow globes; dartboard; limited edition gold stamp, commemorative stamp book; endless thousands of autographed photographs; film cell art including Mr. Spock and Captain Kirk pictured next to the Golden Gate Bridge surrounded by four film cells; sets of movie posters; *Enterprise* telephones and telephone and address books; silver coins; ties; the Spock decanter; commemorative spoons; pins; matchbooks; plastic rings; dice; numerous different jigsaw puzzles from twenty-five pieces to a thousand pieces; *Enterprise* earrings; belt buckles; a pocket knife; lunch boxes; a rubber doormat and a mouse pad; photon torpedo candies, numerous key rings and key chains; bookplates and bookmarks; wanted posters; wrapping paper; party invitations; cocktail napkins; dozens of different Halloween costumes "for children of all ages," latex masks and Spock ears; life-size cardboard stand-ups; a command bridge model; Frisbees; kites; View-Master sets; wrist communicators; sticker sets and sticker books; a disc gun; water pistol; space flashlight; yoyos; hand-held electronic games; Spock bop-bag; interactive VCR board game; *Star Trek* the game; *Star Trek* trivia game; Silly Putty; freezicle kit; Super Phaser Target Game; easy painting sets, coloring books, activity books; marbles; pen and pencil sets and pencil boxes; handheld pinball game, window scenes set, soft poseable figures; Mego play bridge; Klingon Disruptor Figure; *Enterprise* glider; bread cards; puzzle boards, sticker books; telephone cards from dozens of countries around the world, including the United States, Germany, Chile, Estonia, Holland, and Austria; piggy banks; CD holders and albums; coasters; holograms; velvet paintings; motion-picture props; fan club and convention magazines; kitchen aprons, lighters; bobble-head dolls; a wallet, raincoats and umbrellas; swivel belt-clip phaser holster . . .

Star Trek grew to become better known than any television series in history. It was broadcast on network television for only three years, there were only seventy-nine episodes, but for reasons that many wise men have tried for many years to explain, it eventually gained a great and extraordinarily loyal following. Small fan clubs grew into conventions that attracted as many as twenty thousand people, many of them dressed as their favorite characters and villains. It has generated more than two billion dollars in merchandise sales, Google lists 1.3 million sites for *Star Trek* merchandise, and at any time eBay generally has more than twelve thousand items for sale. And the actors, in particular myself and Leonard

Nimoy, became among the most recognized people in the world.

For example, just before the shah of Iran was deposed in 1979 I was invited by his government to participate in a photography safari, in which we would shoot pictures of a black leopard at night. The shah had set up wilderness preserves to allow animals native to that area to survive and prosper. So we drove several hundred miles outside the capital of Tehran to this beautiful wilderness. We drove along the Caspian Sea where fisherman were using techniques a thousand years old to catch sturgeon. And finally we came to this small village on the seacoast. The area we were in had been part of the Ottoman Empire; for centuries nomadic tribes had swept down from Russia to stop there on their wanderings. The village in which we stopped had possibly been an oasis at one time, but now it consisted of a single street with perhaps three stores and a kabob house. Our guide asked if we wanted to stop for a kabob. Well, of course we did. This was truly outside civilization as I knew it to be and I wanted to experience as much of it as possible. We walked into this restaurant, it was a shed really, it had no more than six uncovered wooden tables and badly worn chairs. There were several men sitting there, one of them a Turkoman, a large man made larger because he was wearing the traditional Turkoman garb: the tall black bear hat, a red jacket with sashes through it, and high black boots. He looked right at me for a moment, then turned and looked toward the back of this small room. There was a small black-and-white television set sitting on top of a cabinet — and that set was showing *Star Trek.* This Turkoman waved his kabob through the air and declared, as if it were perfectly normal to see me sitting in a kabob house in a village on the Caspian Sea, "Captain Kirk!"

Star Trek was the most wonderful thing that ever happened to me. I look back upon it as the miracle that changed my life. In fact, it has changed your life, too. All the extraordinary opportunities I've been given since that time can be traced directly to that series. So if I hadn't done *Star Trek* none of the things that followed would have happened, therefore you wouldn't be reading this book. To fill the time you're spending reading it, you would have had to find other things to do. And your life would be different.

It continues to astonish me how many people know it so well. And know me. In 2001 I was producing and directing a low-budget film named *Groom Lake.* We were shooting in the small town of Bisbee, Arizona, which is about twenty miles from the Mexican border and a popular crossing point for illegal immigrants. One night while I was working, my now-wife, Elizabeth Shatner, was invited by a border patrolman to ride along the border on horseback with him.

It was a very unusual experience, she told me. So several nights later Liz and I went on patrol along the Mexican border. We began by driving deep into the Sonoran Desert until we reached a campfire where horses were waiting for us. Even though we were in the desert it was very cold and we were wearing heavy jackets and Western hats. There was no moon that night and we could barely see twenty feet in front of us. The agents gave us their night goggles; when we put them on everything appeared in a greenish tint. Then we rode into the night. The agents stayed on foot; we trailed about fifty yards behind them.

In a sense this was like a sad game in which everyone was playing a role. The agents knew from experience where the Mexicans were going to try to cross the border. Suddenly the agents started running and our horses started galloping behind them. Within minutes the agents had rounded up about twenty-five Mexicans who had just crossed the border. By the time we got there the Mexicans were squatting on the ground, listening to the agent. "Look," he told them. "You're going back across the border. Don't come back this way."

Liz and I were sitting up on our horses, bundled into jackets, hats on our heads, wearing these goggles that covered most of our faces. And suddenly, one of these illegal immigrants looked at me, first with curiosity, then with recognition, and said finally in a heavily accented English, "That is Captain Kirk?" Then he smiled and asked, "We have autograph?"

Obviously I never dreamed that any of this would happen when I did the pilot. If I had I would have done it much sooner. *Star Trek* was created by an experienced television writer named Gene Roddenberry. In his proposal to NBC he described his show as *Wagon Train* — a very successful Western series about the adventures of a wagon train as it rolled west — to the stars. Initially Roddenberry wanted Lloyd Bridges to play the lead role of Captain Pike, and when Bridges turned him down the part went to Jeffrey Hunter, who was best known for playing Jesus Christ in the movie *King of Kings.* The pilot also starred an actor named Leonard Nimoy playing an alien named Mr. Spock. As Leonard remembers Roddenberry telling him, "I've got this alien and I want him to look kind of satanic." Basically that consisted of a severely curved eyebrows and large pointed ears.

NBC turned down the *Star Trek* pilot, complaining that there wasn't enough action in it, that it was "too cerebral." It required the audience to think too much. But the concept was so intriguing that the network agreed to pay for a second pilot. Apparently Hunter's wife began making all kinds of demands on Roddenberry, who finally fired him. To replace him he needed an actor who was not too cerebral. So he offered the role to Jack Lord, who later starred in *Hawaii Five-0.* Supposedly Jack Lord asked for 50 percent ownership of the show. That's when Roddenberry called and asked me to look at the pilot with him. I guess he felt I was the perfect choice for the lead role in a show that wasn't too intelligent for its audience and whom he didn't have to pay a lot of money. And for me, all I had to do was replace Jesus Christ.

The first pilot was a wonderful, magical story in which Jeffrey Hunter is lured to a planet by an alien species in hopes that he will mate with a deformed human female who had survived a crash landing there. To convince him to produce children with her, they transformed her into various types trying to figure out what would attract him. Psychologically it was very interesting. But it was much more than interesting. It was original.

It's very difficult all these years later, after *Star Wars* and *Close Encounters* and all the other space stories, to appreciate how extraordinarily innovative it was. The genius of Roddenberry's *Star Trek* was that its characters were normal people — even the alien Spock — who had normal relationship problems — when they weren't busy saving the universe. After watching the pilot I told Roddenberry that I thought the characters took themselves much too seriously. They made everything they did seem so monumental. Something as simple as "Turn left," became: We are about to execute an extremely difficult maneuver that we have been carefully trained to do but accomplishing this incredibly risky task will require every bit of our ability and intelligence and we have no way of knowing what the impact of this attempt will be upon the universe. These guys have been on this voyage for years, I told him. Sometimes a left turn is simply a left turn. It's just another workday until something dramatic changes it. I see it having more humor, more fun.

"Okay," he agreed. "I go along with that."

Roddenberry changed the name of the captain from Pike to James T. Kirk — after considering other names like Hannibal, Timber, Boone, Flagg, and Raintree. I tried to provide Kirk with the sense of awe and wonder that had been missing in the pilot. Kirk was a man who marveled and greatly appreciated the endless surprises presented to him by the universe after making that left turn. He didn't take things for granted and, more than anything else, respected life in every one of its weird weekly adventure forms.

And if every once in a while he could slip a whoopee cushion under the behind of the supreme commander of the Evil forces, figuratively of course, that would be okay too.

In the second pilot Captain Kirk and Spock immediately developed the chemistry that had been missing in the pilot. Mr. Spock was half-Vulcan, an alien struggling to suppress his human emotions — his choices and decisions were all based on logic. If his commander also was serious and somber, as it had been originally written, Leonard had nothing to play against. As he remembers, "The writers couldn't get a handle on the difference between Pike and Spock, so Spock came off as this weird kind of colorless character who was little more than a competent first officer."

But when Kirk was rewritten as a man with very human emotions, as well as a sense of humor, the character of Spock emerged. The broad range of emotions displayed by Kirk was a perfect contrast to Spock's lack of emotion. We expected that viewers would find Spock strange and interesting, while at the same time Spock was finding human beings — Kirk in particular — strange and interesting. He was always curious about why Kirk did things that were not logical. This was probably the first time that viewers could look at themselves through an alien's eyes.

One of the reasons the relationship worked is that Leonard's acting style and mine were as opposite as Kirk and Spock. As Leonard explained, "Bill has always been a very externalized actor, he just opens his arms completely to the audience. By the time this show began I'd been a working actor for seventeen years, I'd been teaching acting for five years, and my style was much more internalized, each action I took and every word I spoke seemed considered, thought out.

"The best thing that Gene Roddenberry gave to me when he offered me the part was to tell me that this character would have an internal struggle. That part of the Vulcan dynamic would be the need to find logic in often illogical situations."

When we began filming I didn't know any of the other actors. The only member of the cast I'd worked with previously was Leonard Nimoy, although I was unaware of that for many years; we'd both appeared in an episode of *The Man from U.N.C.L.E.* We may have appeared in a crowd scene together, but we had no dialogue and we definitely did not get to know each other. In addition to Leonard, DeForest Kelley played Dr. Leonard "Bones" McCoy, James Doohan was our Scottish chief engineer Scotty, George Takei was our Asian helmsman and weapons officer Sulu, and Nichelle Nichols was our African-American female officer of the deck, Uhura. Our Russian navigator, Chekov, played by Walter Koenig, did not join the cast until our second season.

Desilu Studios did not spend a lot of money on the show. Our special effects were primitive. Outer space was a black cloth with holes in it lit from behind. Our technical crew used anything they found lying around that looked interesting and called it something else.

On September 8, 1966, for the first time we entered "Space: The Final Frontier. These are the voyages of the Starship *Enterprise*. Its five-year mission: To explore strange new worlds. To seek out new life and new civilization. To boldly go where no man has gone before."

Do you think Francis Scott Key knew he had written America's national anthem when he jotted down a few words? Do you think Christopher Columbus knew he would soon discover a new world when he sailed? Did Michelangelo know he was going to create one of history's greatest masterpieces when they told him the Sistine Chapel ceiling needed a paint job? And do you think Gene Roddenberry knew that the space suit worn by Dr. McCoy in an episode of *Star Trek* called "The Tholian Web" would one day be auctioned off by Christie's for $144,000?

Probably not, at least based on our first reviews. According to *Variety,* "*Star Trek* . . . won't work. Even within its sci-fi frame of reference it was a . . . dreary mess of confusion . . . a long hour with hardly any relief from violence, killings, hypnotic stuff, and a distasteful, ugly monster.

"William Shatner . . . appears wooden . . ."

Well, apparently we'd licked the "too cerebral" problem. And not to be critical of the review, but aren't monsters supposed to be distasteful and ugly? That's why they're called monsters. What kind of monster would be "a tasteful, attractive monster"?

I wasn't at all concerned about our reviews. The many excellent reviews I'd received during my career had not made me a star. So what damage could a poor review do to me? But over the next few weeks Leonard Nimoy's character, the highly logical Vulcan Mr. Spock, began receiving most of the attention. Spock fan clubs were formed. Magazines started writing stories about him and the network sent Roddenberry a memo wondering why Spock wasn't featured in every story. In other words, the ears had it.

Wooden? Me, wooden? Not that I took it personally, of course. Or even noticed.

I've often heard it said that acting is not a competitive sport — but never by actors. Believe me, I've sometimes thought it might be a good idea at the start of every production to have the actors meet in the middle of the stage to go through the rules with the director: No stepping on another actor's lines. No upstaging below the belt. And after you've said your lines go to a neutral corner. The truth is that every good actor has an ego. Actors are ambitious people. And every moment center stage can lead to the next job. The day I reported to work on the first episode of *Star Trek* I was already wondering what would come next. And so was every other member of the cast. I was supposed to be the star but Leonard Nimoy was getting more attention than I was. It bothered me so much that I finally had a discussion about it with Gene Roddenberry. "Don't be afraid of having other popular and talented people around you," he said. "They can only enhance your performance. The more you work with these people, the better the show's going to be."

He was absolutely right, and from that day on it never bothered me. Although perhaps when Leonard was nominated for an Emmy as Best Supporting Actor — in three consecutive years — while I was not nominated I did get a little envious. I remember wondering, why is that not happening to me? Here I've sacrificed so much and yet someone else is receiving the acclaim. It did bother me. It bothered me a lot.

. . . *Star Trek* refrigerator magnets; Federation uniform pins; ladies' jumpsuits; draw-string bags; backpacks; a briefcase; wooden plaques; various patches . . .

Eventually Leonard and I would become best friends but at that time we didn't know each other at all and didn't really get along. We actually had one pretty loud argument. The process of getting Spock's ears just right had been difficult and expensive. Finally the head of the makeup department, Freddy Phillips, paid out of his own pocket to get the right pair of ears made. Leonard felt Freddy had prevented Spock from becoming some kind of visual joke, so when a national magazine wanted to do a photo story about his makeup process, featuring Freddy, he agreed. But nobody told me about it.

We began filming every morning at 8 a.m. Leonard reported to makeup at about 6:30, but I got there about forty-five minutes later. One morning I came to work and found the photographer in the makeup room snapping away. I didn't like that at all; I was concerned all of my little makeup secrets were going to be revealed. And no, I can't tell you what they are. That's why they're secrets. So I asked someone, justifiably, I thought, "What's this photographer doing in the makeup room?"

The photographer quietly left the room. Leonard and Freddy waited for him to return but he never came back. Eventually Leonard was told that at my insistence an assistant director had forced the photographer to leave. Leonard was furious. He immediately came to my trailer to confront me. "Did you order the photographer out?" he demanded.

"Yes," I admitted, explaining, "I didn't want him there."

Leonard recalls this conversation much better than I do. As he remembers, he told me, "It was approved by Roddenberry. It was approved by the head of the studio. It was approved by publicity."

To which I apparently replied, "Well, it wasn't approved by me!" Why I responded this way I certainly don't remember. But I'm certain my envy must have had something to do with it.

"You mean to tell me that I've got to get approval from you to have my picture taken?"

This probably was the moment that impolite language was used. Leonard angrily returned to his own trailer and refused to go to work until Gene Roddenberry arrived and settled this argument. On a TV production schedule this is an expensive crisis.

Roddenberry was able to calm the situation down and eventually Leonard and I made peace.

Generally the bonding that takes place on a set is enormous. A group of disparate people come together for a prolonged period of time, usually working under tremendous time, financial, and career pressures, and become a single unit. Almost a family. And when the production ends you promise each other that you're going to keep in touch, that your friendship is extremely important and you just can't wait to see them again. Two weeks later you're working with your new family on another set.

But on the *Star Trek* set Leonard remained aloof. Certainly part of the reason for that was to maintain the integrity of his character. Spock was an outsider and Leonard worried that if he got too friendly with the rest of the cast he might unconsciously close that distance. He also felt very comfortable playing that role. "I was totally at home in that character," he told me. "I'd felt so alienated as a Jewish kid growing up in an Italian neighborhood in Boston. So I learned how to stay within my own framework. To stay out of harm's way, out of direct confrontations because generally they didn't work out well for me. I had a physical fear of being beaten up, or hurt, or emotionally injured in some way. So I learned how to cope with being different, with being the other. And that was the same challenge faced by Spock. I knew that feeling so very well.

"Playing that character ten hours a day, five days a week, made it very difficult for me to turn it on and turn it off. I just couldn't step out of the character between takes."

The perfect word to describe that is alienation.

Leonard was extremely protective of Spock. As any actor who has worked in a television series understands, the producers, directors, writers, and members of the crew often change for each episode, only the characters remain consistent. "The actor is the caretaker of the character," is the way he explained it. "Nobody else can be counted on. You have to be able to say to the writer, 'You can't have me say, "Let's make hay under the Vulcan moon," because three episodes ago we said that Vulcan has no moon.' So my energy went into providing that consistency and continuity."

And perhaps the other reason that Leonard remained aloof is that he was an alcoholic. Truthfully, I didn't know it at the time. But certainly I was aware of the fact that he maintained a cool distance from the rest of the cast. As he admits, "I was in bad shape when we were making *Star Trek*. My marriage had fallen apart and at times I was very despondent. So I would go home every day and drink. On weekends I would tell myself I'll have a beer at ten o'clock. By two o'clock I was drinking hard liquor and by five o'clock I'd be passed out.

"As many alcoholics can do, I hid it at work. I never allowed it to affect my work. And as long as I never drank while I was working I had this illusion of control. I lied to myself a lot: I don't work drunk, I don't drink at all in connection to my work. I can wait. When I was performing in a play my first drink would be when the curtain came down. But that drink had to be there. When I walked into my dressing room I wanted an ice-cold gin on the rocks waiting for me. When I directed the movie *Star Trek III* my secretary knew that as soon as I said, 'Cut. That's a wrap,' I wanted a drink. And then I would drink constantly. Once I had that first drink I would not stop drinking until I passed out or fell asleep.

"I thought I was smart. I thought I was able to hide it successfully. But alcohol is smarter. When I was in need of a drink and it wasn't there I could get very upset. I did a lot of college lectures, many of them in small towns. When I checked into the motel in the afternoon one of the first things I asked was how late their bar was open. That way I knew what time I had to finish and get back there. Well, in some of these towns if there's nobody in the bar on a weeknight they'll tell the bartender to lock up and go home. And every once in a while I'd come back to the hotel and the bar would be locked. I wanted my drink. I'd go to the front desk and say, 'You told me the bar would be open until ten o'clock. Open the fucking bar!' *Because I'm in trouble* was the unspoken subtext. And security would get me a bottle of scotch. When going out I would choose restaurants that I knew had a full bar. I loved going to the theater in London because they allowed you to drink before the show and during intermission.

"This went on for many years, the entire time I believed I was in control. I can handle this. If necessary for professional reasons I could go a week without a drink. But eventually I started waking up in the morning thinking, why do I want to live today? And that's when I first became concerned.

"I married my wife, Susan, in 1989. I was

still drinking, but I was deliriously happy with her. And one day I was talking to her about how different my life was with her and how happy I felt, and she asked me, 'Then why do you drink so much?'

"And I thought, you know, she's right. I don't have to do this anymore. So she called a friend and within hours, on a Sunday night, someone was here from Alcoholics Anonymous. I remember he said to me, 'You cannot drink a little.' We talked for two hours and the next night I went to my first AA meeting, which was a thrill. I haven't had a drink since we had that conversation that night."

Years later Leonard's alcoholism, about which I knew nothing while we were making *Star Trek,* would come to play a central role in my life. And it would bond us together in a way that I never could have imagined — particularly when he was getting all that attention. Not that I minded the character with the weird ears taking the attention away from the noble Captain Kirk, of course.

Wooden? I barely even remember sitting at the kitchen table on a rainy morning, eating three slightly undercooked eggs over easy, reading that review while Gloria, who was dressed in a pale green cotton top, got the girls ready for school. As a professional actor, those things don't bother me. And that particular review has continued to not bother me for more than four decades.

A series begins to work when the personalities of the characters, and the relationships between those characters, become clearly defined to the viewers. So you don't need an explanation about the meaning of each line or gesture. Leonard always pointed to the end of an episode entitled "The Devil in the Dark" as the moment that perfectly captured the relationship between Kirk and Spock. After we'd successfully saved a creature named the Horta, who seemed to be attracted to Spock, I told him that he was becoming more human all the time. He considered that, then responded, "Captain, there's no reason for me to stand here and be insulted." Then walked off the bridge of the *Enterprise*.

Certainly no television show in history has been so thoroughly chronicled and analyzed as *Star Trek*. There are people, Trekkies, who can quote entire shows, entire seasons, people who know these characters better than their own families. University courses have been taught about the show. Books have been written about the philosophy and ethics of our plots. But when we were making the show all we were concerned about was being renewed for the next season. Another season meant twenty-six weeks of regular paychecks. Our ratings were never tremendous, but our audience was extremely loyal. I think we realized the show was successful when key phrases we used began seeping into the general culture. I'd walk through an airport and people would recognize me and say, "Beam me up, Scotty," or "Live long and prosper." On other shows comedians were promising to "Boldly go where no man has gone before," and traveling at "warp speed," and issuing their own "prime directives," while kids were talking about our futuristic props; our gunlike phasers — which could be put on stun rather than simply killing our enemies, and flip-up communicators which looked precisely like the flip-phones that would be invented almost four decades later, as if they were real.

The general consensus among respected philosophers is that *Star Trek* was successful and has endured because our stories focused on universal themes — which of necessity took place elsewhere in the universe because they were about subjects that couldn't easily be tackled by traditional programming. Gene Roddenberry once said that the real mission of the *Enterprise* was to search for intelligent life on the other side of the television set. While the grand theme of our five-year mission was always good versus evil, we also did stories about racism, sexism, authoritarianism, class warfare, imperialism, human and parahuman and alien rights, and the insanity of war. Nichelle Nichols and I shared the first interracial kiss on American television — which several Southern stations refused to broadcast — although we were compelled to kiss by space aliens controlling our minds. Which was certainly one of the most creative excuses to kiss a beautiful woman I'd ever heard.

Before our first show was broadcast the cast met with the media. When Leonard was asked about the character of Spock, he responded that we were doing something very different than the typical science-fiction story. "This is an intelligent character, a scientist, a being with great dignity." As the same reporters watched the next day, we filmed a scene in which Spock was lying in a bed in sick bay, green blood dripping from his head. I rushed in and asked urgently, "What happened, Spock?" to which he replied, "Captain, the monster attacked me!"

Gene Roddenberry never referred to

himself as *Star Trek*'s producer, rather he was . . . the creator. And ironically it was Gene who brought Leonard and me closer together. Roddenberry was a quirky guy whose greatest invention was the character of Spock. After the first thirteen episodes writer/producer Gene Coon was brought in and Roddenberry became the executive producer, meaning he was more of a supervisor than working on the show day-to-day. After that his primary job seemed to be exploiting *Star Trek* in every possible way.

After we had been on the air for a couple of months an agent called Leonard and offered him two thousand dollars to make a personal appearance somewhere in Massachusetts on a Saturday afternoon. From that amount the agent would take his ten percent fee. At that time Leonard was earning $1,250 a week so this was very exciting. His problem was that in order to get there in time for the lecture on Saturday he had to be on the 6 p.m. flight Friday afternoon out of Los Angeles. That meant leaving the set an hour and eighteen minutes before we finished. Technically that wasn't a problem. With enough notice we could easily film around him. So he asked the producers for permission to leave early that Friday. "Two or three days went by," he remembers, "and

I hadn't heard anything. The agent wanted me to make a commitment. Finally I was told that Gene Roddenberry wanted to see me. I went up to his office. 'I understand you want to get out early?' he said.

"I told him that was true, 'I've got a job offer on Saturday for two thousand dollars.'

"Then he said to me, 'I've just started a company called Lincoln Enterprises. We're going to do some merchandising of *Star Trek* memorabilia, but we also want to represent actors for personal appearances. I'd like to represent you for this appearance. And the fee is twenty percent.'

"I shook my head, then told him that I was already paying an agent ten percent and that I didn't understand why I had to pay him too.

"He looked at me and said, 'The difference between your agent and me is that your agent can't get you out of here at five o'clock on Friday and I can. And all it'll cost you is twenty percent.'

" 'Gene, I can't do that to this agent,' I said. 'He got me the job.'

"And then he said, and I will never forget his exact words, 'Well, you're just going to have to learn how to bow down and say master.'

"I told him, 'You got the wrong guy,' and

walked out of his office. Eventually he backed down and I made that plane, but while we worked together for years afterward that was the end of any semblance of a friendship between Gene Roddenberry and myself."

The relationship between Leonard and the producers got so bad during the first season that they actually sent him a memo informing him that he was not permitted to use the studio's pens and pencils.

Gene and I had a similar argument about a small medal of honor he wanted me to award to a member of the crew on the show. It had absolutely nothing to do with the plot — and everything to do with the fact that this medal was going to be sold by Lincoln Enterprises. The actors' contracts called for a minimal participation in merchandise revenue and this was just a clever way to get around that. I refused to have anything to do with the pin — so then they began working on Leonard to wear it, finally pressuring him into doing it.

Roddenberry sold everything. To check the lighting of each scene the cinematographer would shoot what was known as a light strip. It was usually about ten frames times the number of scenes we'd shoot in a day. Maybe a hundred frames a day. Most people threw them out. Not Roddenberry. He cut out the individual frames and sold them as a piece of *Star Trek.* He was selling our images.

Each Christmas the editors would put together a gag reel to be shown at our Christmas party. It's ten minutes of jokes and bloopers, some of them intentional, many of them not; it was actors at play and actors making mistakes, and it was never, ever meant for anyone except the cast and crew to see. For example, we had one scene that showed Spock shooting an arrow — immediately followed by a scene showing Kirk being carried into a cave by members of the *Enterprise* crew, with an arrow sticking out of my crotch. Several years later I was in Mammoth and someone asked me if I'd seen the *Star Trek* gag reel being shown at a local pub — Roddenberry had spliced together two or three of these private reels and sold them.

The battles both Leonard and I fought against the studio actually pushed us together. Eventually we were able to negotiate contracts that included a "most favored nation" clause, which basically meant that whatever perk or payment or privilege either one of us got, the other one would be entitled to the same treatment. Leonard and

I became friendly, although certainly not best friends. In fact, I actually believed the entire cast got along quite well. Many years later I discovered that we weren't getting along at all and that apparently I was the cause of it.

After we'd shot about half the shows for our second season we began hearing strong rumors that the five-year voyage of discovery was about to come to an early and abrupt ending. NBC was preparing to cancel the show. To prevent that from happening two very loyal fans and friends of Roddenberry, Bjo and John Trimble, initiated a letter-writing campaign. Bjo obtained mailing lists from the World Science Fiction Convention and from notable science-fiction bookstores, as well as fan letters written to the cast. "I just got a call from Gene Roddenberry," she wrote. "[T]here has been no word on renewing the show for next season, and in fact, it is highly likely *Star Trek* will die if something isn't done . . .

"If thousands of fans just sit around moaning about the death of *Star Trek,* they will get exactly what they deserve: *Gomer Pyle!* . . . So pass the word and write some letters, people." Some letters? As a result of this campaign NBC received — trumpets blare here — more than one million letters urging the network not to cancel the show. NBC announced, "*Star Trek* will continue to be seen . . ."

A very logical decision, Captain.

Perhaps more important, the people who wrote these letters suddenly had an emotional attachment to a television program unlike any viewers ever before. They had actually influenced a network's programming decision. They had ownership; *Star Trek* really had become their show. This marked the beginning of the most unusual relationship between viewers and a TV series in history.

NBC scheduled the show for Monday nights at 7:30, the perfect time slot for us because our audience consisted primarily of teenagers, college students, and young adults, science-fiction fans who would be home at that hour. But when George Schlatter, the producer of NBC's top-rated *Laugh-In* — which would have to be moved a half-hour from its 8 p.m. starting time — objected, the network moved us to Friday nights at 10 p.m.

It was no *Bonanza* — for *Star Trek* this was the worst possible time slot. No one in our universe was going to stay home Friday night to watch television. Our audience was out on Friday nights. Not home, *no esta en la casa,* gone, away. Those people who would be at home weren't going to be watching science fiction. Even then NBC reduced our budget, paying $15,000 less per episode than it had during our first season. That meant that we could no longer film on location, we couldn't pay guest stars, and one of every four shows had to be done entirely on the *Enterprise.*

Our first show that third season might have been a tribute to the NBC executives who so mishandled this show: it was about a society in desperate need of a brain. It was entitled "Spock's Brain" and took place on Stardate 5431.4. I don't know what day of the week that would have been — but I can assure you it was not a Friday night at ten o'clock. Because even aliens are busy Friday nights at ten o'clock. In this story a beautiful alien woman beams aboard the *Enterprise* and steals Spock's brain, turning him into a zombie, and causing Bones to have to utter one of the worst lines of all seventy-nine episodes, "Jim. His brain is gone!" We had twenty-four hours to find Spock's brain somewhere in the entire universe, then reinsert it in his head. Naturally Spock comes along with us, showing all the emotion of . . . Spock. Eventually we discover a race that needs his brain to control its planet's life-supporting power systems. McCoy operates to reinsert Spock's brain — during which Spock awakens and instructs him how the parts should be properly connected. In the dramatic highlight of the episode we are all standing by the operating table, waiting anxiously to see if Spock will survive this operation. Suddenly, Spock opens his eyes, looks at me and blinks several times, and then says in absolute astonishment, "Friday night at ten o'clock?"

Perhaps he didn't. But it was true, of course. The show was canceled after three seasons on the air. In January 1969, we filmed the final episode. It had been a good job, a good cast, but it was over. During the three years I'd worked on the show my life had changed completely. Gloria and I had finally separated and, early one afternoon in 1967, as we were filming an episode called "Devil in the Dark," I received a phone call telling me my father had died of a heart attack while playing golf in Florida.

There is no way to prepare for the death of a parent. It is a knot in time into which all the emotions you've ever felt about that relationship come racing together. It is the ultimate unfinished symphony, with the loose ends of life and loves to somehow be bound together. Well, all of that hit me — and I had work to do. We were in the middle of a scene and it had to be finished. I owed it to my fellow actors. The first plane to Florida didn't leave for several hours, so rather than wait in an airport I decided to work, hoping the familiarity of my work would provide me with at least a few moments of peace.

Working that day was very difficult. I'd spent my career masking the reality of my own feelings, and instead presenting to the camera the emotional life of the character I was playing. As an actor you learn to do that, to blank out everything except the persona of the character you're playing, and that's what I tried to do because that's what I had always done. I also knew that if I faltered it would be on camera as long as film lasted. Sooner or later the pain I was feeling would go away — but the impact of it on my performance would be recorded on film forever. So I persevered. I worked. When we'd rehearsed this scene in the morning I'd known all my lines, but when we filmed in the afternoon I just couldn't remember them. I remember being stoic, while Leonard remembers me saying over and over, "Promises not kept, promises not kept. Things that he wanted to do . . ."

That night I flew to Miami to pick up my father's body and bring him home to Montreal.

The result of that was the last serious argument Leonard and I have ever had. In this episode workers on a mining planet were being killed by a creature who lived in their caves. The creature, called a Horta, was a strange-looking beast operated by a guy inside the suit crawling on the floor. As Spock discovered during a painful mindmeld with the Horta, it was the last of its race and was simply protecting its eggs. It was saving the species. Eventually I was able to forge a peace between the miners and the Horta, which agreed to tunnel for the miners, who in return agreed to protect its offspring.

While I was gone Leonard had a scene in which he performed a mind-meld with the wounded Horta. The danger of a mind-meld is that Spock literally felt the intense pain being felt by the Horta. So in this scene he had to get down and put his hands on it and cried in pain. Pain . . . pain . . . pain. It's a difficult scene for an actor to make believable.

When I returned from my father's funeral the set was very somber. People were being very sympathetic, which I appreciated, but I wanted everyone to know that I was dealing with it and I was fine. I wanted to relieve some of the tension on the set. The first thing I had to do was figure out how to react to Leonard's mind-meld. I looked at the footage and then told him, "Show me what you did."

He explained, "Well, I went over here and I put my hands on her and I said, 'pain, pain, pain.' "

I shook my head. "It was bigger than that. Can you show me exactly what you did?"

This had been a difficult scene for an actor, but as a favor to me Leonard got back into position and did the scene. He didn't just go through the motions, he felt the emotion. He screamed out, "Pain. Pain. Pain."

And I said glibly, "Can somebody get this guy an aspirin?" I thought everybody would have a good laugh and we would go back to normal.

Leonard did not think it was funny. He was furious. He thought I'd set him up and then betrayed him for the amusement of everyone else on the set. I had toyed with his commitment to his character and the show. For a laugh at his expense. An actor had betrayed an actor, the worst thing you could do. He told me later that he was done with me, that he thought I was a real son of a bitch. He didn't say a word to me for more than a week.

Many *Star Trek* plots revolved around beautiful women, although often we discovered these women were actually alien life forms or computer-generated mind images intended to make us compliant. The ole man-trap strategy. But during an episode in the third season entitled "Elaan of Troyius," which guest-starred France Nuyen as an arrogant princess, I told Spock, "Mr. Spock, the women on your planet are logical. That's the only planet in the galaxy that can make that claim." In many ways I think that summed up the difficulties that I had understanding women.

Admittedly, I wasn't good at being married. I didn't know how to make a real commitment to another person. On some level I believed that because I was paying the bills, I should make all the decisions. Holding the purse strings meant having the power. So my marriage to Gloria became very lopsided. I know now that when you take away someone's self-worth their whole entity is lessened. The person you fell in love with slowly disappears, replaced by . . . by frustration, anger, disenchantment, and tremendous resentment. And then you get angry with them for no longer being the person you married. It's considerably more volatile when two actors marry but only one has a successful career.

I was working so hard to support my family and resented Gloria because I was getting so little joy out of my marriage. She resented me for . . . for probably many reasons. So Gloria stayed home with our girls and it seemed like each week new and beautiful — and seemingly available — women showed up on the set. We had separated emotionally years earlier, but while we were making *Star Trek* I physically moved out of the house. Eventually she filed for divorce.

Divorce is simply modern society's version of medieval torture. Except it lasts longer and leaves deeper scars. A divorce releases the most primitive emotions; the ugliest, raw feelings. Emotionally wounded people do their best to inflict pain upon the other party, but rather than using claws they use divorce lawyers. My marriage to Gloria didn't simply end, it was ripped apart. It left only sharp edges. And poverty.

When the show was canceled the three anchors that had bound me to responsibility had been cut loose. My job was done. My marriage was done. And my father had died. I was floating free. I had no firm direction, no emotional compass. I was just drifting with the currents. I took affection anywhere I could find it. It seemed like there was always someone around who had her own needs to be fulfilled, so lust and romance and passion all began playing a more important role in my life.

I had assumed that the day we finished shooting *Star Trek* was the end of my association with Captain Kirk and the *Enterprise* — and its crew — forever. When a Broadway show ends its run it's done forever; the producers burn the scenery and there is no recorded copy of the show. It exists only in memories. But television shows are different; television shows are syndicated, sold to local TV stations, which broadcast them over and over.

Paramount had no concept of *Star Trek*'s true value. It was just another failed series. To try to recoup some of its cost they sold it very inexpensively to local stations, who bought it because it was inexpensive and had a proven, loyal audience. The syndication market was just beginning to expand and *Star Trek* was the perfect product. In cities all around the country stations began showing it when the core audience was home. Old fans didn't want to miss an episode and they brought new fans with them to the living room. The ratings were terrific, especially for the price Paramount was asking, so more local stations bought it. And then television stations in other countries began buying it. In our second season we did a wonderful episode entitled "The Trouble with Tribbles." Tribbles are adorable balls of fur that rapidly reproduce reproduce reproduce reproduce. They reproduce faster than a renegade copy machine; and once they start there is no stopping them them them them.

That's what happened to *Star Trek*. No program in television history had ever tribbled like this. It just kept tribbling and tribbling and tribbling. Leonard realized it long before I did. He was touring the country starring in the one-man show he'd written, *Vincent,* the life of Vincent van Gogh as seen through the five hundred letters he'd written to his brother. And he found that no matter where he went — Billings, Montana; Cedar Rapids, Iowa; Rapid City, South Dakota — wherever he went the only thing the local media wanted to talk about was *Star Trek.* "It was just all over the place," he remembers. "I was becoming very aware that it was invasive — and pervasive — in the culture. The media started writing about the success of the show in syndication, which encouraged even more local stations to buy it. In some cities it was running six nights a week. Stations were running marathon *Star Trek* weekends. We were hearing stories about colleges changing course schedules in the afternoon to eliminate a conflict with *Star Trek* reruns."

It was impossible to truly grasp what was happening, because nothing like it had ever happened before. A failed television show was becoming a cultural phenomenon. While we were making the series I had often been recognized, but suddenly it started happening all the time and in strange places. People would come up to me in airports and recite ten pages of dialogue word-for-word from a specific episode they loved — and I would have absolutely no concept of what they were doing. I remember in the early 1970s I was working on a television show and got hurt. They rushed me to the hospital to take X-rays. Fortunately, my most serious injuries were some very bad bruises. But just to be certain the doctor asked for a urine specimen. He wanted to make sure there was no blood in my urine, no internal bleeding. I was lying in bed and he handed me a bottle and asked me to fill it. I was too sore to move, so he pulled the oval curtain around the bed to give me some privacy. And just as I started peeing into the bottle a nurse opened the curtain to see what was going on. She looked at me peeing into the bottle, then her face just lit up with joy and she said, without pausing, "I'm your biggest fan."

And to which part of me are you addressing that compliment, madam?

While I was very pleased that *Star Trek* was finally getting the attention it deserved, financially it wasn't doing me any good at all. The actors received only a small royalty for the first few reruns, but nothing after that. There had been some benefits, of course. For example, it was while *Star Trek* was on the air that I had launched my renowned singing career. Until that moment my singing career had been limited to auditioning once for a Broadway musical and being told by the director to focus on acting. But in 1968 Decca Records asked me if I was interested in doing an album. I hesitated, I wasn't a singer — but then it was pointed out to me that the first note of the musical scale is do.

During appearances on several talk shows I had spoken the lyrics of several popular songs without causing any permanent damage. But on my *first* album I wanted to do

247

more than that, I wanted to explore the unique relationship between classic literature and popular song lyrics. I wanted to emphasize the poetry of language, in both its written and musical forms, used to express the extraordinary range of human emotion. That was my concept for this album.

What I decided to do was find a selection of beautiful writing and use that as a lead-in to a song that complemented it. Or at least served as a corollary. For example, I would use a selection from *Cyrano de Bergerac* ending, "I can climb to no great heights, but I will climb alone," to segue into Bob Dylan's "Mr. Tambourine Man," which had been interpreted to be Dylan's allusion to his experiences with LSD — and I would perform it as a song sung by an addict bemoaning the fact that he is incapable of surviving without his drugs. In much the same way Hamlet's classic speech, "To be, or not to be," led directly into "It Was a Very Good Year," made famous by Sinatra.

It all made perfect sense to me. But apparently it was a bit obtuse for some other people. Okay, for many other people. All right, for most people.

The album was called *The Transformed Man* and Johnny Carson invited me on *The*

Tonight Show to promote it. I decided to do the Cyrano-Tambourine Man cut on the show. It went very well in rehearsal, but it was six minutes long. Producer Freddy de Cordova told me I had to cut it down to three minutes. "Just choose the literature or the song," he told me. Hmm, I decided I would talk the song, which would be more commercial and certainly more popular.

Here, let me talk a few lines for you: "Hey. Mister. Tam. Bour. Ine. Man. Take me for a trip. Upon your magic swirling ship. My senses, have been stripped. My hands can't feel to grip. My toes too numb to step . . ."

As I finished this song I glanced over at Johnny Carson, who had a look of astonishment on his face vaguely similar to the look on Spock's face when his brain was missing. Without the literary lead-in, I was singing the song as a drug addict looking for a fix. Hey, where are you, Tambourine Man? I need you, I'll follow you anywhere.

The song was inexplicable to the audience. What the hell is that guy doing? The reviews were very mixed; while some critics wrote that it was the worst album ever produced, others felt just as strongly that there had never been an album like it ever before.

I didn't mind. I'd pushed the envelope,

perhaps I'd pushed a little too far, but I'd tried. I'd taken a creative risk. I'd tried to do something unique, something very different. And I'd learned very early in my acting career that you can't improve without taking risks, and sometimes that means making mistakes. The good news was that now I knew for certain that I had a lot of room to improve. I mean, a lot of room.

Years later, decades later, my debut album *The Transformed Man* would lead directly to one of the most successful commercial ventures of my career — and another album! But the only reason I was permitted to . . . let's call it singing . . . sing on television was because of *Star Trek*'s loyal fan base.

The end of the initial run of *Star Trek*'s seventy-nine episodes was actually the beginning of an entirely new phenomenon. For me, *Star Trek* was done. The only thing I expected were a few pitiful checks for the first few reruns. At that time there was no such thing as residual payments. Two or three years later the Screen Actors Guild was able to forge an agreement with producers that actors would be paid each time a show was broadcast. So none of the actors on *Star Trek* ever received a residual check.

After my divorce from Gloria I was just about broke — once again eighteen hundred dollars in the bank became my goal — and I began looking for work. I had three kids and an ex-wife to support. I had absolutely no idea that the show was about to become a much bigger hit in syndication than it had ever been on network television. There have been many attempts to explain the reasons that so many people connected so strongly to *Star Trek*. But certainly at the core of it there was one simple truth: It was fun. Just as sports serves as a common denominator for many people, and just as strangers can bond over discussions of their favorite movies, *Star Trek* became a language that bound together a large group of people with common interests. It became a sun with great gravitational pull that drew all kinds of people to it, where they could meet others just like themselves.

Wearing costumes.

The very first unofficial *Star Trek* convention apparently was held in the Newark, New Jersey, public library in March 1969, when a small group of *Star Trek* fans got together to celebrate the show. At this gathering they sang folk songs inspired by the show, showed slides of the *Enterprise* set, had a panel discussion about the *Star Trek* phenomenon, and gave a brief lecture about the connection between *Star Trek* and science.

Around the country, and eventually around the world, small groups of fans of the show were getting together to watch the reruns or just talk about it. These weren't commercial events, nobody was making any money from them, people just wanted to get together to honor the show. But in January 1972 the first official *Star Trek* Convention was held at New York's Statler Hilton Hotel. Gene Roddenberry was there and NASA sent an eighteen-wheeler filled with scientific displays. The organizers were actually shocked at the number of people who showed up; at most they expected a couple of hundred people; instead, a thousand people were there. The vendors had brought enough merchandise for a weekend — but by Friday afternoon many of them had already sold out. The conventions took just a little longer to tribble. In 1973 three conventions were held, two years later there were twenty-three conventions. In Chicago, organizers planned for ten thousand people — instead, thirty thousand Trekkies — that was what they called themselves — showed up. A year later there was an average of a convention a week; security actually had to close the entrance to a convention at the

Los Angeles Convention Center in 1976 because there was no more room inside. By the early 1980s as many as four hundred *Star Trek* conventions were held annually.

I vaguely knew that these conventions were taking place but I really didn't want anything to do with them. That was my past, I'd done that. Truthfully, I wasn't in touch with anyone from the show — even Leonard. I certainly did not want the highlight of my career to be three years as Captain Kirk in a failed science-fiction TV show. My focus was on the future. The very near future. The end-of-the-month future when the bills had to be paid. And truthfully, the whole thing made me uncomfortable. I didn't want anything to do with a group of obsessed people who paid to get together — some of them wearing costumes — to talk incessantly about a TV show that had been canceled. It wasn't logical.

. . . autographs, certificates, trash cans, collector's albums, calendars, lamps, bed covers, computer games, miniatures, Snoopy as *Star Trek* characters, wallets . . .

I attended my first *Star Trek* convention at New York's Americana Hotel in November 1975. Did I mention that the first — and last! — notes of the musical scale are do? The money they offered me to attend this convention was . . . do I dare? Yes, I do! Out of this world! I didn't prepare any remarks. Just be yourself, the organizers told me, Captain Kirk. But when I walked onstage to thunderous applause I was stunned. I had expected perhaps a thousand people, but the room was completely filled. As far as I could see people were jammed together, they were on the sides, in the balconies, sitting on the floor in front of the stage. They were ready to hear words of wisdom from James T. Kirk and I didn't have anything of importance to tell them.

It didn't matter; the audience was an actor's dream. They responded to my slightest smile. I had them in the grip of my phaser. Eventually I would develop a little bit of a routine; for example, I would tell them about the day Dee Kelley came to the set and was crying. Dee was a wonderful man and clearly he was very upset. "Dee," I asked with great concern, "what's the matter?"

It was his beloved Chihuahua, he told me. This little dog who had meant so much to him had died tragically.

"Oh, Dee," I said. "I'm so terribly sorry. I love dogs and I know the pain of losing a dog you love. How did it happen?"

And through his tears he told me, "Well, I

let her off the leash in my front yard and she was running around, she was so happy, and then she ran into the sprinkler head and died."

Naturally, I laughed. And Dee didn't speak to me for two years.

But at that first appearance I didn't have a speech, so I fumbled around for a little while and, in desperation, I asked hopefully, "Does anyone have a question?"

Instantly eight thousand hands went up. I knew I was home free. Questions I could answer, and if I didn't know the answer I could always make up a good one. Except when their questions were so specific I barely understood the question, much less knew the answer. I learned very quickly that most of the people who attended these conventions understood the universal joke — and simply wanted to have a good time. It was playtime for adults. As a volunteer at the very first organized convention once admitted, "If the man from the funny farm came to take us away right now, there'd be absolutely nothing we could say in our defense."

After that I did start attending conventions, often appearing onstage with Leonard. It was while appearing at those conventions that we started to become really friendly. While the cast of the original series, and then the cast of *Star Trek: The Next Generation* were the biggest stars, pretty much anyone who ever appeared on the show could be invited to appear at a convention. True fans didn't care, even the slightest connection to the show was sufficient: Ladies and gentlemen, let's hear it for the doorman on the *Enterprise!* Yeaaaaa!

My mother and my sister, Joy, were even invited to appear at a *Star Trek* convention.

Truthfully, while I attended several conventions, I did not fully appreciate the passion that the fans felt for the show. To me, it was a TV show; a show that I had enjoyed doing and I was very proud of, and certainly I was grateful for everything that had happened to me because of it, but it was a TV show. Then, in December 1986, I was asked to host *Saturday Night Live.*

The opening skit was a parody of me addressing a *Star Trek* convention. Facsimile trekkies were asking me questions I'd actually been asked, "Um, like, when you, um . . . left your quarters for the last time? And you opened up your safe? Um, what was the combination?"

Finally, in this skit, after a decade of attending conventions and being asked hundreds of these inane questions, I'd had enough. I finally told these people exactly what I had been thinking for all those years. "You know, before I answer any more questions, there's something I wanted to say. Having received all your letters over the years, and I've spoken to many of you, and some of you have traveled, y'know, hundreds of miles to be here, I'd just like to say . . . **get a life,** will you, people? I mean, for crying out loud, it's just a TV show. I mean, look at you! Look at the way you're dressed! You've turned an enjoyable little job, that I did as a lark for a few years, into a colossal waste of time!

"I mean, how old are you people? What have you done with yourselves? You! You must be almost thirty . . . have you ever kissed a girl? I didn't think so. There's a whole world out there. When I was your age I didn't watch television. **I lived!** So . . . move out of your parents' basements! And get your own apartments and **grow the hell up!** I mean, it's just a TV show, dammit, it's just a TV show!"

It was meant to be a joke. I was kidding. I was just having a little fun, making fun of myself and the whole phenomenon. I mean, please. What kind of reader are you to think I was being serious? Get your head out of those books and watch more television!

Then you'll know that *Saturday Night Live* is a comedy show, not a documentary. In fact, if you want realism, then go ahead and rent the DVD of my miniseries *Invasion, Iowa,* in which I took an entire movie crew to Riverside, Iowa — the town that promotes itself as the future birthplace of James T. Kirk — and faked the making of a science-fiction movie while we were really playing a practical joke on the entire town! Now that's a real fake, unlike this skit on *Saturday Night Live.*

When I read the script I decided the best way to make it funny was to play it seriously. If I had been nervous about doing it, if I had been worried about the reaction of *Star Trek* fans, I would have played it very broadly, as a comedian. Instead, having been to enough conventions to know that most Trekkies were able to laugh at themselves, I did it as an actor.

And most of them realized it. Most of them loved it. Most of them. In fact, at conventions they started telling each other, "Get a life." And eventually, when I wrote a book about the phenomenon of *Star Trek* conventions, it was titled *Get a Life.* Which, naturally, was sold at conventions. And coincidently is currently available at www .WilliamShatner.com for the bargain price of only $7.95.

In a very strange way, doing that sketch allowed me to erase some of the distance I'd kept from the Trekkies. With that sketch, as well as some of the others I did on *Saturday Night Live,* I think they appreciated the fact that I had a sense of humor about myself that perhaps I had not shown very publicly before. I not only could take the joke, I could make it.

The conventions had become a grand show in themselves, complete with costumed characters, panel discussions, trivia contests, speeches, screenings, and those guest appearances. We were treated like rock stars. I was told that there were female Trekkies who kept lists of all the members of the cast with whom they'd slept. I was told this! Told it! But I knew that if I ever ended up on a list the news would circulate at warp speed. It actually put me in the odd position of having to find a way of saying no to a woman without being insulting.

Not that I was shy around women. Truthfully, I have always enjoyed the company of women. During much of this period I was single and I certainly had opportunities to be with many women and I grasped a great many of those opportunities. Never at warp speed. Admittedly, there were times when the woman I was with said, "So this is what it's like to be in bed with Captain Kirk." That was definitely a downer, in every sense of the word.

Although none of them ever asked me afterward, "Did the universe move for you, too?"

Among the lessons I learned was the price of my new celebrity. For example, I was very privately dating a young actress and suddenly a photograph of the two of us appeared in the tabloids. I was thunderstruck; this was a part of my life I did not want my young children to know anything about. I couldn't figure out who could have seen us together, and where and when and how. The woman was just as upset, telling me that she was sick about it. So I stopped seeing her for about six months, and then gradually resumed our relationship. Within a month a second story appeared — only then did I realize that this girl was feeding the story and pictures to the paper to further her career.

While my celebrity made women available to me, I had learned to wonder why these women were available to me. What was their objective? Everything that I do, that any actor does, can potentially impact their career as well as have legal and even economic consequences. I learned to be very careful. I even had to be careful where I looked when I was in public. In the days before cell phone cameras it was slightly more difficult for a photograph to be taken without my knowledge, but now, now every minute I'm in public I am aware that someone might be snapping a picture. So eyes straight ahead.

Years after going off the air *Star Trek* was more popular than it had ever been. Fans couldn't get enough of it. It was generating millions of dollars in merchandising — of which the cast got almost nothing. But after only seven or eight years Paramount suddenly realized it owned an extremely valuable intellectual property and was doing nothing with it. Somebody came up with an interesting concept: let's do a TV show! Eventually that concept became six major movies, but that would be later in my career.

Captain James T. Kirk eventually became one of the best-known and most easily recognized characters in the history of American entertainment. One night, for example, decades after the show went off the air, I was watching a TV show. A scene took place in a lawyer's office, and as the camera panned across the room I noticed that hanging on the rear wall, just over the main character's shoulder, was a framed photograph of Captain Kirk. I literally had become part of the furniture.

But the incident I remember most took place in the early 1980s, as I was driving to the Academy Awards with my second wife, Marcy. We were on Wilshire Boulevard in Westwood, a very main road. There was a lot of traffic and directly in front of us two cars were jockeying for position. As I watched, it was clear that this was a serious case of road ego. These drivers were both recklessly swerving in and out of traffic, trying to cut off the other's car. Finally the two cars ended up right next to each other. I could see the passenger in the car on my left leaning out his window and screaming at the driver of the second car, who apparently was screaming right back. And then he just took a deep breath and spit at the driver. That was it. The second driver swerved in front of the first car, cutting him off, and slammed on his brakes. His door flew open and he jumped out of the car. The passenger swung open his door and got out. They started screaming at each other and finally one of them threw the first punch. They started pummeling each other. An incident of road rage had escalated into a dangerous fight.

It was terrible. Marcy and I were going to be late for the Oscars.

I got out of the car. I grasped the arm of one of the brawlers to alert him that I was there. I didn't want to get hit by a wild blow. I held up my hand in front of the second man and said firmly, "I'm breaking this up."

It seemed obvious that both men had been driven by their machismo to get into it a lot deeper than they liked — and were happy that someone was stopping them. The second man glanced over my hand at my face. He seemed shocked. "Captain *Kirk!*" he said.

Almost instantly both men relaxed. The anger just drained right out of them. Of course they had to stop — Captain Kirk had taken charge of the situation!

That was the power of the *Star Trek* franchise. While we were doing the show, Leonard, more than anyone else, worried about being typecast. "When the part was first offered to me," he remembers, "I had a conversation with Vic Morrow, who had starred in the successful series *Combat!* I told him I was concerned about what playing this character might do to my career. He told me, 'You have three choices. You can do it in total makeup so nobody knows who's underneath the makeup, or do it for

263

the money and when it's over you take the makeup off and you're ready to go to work, or you can do it recognizably and hope it helps your career.'

"I didn't want to hide inside the character. I thought, if this thing works I want people to know that this actor did it. I was proud enough to want the credit for giving that performance."

But in its initial run *Star Trek* had not been successful enough for any of the actors to become typecast. *Star Trek* was just a few lines on our résumés and an occasional small check. Probably Leonard had a little more difficulty than anyone else because his character was so unique. When the show was canceled all of us went back to the work of being an actor. Leonard, for example, began touring with his play *Vincent,* and eventually joined the cast of *Mission: Impossible* for two seasons.

It was only after the show unexpectedly became an international hit that all of the actors became well known and strongly identified with their characters. But by the time that happened all of us were hard at work on a variety of other projects. So until I began appearing at conventions and making the *Star Trek* movies I hadn't seen any members of the cast besides Leonard since the day I had walked off the set for the last time. We'd worked together on the television series and on six *Star Trek* motion pictures, and then we'd gone in different directions. That's what an actor's life is like.

I had always assumed my relationships with everyone else in the cast were fine. Maybe we hadn't become good friends, but to my memory there had not been any difficulty, any bad feelings. And truthfully, for most of my life I've had very few close friends. I've had many acquaintances, there are so many people whom I've liked and admired, but almost no one beyond my wives with whom I felt comfortable talking about the things that mattered. So the fact that I hadn't maintained friendships with any other members of the cast seemed very normal to me. That's why I was shocked many years later to learn about the deep animosity several members of the cast had toward me.

In the early 1990s I had just finished interviewing Nichelle Nichols for a book I was writing, *Star Trek Memories,* when she told me, "I'm not finished yet. I have to tell you why I despise you." As this wasn't *Saturday Night Live* I knew she was serious. Despise me? I didn't understand that at all. That possibility had never even occurred to me. She began explaining, telling me that while we were making the series I had been completely self-absorbed; not only hadn't I been supportive of the other actors, at times I'd even been responsible for them losing time on screen and even took lines away from them.

When I considered this, I realized she probably was right. I was the star, Leonard Nimoy and I were in the middle of almost every scene, Dee Kelley was also in the majority of the scenes, so it hadn't even occurred to me that Nichelle and Walter Koenig, George Takei, and Jimmy Doohan had to fight for every minute on camera. Their careers depended on it. I was so intent on telling the story that I never focused on their needs or desires. The only thing I could say in my defense was that I never intentionally tried to hurt another actor. Perhaps I was ignorant, but I was never mean.

I discovered that the rest of the supporting cast felt very much the same way, but only Jimmy Doohan refused to speak to me. Doohan was particularly critical of me, both as an actor and a person. Obviously there wasn't anything I could do but take it. While I thought his comments were extreme and truly unjustified — and maybe even petty

— I certainly wasn't going to get into an argument with him. The fact is that Leonard and Dee Kelley and I worked full days five days a week, while the other members of the cast came in as they were needed. When the show ended, as far as I knew, everybody was satisfied. Then the conventions started and the actors would go to the conventions and get standing ovations. Slowly, I think, the supporting players began to consider themselves lead actors and no longer wanted to take a backseat. In some ways their perception of reality changed. But even after being criticized I do think of the cast with affection on some level.

And at least *they* didn't call me wooden!

What I would rather remember is that working together — all of us — we had made entertainment history; we'd created a multibillion-dollar franchise with beloved characters that has been seen, and reseen, and rereseen, and . . . and in doing so we'd made an indelible impression on American culture and changed countless lives. The Smithsonian Institution has held a major *Star Trek* exhibit and the Las Vegas Hilton is the site of *Star Trek: The Experience,* a themed attraction featuring rides and a show. Dee Kelley, Dr. McCoy, used to say that his greatest thrill was the number of people who told him that they had entered the medical profession because of him. Similarly, both Leonard and I have often been told by people that they had become an engineer because of *Star Trek,* or a physicist, or an astronomer, or a pilot. Astronauts have told me they first started dreaming of going into space when they watched the show.

Just imagine what the world would be like if the other series pilots I'd done had made the same impact on society as *Star Trek.* If *Alexander* had been successful tens of thousands of people would have become soldiers and armies would have swept through the Middle East and then . . . Well, if *For the People* had achieved the same level of success as *Star Trek* we would have become a nation of countless lawyers and I'm certain you can imagine what the result of that would be!

Fortunately, it was *Star Trek.* Naturally, we had a very special relationship with the American space program. As it turned out, a NASA executive discovered that every time they launched a manned rocket our ratings went up, meaning people were very interested in space; and when our ratings went up Congress voted more money for the space program. In fact, the prototype space shuttle, which was used primarily to perform tests in the atmosphere, was named the *Enterprise.* NASA officials often invited us to launches, and finally I decided to go to one of them. They treated me as space royalty, eventually allowing me to sit inside the LEM, the moon landing module, with an astronaut. I was lying in the hammock-like seats pretending to be flying this module, looking out of the small windows at the universe displayed around us just as the astronauts would see it. The astronaut, who was teaching me how to fly this craft, told me to look at a certain section of the star system — and as I did, flying beautifully across the entire horizon came the Starship *Enterprise.*

As I climbed down from the LEM several thousand NASA engineers started applauding. Several of the brilliant men and women who actually had designed and built this craft that would soon land Americans on the moon came forward to present me with an intricate scale model of the *Enterprise* that they had spent hours putting together. As they told me how difficult it was to complete, the model broke into pieces. I looked at it, and when the laughter subsided I pointed out, "It isn't rocket science, you know."

Perhaps the most memorable story I've heard about the impact of the show was told to me by a limo driver. He had picked me up at my home to take me to the airport and we'd driven only a short distance when he pulled the car to the side of the road and stopped. "I have to tell you a story," he said.

Oh man, I thought, what's going to happen now? There are certain encounters all well-known people have with fans that are less than pleasant. Sometimes they are dangerous. My hope was that this was the usual, "I've written a screenplay that would be perfect for you and I know you'll want to hear all about it. That's why we were brought together. Okay, page one, scene one. A beautiful day but storm clouds are gathering . . ." But this wasn't one of those stories at all. "When I was a prisoner in Vietnam," he began. He had spent several years in a North Vietnamese prison camp. He told me the most terrible story about being chained in cages, tortured, beaten, and deprived of food and water. But one of the few things that kept him going, he explained, that kept them *all* going, was that they kept themselves alive mentally by playing the *Star Trek* game, in which they would play our roles. By constantly changing roles and doing different segments from memory, they kept their sanity and hope alive. *Star Trek* had enabled him to survive, he told me, and he just wanted to thank me.

By the time he'd finished telling me that story both of us had tears running down our faces. And he hadn't written a screenplay.

It's just astonishing that a television show would have that kind of power, that it could affect scientists and soldiers and be celebrated from the Smithsonian to Las Vegas. But there was just one more little thing that ensured Captain Kirk would survive the end of the voyages of the *Enterprise*. In the mid-1970s director John Carpenter was creating the character of Michael Myers for his horror film *Halloween*. After briefly debating using a clown mask, production designer Tommy Wallace bought a $1.98 Captain Kirk mask from Burt Wheeler's Magic Shop on Hollywood Boulevard. Then he widened the eye holes and spray-painted the mask kind of a bluish-white. Michael Myers was born.

I have often gone trick-or-treating with my children and later my grandchildren. The concept of going door-to-door collecting candy has always been appealing to me. One year I was visiting my daughter Leslie and wanted to go out trick-or-treating with my grandchildren — but I had no mask or costume to wear. Hmm, now what could I possibly do?

It was absolutely perfect. I put on the William Shatner mask and disguised myself as myself. Everybody who opened their doors recognized me, but nobody knew who I was.

I never forget how much I owe to *Star Trek* — the longevity of my career, so many wonderful experiences at conventions and other events, the checks that enabled me to finally get more than eighteen hundred dollars in the bank, and almost two very large bowls of really good Halloween candy.

Six

Let me tell you how death gave birth to an idea: after I brought my father's body back with me to Montreal I had to pick out the coffin in which he would be buried. My father had come to Canada as an immigrant in the early years of the twentieth century. He'd struggled all his life to bring his entire family over from the old country. So he knew the value of a dollar and that's what he taught me.

I was standing in the showroom looking at different types of coffins. What do I know about coffins? What features are included? What options are available? I knew nothing at all about coffins. And as I looked at the rows of coffins beautifully displayed I could sort of hear my father's voice, telling me, "What, Billy, are you kidding? Forget about that lead-lined stuff, what am I going to do with that? Just get me a nice simple wooden coffin." Which turned out, of course, to be the most reasonable.

I bought that coffin and my father lay in it. During the funeral service, as the rabbi was giving the eulogy, I turned to my sister sitting on my right and I said, "Joy, Daddy would have been very proud of me. I got a great deal on his coffin."

She thought about that for a few seconds. "Why?" she asked. "Was it used?"

I laughed, then turned to my left and told that to my other sister. She passed it along and soon most of the people in the chapel were laughing while we were grieving for this wonderful man. It struck me then how grief and laughter fit so easily side by side, and I never forgot it.

Many years later, in August 1999, I was sitting shiva for my third wife, Nerine Shatner, who had died tragically. For those who don't know, it is an important aspect of Jewish tradition that after the death of a loved one his or her family sits shiva for a week. During that time friends come to the house to pay their respects and console the family. There's always a lot of food, people tell stories about the deceased, and often there's loud laughter. It's a truly wonderful tradition that really helps people get through the extraordinary pain that comes with the loss of someone you love.

During this period I was standing in my kitchen with several good friends, thinking about the eclectic group of people who were there at that moment. I opened the refrigerator door and this idea came to me: what if a group of struggling young comics agreed to show up at the homes of Hollywood celebrities sitting shiva where they knew they would get a very good meal and perhaps meet an agent? Basically, they plan to use the occasion of sitting shiva to audition for whoever was in the house. Nobody walks out on shiva.

I turned from the refrigerator and within two minutes had expounded an entire outline of a story about grief and laughter. I continued developing that concept for several years and by 2007 I had a very good movie script that I began producing.

So should anyone ask you where great ideas come from, you now know the answer: great ideas come from William Shatner's refrigerator.

Obviously I don't know where ideas come from, but I do believe everyone has a unique vision. Given the freedom to create, everybody is creative. All of us have an innate, instinctive desire to change our environment, to put our original stamp on this world, to tell a story never told before. I'm absolutely thrilled at the moment of creativity — when suddenly I've synthesized my experiences, reality, and my imagination into something entirely new. But most people are too busy working on survival to find the opportunity to create. Fortunately, I've been freed by reputation, by the economics of success, and by emotional contentment to turn my ideas into reality. I've discovered that the more freedom I have to be creative, the more creative I become. Rather than diminishing as I've gotten older, my creative output is increasing.

The concept of *The Shiva Club,* as I've named this movie, is a simple one: grief can be funny. But it's as much about dealing with mortality, a subject I've spent considerable time thinking about. And I've come to realize that among those things I most value about life is the joy of discovery. Whether it's the taste of food or wine, the taste of friendship, of the woman I love, of an adventure, or the taste of the thrill — all are wonderful tastes of life. I know that the people who live the longest and the richest lives are looking ahead and not behind. So I immerse myself in new experiences, I dive as often as possible into the river of life. I don't understand the concept of retirement. It's not a bad thing to savor your memories, it can be wonderful and warming, but not at the cost of losing your excitement about the future.

I don't want to die, yet I continually put myself in truly dangerous situations. I seem to have an on-off switch, and when it goes on, I lose sight of the potential consequences of my actions. I take risks that I shouldn't take, but I can't seem to help myself. My family has accepted the fact that they can't stop me. In fact, once, as a Father's Day gift, my daughter Leslie and her husband, Gordon Walker, gave me a certificate to go skydiving. This wasn't something I'd ever spoken about wistfully, but they decided it would make me happy to jump out of an airplane. And of course it did, although admittedly I screamed all the way down.

I don't know why I put myself in these situations, but I continue to do so. Perhaps because I'm afraid I'm going to miss something? So sometimes I find myself in the middle of a precarious situation, wondering, what the hell am I doing here? Am I crazy? In 2005, for example, I agreed to participate in the largest paintball fight in history to raise money for my therapeutic riding program. I had a wonderful idea — well, it seemed like a wonderful idea at the time — I would film the entire event and sell the DVD to raise even more money. But if it was going to be good entertainment it needed to have a spectacular opening. I've got it! This epic paintball battle was going to take place in Joliet, Illinois, and I would paramotor up the Ohio River and land on the playing field.

Can you really do that? the organizers asked me.

Why not? I responded. Once again, I was about to find out exactly why not. The preparations went very well. Four thousand people paid one hundred dollars each to participate. I was going to be the captain of one team, the greatest paintball player in the nation was going to be the captain of the opposition. I had been paramotoring several times; basically, you put a seventy-five-pound engine with a propeller and a parachute on your back and take off. It's a glorious experience — I've flown with flocks of birds — but it also can be very dangerous; people have died doing this. Generally you fly about a thousand feet high at ten or fifteen miles per hour, holding a dead man's throttle in one hand and the controls for your parachute in your other hand. By holding down the throttle the propeller creates the wind in your parachute that keeps you aloft; when you release the throttle the engine stops and you float down and land gently. In theory.

I took off about ten miles from the playing field. It was a beautiful morning and I was following the Ohio River. I was about six hundred feet high and my hand began to sweat because I was unfamiliar with the equipment. The throttle began to slide out of my hand and I dropped to five hundred feet. It was then I noticed that there were potentially lethal power lines alongside the river. I began to sweat a little more. If necessary, I thought, I could land in the river, I'm a strong swimmer — but then I realized I was not a strong swimmer with a seventy-five-pound engine strapped to my back and wrapped in a parachute. I descended to four hundred feet.

The only thing keeping me in the air was that throttle and I was holding it down with my pinkie. I didn't have enough altitude to release my grip and quickly grab hold again to restart the engine — besides, I was too nervous to attempt that. So I just held on with my pinkie, pressing down as hard as I could, literally holding on for life. And suddenly I realized I was in the middle of another why-am-I-doing-this moment. Why am I risking my life for a stunt?

I barely made it over the river. As I looked

down and saw the thousands of people gathered there for this paintball war looking up, for the first time it occurred to me that all of them had exactly the same thought in mind: I'm going to shoot Captain Kirk.

The object of a paintball war is to compile points by shooting enemy soldiers, capturing his flag, and shooting his commanding officer. Shooting me. The primary rule governing the battle is that there is no primary rule: everything is legal. You can cheat, lie, do anything you can to score points. For example, I had paused for lunch when one of my soldiers walked into my tent — and confessed he was actually a spy sent to shoot me. He'd changed his shirt to get through my lines. "But I can't do it," he said. "I love you and I can't shoot you."

"Yes, you can," I said, and so our plot was hatched. He took me prisoner and we marched back to his headquarters. Unfortunately, as we got close I began to feel a sharp, throbbing pain in my left arm. It had been an amazing day: after flying in a paraglider I'd been running around in the heat all morning, wearing very heavy protective clothing. I was covered with sweat. I sat down in the shade and leaned against a tree. My breathing became loud and labored. "I think I'm having a heart attack," I said with astonishment.

The action stopped as the news spread quickly: Shatner's having a heart attack. Instantly, people came running from all over. Somewhere behind me I could hear someone calling for an ambulance. Finally the commander of the enemy came over to help me. It was obvious he was very concerned. He leaned over, and asked, "How you feeling, Bill?"

"Fine," I said, smashing him in his chest with the two paintballs I was hiding in my hand. "Gotcha!" Hey, it's not my fault they forgot I was an actor. Captain Kirk lives!

The truth is that for some inexplicable reason physical fear has never bothered me as much as emotional fear. I have never worried very much about getting hurt, while I have spent many a sleepless night being terrified of failure. Terrified I would never get another acting job, terrified I wouldn't be able to fulfill my responsibilities. During these times my daughters would refer to me as Black Bill, as in: "Dad's being Black Bill," meaning I was in a dark mood. I withdrew, I didn't want to talk to anyone. After *Star Trek* was canceled, for example, I went through one of the most difficult periods of my life. I wasn't particularly worried about myself; I'm a resilient person, I knew I would be fine, but I spent many sleepless nights worrying about how I was going to support my ex-wife and my three daughters.

Star Trek was mostly perceived to have been an interesting and expensive failure. It had lasted only three seasons; we had just barely made enough shows to allow it to be sold in syndication. But as far as I was concerned, I'd put away my phaser forever. My greatest regret was that it did not lead to any other substantial offers, so I really had to start all over again. Leonard accepted a starring role on the already successful series *Mission: Impossible,* a role he played for two seasons and very quickly grew to despise.

Once more, I was broke. I needed to earn some money very quickly, so I decided to perform in a play on the summer circuit. I went on tour in a very flimsy British sex comedy entitled *There's a Girl in My Soup.* When it had opened on Broadway Edwin Newman described it as "the sort of English play that prevents American theater from having a permanent inferiority complex." I played an aging bachelor pursuing a beautiful young woman whose greatest talent was her microskirt. It was a perfect play for the suburbs. We played a different theater each week. To save money, I'd bought myself a ramshackle pickup truck, put a camper-shell in the rear bed, and drove it cross-country with my dog. Each week I'd park the truck way in the back of the theater parking lot and live in it. Just an actor and his dog, living in the back of a truck. It was depressing beyond any imagination. I was absolutely broke, terribly lonely, terrified of failure, and starring in a comedy.

During the day I would do whatever publicity the theater management asked me to do. After each performance I would wait outside to greet the audience and thank them for coming. And then I would go home to my truck. This was the difference in life between comedy and tragedy: when I had been starting my career, if I'd been this carefree bachelor living in a truck, inviting women over to see my carburetor, it would have been a very funny situation. Instead, I'd been a working actor for decades, I'd starred in three failed TV series, and I was a divorced father of three children living in the back of a truck. That was a tragedy.

A summer later I co-starred with Sylvia Sidney and Margaret Hamilton in a Kenley Players production of *Arsenic and Old Lace*. The producer, John Kenley, had been very successful on this straw-hat circuit by bringing television stars to his theaters in Ohio.

As those who worked for him know, John Kenley was a . . . an . . . interesting man. Or woman. Or both. He would spent summers in the Midwest as a man and the winters in Florida as a woman named Joan Kenley. When Merv Griffin wrote that John Kenley was "a registered hermaphrodite," Kenley responded, "I'm not even a registered voter." Although in his autobiography Kenley admits, "Androgyny is overrated."

I do remember that at the cast party following our opening, John Kenley insisted on the first dance — with me.

Nobody was even pretending I was going to be a star anymore. Those days were over. I had made the transitions from young male lead to leading man to guest star and character actor. When I got back to Los Angeles at the end of the first summer I went to work doing guest-starring one-shots. I appeared on all the popular series; I was a mean drifter on *The Virginian,* an arrogant doctor on *Medical Center* and a dedicated doctor on *Marcus Welby,* a burglar on *Ironside* and a criminal kingpin on *Mission: Impossible.* I was an undercover policeman on an episode of *Playhouse 90* and a private investigator on *Hawaii Five-0.* When the phone rang I said yes even before I answered it. I did Efrem Zimbalist's *The*

F.B.I., Mannix, The Bold Ones, Kung Fu, Iron-side, The Six Million Dollar Man. Name a series, I appeared on it. *Barnaby Jones.* I did the movie pilot for *Owen Marshall: Counselor at Law* with Arthur Hill. I was working for paychecks: I became a frequent guest X on the quiz show *The Hollywood Squares.* I was a celebrity guest on the well-known psychic show *The Amazing World of Kreskin.*

For several weeks after returning to L.A. I lived in a motel, but finally I rented a small and inexpensive apartment on the beach in Malibu. I wanted to be near the beach so when I got my daughters on Sundays we could play in the sand together. The apartment was quite reasonable — perhaps due to the fact that my landlady was absolutely insane.

I saw true madness. This was an older woman occasionally visited by demons. Suddenly my front door would fly open and she would rush screaming into the apartment waving a hammer and chasing a being or an animal that only she could see, then seconds later she'd turn and rush out of the apartment. All without even acknowledging my presence. It was crazy, it was a life out of *Arsenic and Old Lace* — but without the laughs. And then every so often I would

285

come home to find the closet door open and a hole smashed through the drywall in the back, leaving a view of the ocean, or I would find a small object smashed to smithereens. There was an element of danger to this apartment, but I just wanted a safe place to live, a place my daughters could visit. Instead I'd walked into someone else's breakdown.

I worked regularly, but without any satisfaction. Most of these programs are long forgotten, especially by me. On occasion one of these programs is shown on late-night cable but I never watch them. In fact, I've rarely watched any of the shows I've done; a performance is made in the editing room and an actor has no control over the editing process. By the time a show is broadcast there is absolutely nothing I can do to change my performance; someone else has already decided what the audience should see. I don't have the objectivity to simply be satisfied with my performance, so rather than risk frustration, I simply don't watch. I've never seen myself as the Big Giant Head and at most only a few minutes of being Denny Crane.

But every once in a while a very special role came along, a role that poked me in the heart and reminded me why I so loved this profession. A role that allowed me to be an actor. A decade earlier George C. Scott had starred on Broadway in *The Andersonville Trial,* the true story of the post–Civil War trial of the commandant of the particularly horrifying Confederate prisoner-of-war camp. At Andersonville thirteen thousand Union prisoners had died of starvation and exposure; the survivors had been forced into cannibalism. This was the first soldier ever tried for war crimes. Much of the dialogue came from transcripts of the trial. PBS had hired George C. Scott to direct a television version of the Broadway show, and he picked me to play the role of the Union prosecutor that he'd created on Broadway.

I'd met George Scott when I came to New York in *Tamburlaine the Great.* A talented actress named Colleen Dewhurst was a member of that cast, playing a minor role as a native girl. I don't think she had any lines. She introduced me to the man she was dating, a tough-looking, growling New York actor. Eventually they married and divorced and remarried, and at this point Scott was at the very top of his career, having just won — and rejected — the Oscar for Best Actor for *Patton.* So he picked a group of working actors he respected to do this play he loved. The cast included Jack Cassidy, Cameron

287

Mitchell, Buddy Ebsen, Martin Sheen, and Richard Basehart.

The other shows I was doing all worked on a very tight schedule, with very little time to rehearse. On *Star Trek,* for example, we shot each show in six days and finished each day at exactly 6:18. There was no provision for overtime in the budget. So even if we were in the middle of a scene, at 6:18 we shut down and went home. Six-eighteen, done. Most series worked pretty much the same way. We weren't creating art, we were churning out television shows. I showed up on time, performed my role, and went home. If it's Tuesday I'm a doctor with a gambling problem. Six days later I'm a newspaperman introducing publisher Gene Barry to the world of witchcraft. But *The Andersonville Trial* was a very different situation, this was . . . *public television!* This was a prestigious production! I knew it was prestigious because it paid less than network shows.

We had almost two weeks of rehearsal. Rather than being filmed, the show was being done on tape so it would have the look and feel of a stage production. The play itself explored the moral ambiguity of the situation, in which the accused prison commander had apparently tried to get food for his prisoners but had been torn between his duty to the Confederacy and his obligation to his prisoners. I had a scene near the end in which I was questioning the commander, Richard Basehart, about his actions. I'd been a stage and television lawyer for many years, so I knew how to question a witness for the camera. But toward the end of rehearsals Scott sat down with me and said, "You know, the way you're playing that last scene is the way I played it to begin with." But then he proceeded to tell me that his performance had evolved during the stage run. Instead of attacking the witness with the fury of an angry DA, he said, eventually he'd identified with the pain of the commandant who had been caught in this terrible situation. "You know, what I found was that rather than expressing anger, anguish worked a lot better there."

It was only a small suggestion, but it changed my entire interpretation of my character. It added yet more depth to the play. "Gee, George," I said. "I don't think so."

"Just try it," he suggested.

Of course it worked. It was the best piece of direction that I can remember being given in all those years. The program was an artistic success, winning three Emmys —

including the Outstanding Single Program of the Year — and a Peabody Award. As it turned out, this show changed my life — although not as I might have expected.

During rehearsals I'd met a lovely woman named Marcy Lafferty, a young actress George Scott had hired to run lines with the cast. Apparently I was the only member of the cast who took advantage of her — to rehearse my lines. To rehearse my lines! But as Marcy once said, "Bill didn't want to get involved . . . I fell in lust with him."

We dated very happily for a couple of years. My girls liked her immediately, and on weekends we'd take them camping and skiing. Marcy had a wonderful sense of humor and was a ready participant in my adventures. She even willingly went with me to see every single kung fu picture ever made. Our relationship was so comfortable it never occurred to me that we should get married. I'd been married and I wasn't very good at it. But early in 1973 she casually asked one day, "Look, I don't want to rush you or anything, but I can't go on like this. Are we going to get married in the next five years?"

"Well," I said, "what about next week?" This was my first second marriage. I remember reading a newspaper story about the marriage in which Marcy was quoted as saying she was very surprised when I proposed. And I thought, *she* was surprised? During our marriage ceremony I remember hearing a sob coming from somewhere. I turned and looked around curiously to see who was so moved emotionally by my marriage that they were crying. It turned out to be *me*. I was sobbing.

As it turned out there really was only one thing wrong with our marriage. Me. I hadn't learned anything from the failure of my first marriage. Marcy and I had a very passionate relationship; when we were in love, we were really in love, but when I got angry . . . One night, I remember, we were in a restaurant and got into a big argument. I have no memory what it was about, but I was absolutely furious. At that moment I didn't want anything to do with her, so I decided to walk home. Walk all the way home, at least eight miles. Unfortunately, I was wearing new cowboy boots at the time. But I was going to walk home, I wasn't going to give Marcy the satisfaction of accepting a ride or calling a cab. As it turned out those particular boots were not made for walking, they were made for driving in a car. Within the first couple of miles the blisters began forming. My route took me right through Boys Town, the gay section of Santa Monica. I just kept going and by the time I got home my feet were bleeding. But I made it. I proved my point. Whatever that point was.

My youngest daughter, Melanie, remembers Marcy as "the most beautiful, perfect caretaker imaginable. My dad really didn't want to have any more children and she really did want to have children, so I became her surrogate child. I needed a mother and she needed a child and we agreed, 'Okay, you'll do.'"

There's a story actors tell that took place during the Depression, when work was hard to find. A young actor named John Wayne was just beginning his career, playing the first singing cowboy in a series of B-Westerns at Republic Studios. Supposedly he was walking across the lot one day, muttering to himself, when he bumped into the legendary philosopher-comic Will Rogers. "What's the matter, kid?" Rogers asked him.

Wayne shook his head. "Oh, they got me making these ridiculous singing cowboy films . . ."

Rogers listened to Wayne complain, and when he finally stopped he asked, "You working?"

Wayne nodded.

"Keep working," Rogers said, and walked away.

This was my own depression: I was working, I'd made prestigious films, I'd been a Broadway star, a television star, and I'd made some good movies; I'd gotten wonderful reviews, I'd won awards — and I'd ended up living in the back of a truck or renting an apartment from an insane landlady. I was always professional about my work; I was proud to be an actor, so no matter how outrageous my role I treated it with respect: When necessary I became a well-meaning homicidal maniac.

I made a lot of theatrical B-movies and television movies during this period. I knew what they were; the reality is when you open a script entitled *The Horror at 37,000 Feet* you can be certain you're never going to hear those magic words, "The nominees for Best Picture . . ." In many instances I just came in for a few days, did my few scenes, and left. I never saw the picture or read the reviews. Several of these movies were actually quite good, they explored controversial issues, but the majority of them were just terrible. Terrible doesn't begin to express how truly awful some of these movies were. There's an Esperantoese word to describe these movies: Oy! Some of these movies were so awful I wouldn't even sell them in my online store, WilliamShatner.com.

Let me give you an example: One of the first TV movies I did was *Perilous Voyage,* which originally was titled *The Revolution of Antonio DeLeon.* We filmed it in 1968 in San Pedro, California. This film was a disaster; not a disaster film, just a complete disaster. I played a drunken playboy on a luxury cruise ship hijacked and held hostage by a South American guerilla and his followers because it is carrying weapons they need for their revolution. There were several good experienced actors in the cast: Lee Grant, Victor Jory, Frank Silvera, Stuart Margolin, and Michael Tolan. The whole plot hinged on the fact that this guerilla leader, Antonio DeLeon, was so handsome, so charismatic that several women passengers couldn't resist falling in love with him. Supposedly he was a Che Guevara type. A talented, handsome young actor named Michael Parks was hired to play that role. Michael Parks should have been a star, but as it turned out he was just too arrogant.

On the first day of filming he arrived on the set made up to look like a sixty-year-old Mexican bandit out of 1940s B-movie Western. He had a potbelly, a gold tooth, and was wearing a white suit. It couldn't have been more wrong if he had been made up as Santa Claus. The director tried to convince him to play it differently but he was adamant: "This is the way I'm going to play it."

The actors were transported back and forth from the ship on a small speedboat. One afternoon several of us were on this boat when its engine failed. We started drifting out to sea in a strong current — just as a thick fog rolled in. Within minutes we were lost in that fog. We couldn't see more than a few feet in front of us — and frighteningly, we couldn't be seen. We were just outside Los Angeles harbor and there were a lot of large ships moving through the area. I suspect all the actors onboard had a very similar thought: if we get killed which one of us is going to get top billing in the obituaries?

That picture was so awful it sat on a shelf somewhere for eight years before it was finally broadcast in 1976. No one knows what damage was done to that shelf.

I'll tell you how bad it got. I starred in a horror film titled *The Devil's Rain*, the story of a man being pursued through the centuries by Satanists. We filmed in Durango, Mexico, and the cast included Ernest Borgnine — who poked out my eyes and crucified me — Tom Skerritt, Eddie Albert, Keenan Wynn, Ida Lupino, and in his first film appearance, John Travolta.

The technical advisor on this film was Anton LaVey, the founder of the Church of Satan. I don't recall having any conversations with LaVey, although I suppose that is not surprising. What would I have asked him, is this the way Satan holds his fork? I was just so miserable making this film. Durango was such a hellhole, I was vaguely ill from the water, I was homesick, and anxious. But it did include perhaps the greatest chase scene of my career — even more memorable than my chase scene through a car wash in *Impulse* — although in this case it wasn't actually in the movie.

In one scene I was tied to an altar as Ernest Borgnine performed a ritual ceremony over me, preparing me to be sacrificed. I was completely nude except for a piece of ribbon, sort of a breechcloth, covering my groin. Let me state here unequivocally that it is my firm belief that I am the only member of the Stratford Shakespeare Festival to have achieved this point in their career. Also in the cast was a nubile, barely clothed, beautiful young woman. A photographer from *Playboy* was on the set shooting pictures. Apparently this actress was to be featured in the magazine and the producers thought this would be good publicity for the film.

Why I objected to Leonard's photographer in the dressing room as I put on my makeup and didn't object to a photographer on the set while I was wearing a ribbon I don't know. But I didn't. In this scene my hands and my feet were bound to the altar. As the photographer started shooting, this actress softly laid her hand on my arm and then on my chest and then on my stomach and then on my . . .

Click. Wait a second! It suddenly occurred to me, *Playboy!* I realized exactly what they were doing. "Untie me!" I screamed. The photographer began quickly packing up his cameras. As soon as I got free, for the only time in my life, I went after a photographer. "Give me that roll of film!"

"No. It's my film." I grabbed his arm, trying to get hold of his camera. He was screaming, "Get your hands off me! Get your hands off me!" Give me that film. "Get your hands off me." We struggled. It was an unusually absurd moment. I was grappling with a photographer who had taken partially nude pictures of me being groped by an almost-naked starlet while being sacrificed by Ernest Borgnine as the founder of the

Church of Satan looked on dispassionately.

Ah, show business.

I finally managed to yank that roll of film out of his camera and expose it.

At the end of these films I often died in a unique way. In the big finale of *The Devil's Rain,* for example, like the other members of the cast I melted in a rainstorm. In *Sole Survivor,* CBS's first made-for-TV movie, and a truly haunting film, I played a ghost trapped in the Libyan desert with the crew of my World War II bomber. At the end of this one I get put in a flag-covered body bag and taken home to rest in peace. I played a psychotic lady-killer in *Impulse* who gets skewered on a sword by the daughter of the woman I'm romancing. In *The Horror at 37,000 Feet* I get sucked out of an airplane while carrying a lit torch into the plane's baggage compartment to try to confront a druid ghost.

Now, there has been considerable discussion among the true Shatner aficionados about precisely which was the worst movie I ever made. And *The Horror at 37,000 Feet* does have its supporters. This was sort of *The Poseidon Adventure* meets *The Exorcist* plot: a small group of potential future *Dancing with the Stars* contestants, including

Buddy Ebsen, Paul Winfield, Roy Thinnes, Chuck Connors, Tammy Grimes, and France Nuyen are flying to New York on a private plane that, unknown to us, is carrying in its baggage compartment a druid sacrificial stone — and it's hungry! Or it's thirsty. Or lonely or whatever happens to druid sacrificial stones to make them need another sacrifice. I played a drunken architect who eventually finds his nobility by fighting unseen ghosts. Ghosts are very popular in low-budget films, by the way, because they can't be seen!

The most difficult problem I had to overcome while making this film was dealing with a young actress's mother. I've worked many times with child actors, almost always without any problems. But in this picture the child was possessed by the druid ghosts and I had to choke her. There is a skill to convincingly choking someone on camera; you have to make it look real because the camera is close but obviously you can't really choke them. I was very careful, but apparently not careful enough for her mother. No matter what I did, this woman complained. Too hard, too tight, too long. The child was very embarrassed — being possessed by the devil had turned Linda Blair into a star, so if necessary she was prepared to be choked for her art.

It was while I was busy working on these shows and movies, and pretty much unknown to me, that the entire *Star Trek* industry, an industry that would eventually cover the entire civilized world, was slowly coming into being. The original episodes were being syndicated . . .

Let me pause right here again. Did I happen to mention my favorite Italian restaurant? Now, I am aware it has been said about me that I am a man of many great passions and that I do tend to get overenthusiastic about things, that perhaps on occasion I might have even exaggerated. All right, it's true that when I find something that is really special I feel a great desire to share it with everyone. But what's wrong with that? For example, I would argue that among the very few common goals shared by most of civilized mankind is the eternal search for the perfect chicken parmigiana. So when I chanced upon it, should I not convey that discovery to others?

I certainly don't get that enthusiastic about everything, only about things that I believe are the very best in the entire world and only those things that truly matter. For example, Café Firenze in Moorpark is simply the finest Italian restaurant in the world. That's just the way it is. You have to trust me on this, but you have never had better chicken parmigiana in your life. You have to taste it, I mean, you won't believe it. You've never tasted anything like it. What I do when I go there is, rather than ordering, I tell the chef, "Surprise me," and I'm always surprised! Of course, if I wasn't surprised, then I would have been surprised by that. That's how good it is!

My daughters find it amusing when I get really enthusiastic about something. When I insist that they share it with me, or try it themselves. Oh, it's just Dad being Dad again. But when they try it, they discover that maybe I did know something. Let me give you another example. When you leave Café Firenze, there's a gas station several blocks away on the right. I mean, it looks like a normal service center, but in this place they have an air pump that contains the finest tire air I've ever encountered. It's really amazing. Until finding this place I had always believed that all tire air was the same, but for some reason when you put this air in your tires the car rides more smoothly. I don't understand it, what could it be? How could they have improved air? They can't, can't be done, it's just air, but you have to try it. I mean, you must. It's truly superior air.

As I was writing, the original episodes were being syndicated all over the world and wherever it was shown the program gained a dedicated following. There was no real explanation for it, just that people watched it and liked it. This growing popularity hadn't affected my life, I'd already received all the checks to which I was entitled so I wasn't making any money from it. And then in early 1973 Gene Roddenberry called and said he'd sold an animated version of *Star Trek* and wanted me to be the voice of Jim Kirk. And so it began.

This was my first experience doing a voice-over for animation. It's the strangest form of acting I've ever done — although I did do all my own stunts. Since then I've done several major animated theatrical movies. I've always done it alone, without any other actors being present. When we were doing the animated *Star Trek* the director and the sound technicians would come to the set wherever I was working and between scenes we'd go into a bathroom and record my part. Apparently the acoustics in a bathroom are particularly good — and for obvious reasons bathrooms generally have thicker walls.

For movies like *Over the Hedge* and *The*

Wild I did go into a soundproof booth to read my role. I don't know why voice-over actors work alone, but that's the way it's done. At first, someone read the lines with me, but after a point I started hearing them in my head and simply responded out loud.

It's not as easy as it sounds. There are as many as fifteen technicians working with me in the room, and all of them have an opinion about my reading. There is no right or wrong way to do a reading, just opinions. Endless opinions. In *The Wild* I played an egotistical wildebeest who wanted to become a predator — and who had a real passion for choreography. After one take I remember one of the techs telling me gently, "That just doesn't sound like a power-crazed wildebeest to me."

I didn't know how to respond. I didn't sound like a wildebeest? I was tempted to tell him that I was playing it as a Canadian wildebeest, which has a much different accent than your normal wildebeest. Instead, I went back in the booth and did my best possible wildebeest.

Unlike film, which can be expensive, audio tape is very inexpensive. Normally on the first few takes I would be spontaneous, and then I would begin doing variations. Endless variations. Surprisingly, they record the

303

audio first and then draw the animation to fit the voice.

In *Over the Hedge* I didn't work with a wonderful cast that included Bruce Willis, Garry Shandling, Wanda Sykes, Steve Carell, Nick Nolte, and Avril Lavigne. Normally at the end of a picture the entire cast has a party, but when I finished doing my role in this film I popped open a soft drink.

Not working with your co-stars in a movie is actually quite common. In many of these pictures I appeared in only a few scenes, I'd come in for a few days and do my scenes and leave. If the other actors weren't in my scenes there would be no reason or opportunity for us to meet. The one person in particular I remember not working with was Ava Gardner. Growing up, I had been in love with Ava Gardner, who was my fantasy of the perfect woman. I didn't work with her for the first time in my career in *The Kidnapping of the President.*

So when we did the animated version of *Star Trek* I didn't work with Leonard or any other members of the cast. In fact, they eliminated Chekov from the series because they couldn't afford to pay Walter Koenig. The scripts were written by many of the same writers who'd done the original episodes and, in fact, some of them were based on those episodes. For example, we had more trouble with tribbles.

I enjoyed reprising Kirk, perhaps even a little more than I'd expected. He'd been locked away inside me for almost four years, but as soon as I opened my mouth to read his first line he was back. Slipping back into that character was like putting on a comfortable old sweatshirt; it fit. An actor does form a relationship with the characters he or she plays. When I was doing a low-budget movie or a guest-starring appearance on TV there rarely was time to actually get to know the character, it was just a mask I slipped on for a few days and I tried to invest as much humanity as possible into him. But when you're working on a series for several years, on many levels your character actually does come alive, the character takes on its own emotional life, and you experience the emotions of the story through the prism of that character. You don't even have to think about it, you just react. On occasion a character will surprise you, and react in an unexpected way. You also get the freedom within the protection of that character to take actions and behave in ways you never would normally. I liked Kirk. He was a heroic figure, he had a bit of Alexander's nobility but with a nice sense of irony — and an appreciation of a lovely earthwoman.

Mr. Spock also became real on some level of my mind. Of course I know Spock is a fictional character, but I've known him so well for so long that . . . Actually, Kirk knew him so well and valued Spock's friendship so greatly, that it was somewhat surprising that Leonard and I hadn't become better friends. After the series ended we saw each other only when we were making an appearance and never spoke privately.

So I was very pleased that Kirk was back, even if it was only his voice. The animated series lasted two seasons, twenty-two episodes, and won our first Emmy, for Outstanding Entertainment in a Children's Series.

Being Kirk was an island of tranquillity in an ocean of anxiety. It was like coming home. This was a very tough time in my career, I was having to run faster and faster just to stay in place. One of the few positive memories I have from this period, besides meeting Marcy, was that I began to work often with horses.

There is nothing in my background to explain my deep love for horses, whether I'm riding a horse, or communicating with a horse, or simply appreciating the beauty of this magnificent animal. For some reason I found myself enthralled by horses as a child. What could have caused that? I was a Jewish kid from the streets of Montreal. No one in my family knew anything about horses; it was a word that never entered my family's lexicon. But I do remember loving Westerns and loving being in the woods and loving animals. There was a stable near our house and when I was ten years old I went riding there for the first time. I think I had earned this ride by working there. It was obviously a big deal because my parents came to the stable to watch me. I don't think it made a lot of sense to my father, who was a very practical man. Jews didn't ride horses. Name one great Jewish cowboy! My mother was terribly frightened I was going to get hurt. Oy, what does my little Billy know from horses? My sister Joy remembers sitting there with my parents as I climbed up on this horse, kicked it in the hindquarters, and galloped away.

The three of them sat there stunned, their mouths open. My first time on a horse and I was galloping. The only possible reason I might have had for doing that is because that's the way cowboys rode. It never occurred to me not to; in the movies it looked like so much fun. For me it was just a matter of holding on. After that I rode every time I had the opportunity — which was not very often. And I ended up doing a lot of movies in which I got to ride a horse. For *Alexander* I had learned how to ride bareback, but I really learned to ride while doing a movie in Spain named *White Comanche.*

White Comanche was an Italian Western I made during a hiatus from *Star Trek,* in which I played twin half-breed brothers, or one breed, one good and the other evil, who eventually must fight to the death. Clint Eastwood's spaghetti Westerns had become hugely popular and this was an attempt to make a less-expensive version. And when I was offered the part I realized that my childhood dream had come true: I was going to be in a Western! It turned out to be more of a macaroni and very cheesy Western. This was a truly awful experience. I was in the middle of my divorce from Gloria, I was one of the few people on the crew who spoke English, I didn't get along with the director, and the script was dreadful.

How dreadful was it? I think I can probably sum it up by quoting one of my better lines from this picture. After my good character shoots a bad guy he says knowingly, "Next time, don't eat the peyote."

While *Comanche Blanco,* as it was released in Spain, is not available at my online store, WilliamShatner.com, you can get it at Amazon — for the incredible price, ladies and gentlemen, of . . . one cent. Literally, they are selling it for one cent. Truthfully I don't know how they can earn a profit that way, but I've never been strong in mathematics. One buyer, however, did write that he had actually purchased "the upgrade for forty-three cents."

While making this movie I got to ride wonderfully high-spirited Spanish horses. Since each brother needed a horse, I had two horses with very similar markings. One of these horses, whom we called El Tranquillo, was to be used for close-ups. El Tranquillo had to remain calm when the clapboards snapped and the bright lights went on in his face. The horse that we used for long shots was called El Nervisio. El Nervisio was a difficult horse to ride; he'd broken the noses of several stuntmen by stopping short and as the rider's momentum was carrying him forward sticking up his head. Bam, broken nose.

But after about a month El Tranquillo had become crazed by the snap of the clapboard — as soon as he heard it he knew he had to work and he didn't like it. We stopped using the clapboard, instead the director shouted "Action." But he quickly caught on to that. And he became difficult to ride. Meanwhile, El Nervisio got used to me and calmed down. So in the middle of the film we had to switch horses; El Tranquillo was used for long shots and El Nervisio was used for close-ups.

Honestly, I personally would pay a penny for this movie, if just to see the riding. After this I did several other films in which I rode — including one film in which I played perhaps the most celebrated rider in history.

No, I did not play Lady Godiva.

In John Jakes's *The Bastard* I played Paul Revere, riding through village and town — in the mud as it turned out — to warn Americans. It was a small role in which . . . wait, let me do it for you. "To. Arms! To arms! The British. Are *coming!* The British are coming!" In my entire career, that was the easiest dialogue I ever had to memorize.

I got to ride quite a bit in the television movie *North Beach and Rawhide,* which ended with a rodeo. I played Rawhide, an ex-con who runs a correctional ranch for wayward kids, believing that working with horses could have great therapeutic value for them. By the time I did this film I was already involved with the Junior Justice Correction Program, but hadn't yet discovered Ahead with Horses. In the seventh *Star Trek* feature film, *Star Trek: Generations,* I had a scene in which I'm riding with Patrick Stewart. In that film I rode a horse that I'd bred on my horse ranch in central California.

I can just imagine if my father had lived and was reading that last sentence: Billy has a horse ranch? My Billy? What does he call it, the Bar Mitzvah?

Patrick Stewart had very little experience on horseback so I worked with him. I remember the best single bit of advice I ever gave him: Patrick, you should wear pantyhose under your pants because it will reduce the chafing.

As I've learned several times, horseback riding can be dangerous. You don't ride a horse a lot without falling off. I remember how awful I felt when Chris Reeve broke his neck. I knew Chris vaguely, and several months after his accident I went to visit him. As I walked through the glass doors of the hospital in New Jersey I saw him sitting in his wheelchair, breathing with the assistance of a machine, and I thought, what am I possibly going to say to him? I sat down beside him and within minutes we were talking about horses. Horses on the bit, off the bit, all we talked about was horses. He loved them as much as I did.

But for months after that visit every time I got on a horse I thought, is this it? Is this the day I fall off a horse and break my neck? I was just luckier than he was. In 1975 we were shooting the first episode of a series that eventually became known as *Barbary Coast,* although at that point it was called *Cash & Cable.* The series was a combination of *Wild Wild West, Mission: Impossible, I Spy,* and just about every other period detective show ever done. I was Cable. The gimmick was that each week I would have to wear some elaborate disguise. For this episode, though, I was dressed as a cowboy. The first day of filming, the very first day, we were doing a simple stunt, a horse falling. I decided to do it myself. I won't volunteer to do a stunt if it's unnecessary or dangerous — I'm not going to fall off a building in a long shot in which no one can see my face. But if the camera is going to be close enough for the audience to recognize me, I want to do it.

Falling off a horse is not a particularly dangerous stunt. To do it, they dig a soft pit to fall into. When you give the horse its cue, yanking his head around, he's trained to fall flat. The key is to get your leg out from under the horse. You do this stunt with your feet out of the stirrups; the ground is soft and as long as you let yourself relax you'll get away from the horse.

I had never done a falling horse gag before — but I'd seen it done many times. What could go wrong? "This is where you fall," the director told me as we worked out the shot. "When you fall, roll into here. The cameras are gonna be right on your face as you roll in, so we'll get it all in one." Then he had the crew water down the pit to get rid of the dust and soften it for my fall. "Ready, Bill?"

Action. I got the horse running, I yanked the reins, the horse falls. Perfect. And I almost get out of the way. Part of my shin was caught under the horse. The horse struggled to get up, but couldn't, and it was lying on my leg. And I can't get my leg out from underneath. It felt like it was broken.

As it turned out, the dirt in the pit was actually clay; they had watered the clay and it was hardening. The horse kept rolling on my leg. Finally the horse got up. I was shaking with pain, but I was determined to complete the scene. I wasn't going to go through all that and not get it done. So I said my lines. Then, cut! "Bill, are you okay?"

"No. I think I'm dying." My foot was swelling rapidly. My boot had to be cut off. They rushed me to the Emergency Room of a large downtown hospital. I was lying on a gurney in this urban hospital, all around me were victims of shootings and stabbings, cops were walking around. People were moaning and screaming, crying. It was as if I'd been dropped into a scene out of a Tyrone Guthrie–directed Greek tragedy in downtown Los Angeles. I was lying there on a stretcher, dressed in my cowboy costume, my face covered with my full pancake makeup — and nobody even noticed. I was the most normal-looking person there. Actually, I suppose, it could have been a lot worse. Later in the episode we were filming I was costumed as a member of the Ku Klux Klan.

The producers were incredibly concerned. They saw me lying in pain and said with great sympathy, "When do you think you can get back to work?" The doctor put an air cast on my leg. Two days later I was back at work. Limping, but working.

People always tell you when you have an accident while doing something that the best thing to do is try it again as quickly as possible. It's like falling off a horse, they explain, you have to get right back on the horse. In this case I *had* fallen off a horse, which completely ruined that metaphor. But I did get right back on, and through the years I've fallen off several times.

Years later, for example, I *had* been invited to sing five songs nominated for Song of the Year on the very first MTV Movie Awards show. I was scheduled to go into the studio the afternoon before the show. That morning I was out riding with my close friend Danny Giradi at his facility. I was on a young horse, a three-year-old, that was a little skittish. "You know, Bill," he told me. "The type of horse you're on is very sensitive. If you put your hand on their kidney area, their hip area, they're really sensitive."

That was interesting. I reached back, "You mean like this?"

Apparently that's precisely what he meant. The horse bucked, throwing me into the air. I was out cold for more than a half hour. When I came to I asked the woman who was helping me, "What happened?"

"Well, you got knocked out by the three-year-old."

"Oh. Well, what happened?"

"You got knocked out by the three-year-old."

It was like I was walking slowly out of a deep haze, I couldn't process the information. "Really? So what happened?"

Eventually I was taken to a doctor who decided I was all right. But then I remembered I had to record my five songs. I was still covered with dirt and manure and dust but we went to the studio. Knowing that I intended to speak the lyrics, I told MTV I needed some instruments to carry the melody. MTV had provided a xylophone and bongos. That was my accompaniment. "What's my first song?" I asked the lovely woman from MTV.

She said, "I Want to Sex You Up."

Rapidly I came out of my fog. "What's the first song?"

"I Want to Sex You Up."

As I discovered, the lyrics were very simple: "I want to sex you up, I want to sex you up. Sex you up, sex you up, I want to sex you up." Oh perfect, I thought, a love song. With bongos.

It actually was a very funny show. For example, the first MTV Movie Award given for Best Inanimate Object went, I believe, to Vanilla Ice, who just beat out the wallpaper from *Barton Fink*. So naturally my performance was duly appreciated.

I got to ride almost weekly when we were filming *Barbary Coast* in 1975. This was the first series I'd done since *Star Trek,* the original version and the animated version. I played a special investigator, a master of disguise, working for the governor of California on San Francisco's lawless Barbary Coast in the 1870s. My partner, played initially by Dennis Cole, who was replaced by Doug McClure, owned the local casino. I can't begin to imagine the number of different costumes I've worn in my career. I know it sounds glamorous and even romantic; wow! My job was dressing up as a pirate or a lawyer or a cowboy. But this was television, not motion pictures. We didn't have the luxury of new costumes. We had to use whatever was hanging in the wardrobe department — and some of those costumes had been hanging there for years. So in reality I was putting on old clothes that didn't fit and were full of lice, wigs that smelled awful and itched, and shoes that were always too small or too large and caused blisters.

In our two-hour pilot film I worked undercover as a one-eyed pirate and a blind beggar, a well-suited bank examiner and a Ku Klux Klan member, a priest and a Chinese man.

Working on this show made me appreciate the beauty of Spock's ears. Each morning we began with the wardrobe person going through racks of clothes until he found exactly what he wanted; at the same time a makeup man was inventing my makeup. When my makeup was on and I was in costume I'd look into the mirror and get into character. It took about three hours to do the costume, makeup, and preparation. As soon as I got done the assistant director notified the director, "Shatner's ready." They would stop whatever they were doing and move to my next location and get set up. We'd shoot my scene, then cut!

Baaaaaack I went upstairs while they returned to whatever they were shooting. It would take me about an hour to get out of my makeup. My face got raw from peeling off rubber. Then the wardrobe man came back to create my next costume and the makeup man went back to work. Three more hours, shoot my scenes in that character, back upstairs. We did that at least twice every day.

Having the lead in a series is the hardest work in show business. It's physically debilitating, backbreaking, marriage-wrecking, mind-blowing work. It's fourteen to eighteen hours a day on the set, and then when you're done working you begin doing the publicity necessary to promote it.

ABC was extremely enthusiastic about the

series. We were stealing concepts from several of the most popular series on TV. They hung large signs all around the lot, WELCOME TO BARBARY COAST. They spent money decorating the sets. When we began shooting we would have 130 extras crowding the saloon, a piano player and a banjo player in the background, and in the street we had a dozen horses tied to hitching posts. That went on for about six weeks, until our first show was broadcast.

We got poor notices and our ratings weren't very good. The next week I noticed that there were only a hundred people in the bar, the banjo player was gone, and there were eight horses hitched in the street. Our ratings went down again the following week; there were seventy people in the bar and the piano player had been replaced by a player piano. There were four horses in the street and I was doing only one costume change a day. We knew we were in serious trouble when the signs started coming down. Each week the cast got a little smaller, until we were down to ten people standing in a corner of the bar, a drunk was singing in the background, and the hitching post had been removed. I put on one costume Monday morning and wore it for the entire episode. I wouldn't even bother putting on makeup, they just pasted a mustache on my face. We were canceled after thirteen weeks and I was thrilled about it. I had done fifty different characters in thirteen weeks. When the series was canceled I could finally get back to doing what I did best, worrying about getting the next job.

Here I am, *at about 16 years old, standing in front of a future Canadian hockey rink.*
Photofest

Q: Can you find me? *I made my Broadway debut in January 1956, as Usumcasane in* Tamburlaine the Great *with Anthony Quayle and Colleen Dewhurst as the Virgin of Memphis. The show ran for 20 performances. A: That's me on top of the cage.*

Photofest

My first featured role *on American television was in this 1956* Goodyear Television Playhouse *production of Robert Anderson's Broadway show* All Summer Long, *which starred Sandra Church and Raymond Massey.*
Author's Collection

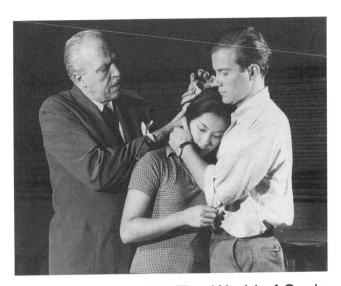

In the Broadway hit The World of Suzie Wong, *gorgeous France Nuyen was in her own world. She and director Josh Logan (above, left) fought so bitterly she refused to speak if he was in the theater. One night I found out that she thought he was in the back when she opened her mouth to speak and nothing came out.*

Photofest

Photofest

I made my motion picture debut *in* The Brothers Karamazov. *The brothers, as described by IMDB .com, were "(A)n elegant officer . . . a sterile aesthete, a factotum who is a bastard, and a monk." The All- Star-except-Shatner cast included our "dad," Lee J. Cobb, Maria Schell, Claire Bloom, and* (from right) *Yul Brenner, Richard Basehart, and me—as the kind- hearted monk.*

Author's Collection

This 1958 publicity picture *was taken at M-G-M while I was making* The Brothers Karamazov. *I was cast as the youngest brother by producer Pandro S. Berman, who supposedly told assistants after meeting me, "Yes, he's the one."*

I've spent most of my life *on TV and movie sets and, truthfully, I've always enjoyed horsing around. I have no idea where or when this picture was taken of me (at left) and a clearly embarrassed horse.*
Author's Collection

Dogs have been the grace of my life, especially Dobermans. I've often taken my dogs into restaurants with me. One Thanksgiving my Doberman, Sterling, stole the turkey. I chased him into the backyard and retrieved it—then served it to my unsuspecting family. When the dog seen here, Kirk, was sick, I consulted a psychic who told me to take him to an acupuncturist—which I did. Another beloved Doberman, China, is buried in the Los Angeles Pet Memorial Park.

Author's Collection

Judgment at Nuremberg, like The Andersonville Trial, *examined individual responsibility during wartime. Although the story was fictional, director Stanley Kramer's decision to include actual Nazi Holocaust films made a devastating impact. Here I'm swearing in witness Judy Garland, nominated for an Oscar as Best Supporting Actress for her role as an Aryan woman whose elderly Jewish lover was executed for their affair.*

Ralph Bellamy *and I created the lead roles of father-and-son defense lawyers in the* Studio One *production of Reginald Rose's* The Defenders, *roles played by E.G. Marshall* (above) *and Robert Reed when it became the classic TV series, on which I made several appearances. In this episode I played an ex-soldier who accidentally killed a man in a street fight.*
Author's Collection

I co-starred *in this 1961 Broadway production of* A Shot In the Dark *with Julie Harris and Walter Matthau, a play based on the French sex comedy,* L'Idiot, *in which I starred on Broadway two years later. In the classic movie version of this play, Peter Sellers played my role—Inspector Clouseau.*

On Star Trek, *Nichelle Nichols and I shared the first interracial kiss in network history, but six years earlier I played a race-baiting bigot in Roger Corman's* The Intruder. *The* Los Angeles Times *wrote it was "the most realistic depiction of racial injustice . . . in American films," and that I was "unctuous and deceitful." We needed police protection while filming in the South. The film failed because too many theaters were simply afraid to present it.*

Photofest

Few things are more frightening *than a face looking back at you through a window—especially when you're in an airplane. I've been fortunate enough to work on material written by many of the greatest science fiction and fantasy writers in history, but Rod Serling's* Twilight Zone *episode,* Nightmare at 20,000 Feet, *has become a television classic.*

Photofest

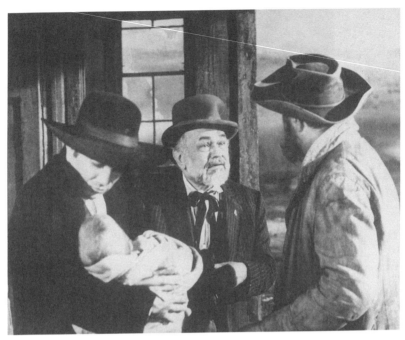

Director Martin Ritt's *1964* The Outrage *was an Old West version of the Japanese classic* Rashomon, *in which the story of a rape and murder is told from several perspectives. Paul Newman starred as a Mexican bandit. I* (left) *played a preacher who loses his faith over this incident. While making this film I became friendly with Edward G. Robinson* (center), *who played a cynical con artist— and offscreen taught me the value of making TV commercials.*

"**Gentlemen**, *I smell of marsh weed, sand, dust, and sweat.*" *Of course I did, because I did all my own riding and stunts playing the title role in the epic* Alexander the Great—*a pilot for a series that ended up being broadcast once, in 1968, four years after it was completed, on the children's anthology series,* Off to See the Wizard.
Author's Collection

Author's Collection

I've piloted *all types of aircraft, from an ultralight to this Cessna. I've parachuted out of planes. I've skydived and put a 75-pound motor on my back and paramotored. For* American Sportsman *I learned how to do aerobatics in a Pitts Special, a short-winged biplane. I did rolls and loops—and had no problem until I tried to land at sunset, and couldn't see the runway. Eventually though, I had to land—the show needed the footage.*

Author's Collection

After the success of producer Herb Brodkin's The Defenders, for which I'd turned down the lead, he developed For the People. This was the first TV series in which I starred, and I played an idealistic, passionate assistant district attorney. We filmed in black and white on the streets of New York, using top New York actors. Our reviews were superb, but CBS put us on opposite Bonanza. We lasted 13 episodes.

Author's Collection

Author's Collection

Many wonderful things *happened to me because of* Star Trek, *but gaining the friendship of Leonard Nimoy is very high on that list. Here Leonard and I savor the fine cuisine served on the Paramount lot.*
Author's Collection

The crew *aboard the starship* Enterprise. (Back row, from left) *James "Scotty" Doohan, Walter "Chekhov" Koenig, Majel "Chapel" Barrett, Nichelle "Uhura" Nichols, and George "Sulu" Takei.* (Front row, from left) *DeForest "McCoy" Kelly, Captain James Kirk, and Leonard "Spock" Nimoy.*

George C. Scott *(in glasses) directed* (from left) *Richard Basehart, Jack Cassidy, Cameron Mitchell, and myself in the powerful 1970 TV film,* The Andersonville Trial. *It was set just after the Civil War and based on actual transcripts. I played the prosecutor of the commander of a Southern prison camp accused of war crimes. We won three Emmys, including the Outstanding Single Program in Drama or Comedy of the season.*

Author's Collection

In the body of my work, *if any body stands out, it is the nude scene I did with Angie Dickinson in* Big Bad Movie . . . *rather* Big Bad Mama, *producer Roger Corman's lower-budget version of* Bonnie and Clyde, *in which I join a gang of bank robbers led by Big Mama and which included her two beautiful daughters.*

The Devil's Rain was your basic "Satanists in America" film. Its climax is probably the second most famous water-melting-actor scene in movie history. It's certainly the only film I know of for which the Founder of the Church of Satan served as technical advisor.

Photofest

In the 1975 TV movie *and subsequent series,* Barbary Coast, *I played Jeff Cable, a master of
disguises who worked for the governor of California
on San Francisco's notorious Barbary Coast in the
late 1800s. With Doug McClure as Cash Conover
(played by Dennis Cole, here, in the TV movie), I
solved crimes by hook and by crooks. The series
lasted 13 episodes.*

Author's Collection

Author's Collection

Few people know *that I was the original Spider-Man—veterinarian Rack Hansen, in the horror classic* Kingdom of the Spiders. *We worked with 5,000 live tarantulas. Of all the stunts I've done, gluing tarantulas to my face certainly is one of the most memorable.*

T.J. Hooker *actually was* with *the force. He was an old-time cop—"I've seen the past," he told the rookie class he taught at the police academy. "And it worked."*
Photofest

Author's Collection

Star Trek V: The Final Frontier, which I directed, was originally intended to be the search for God. Instead, after the studio insisted on story changes and drastically cut my special effects budget, it became the search for an ending.

Photofest

When I was asked *to dance with an orca for an environmental film, I wondered, who leads? As I learned, the killer whale always leads. After this whale spun me around the pool once it then completely surprised me with this great leap over my head.*

Author's Collection

I treasure *this picture. Horses have played an essential role in my life. I have ridden horses, owned horses, and admired horses for as long as I can remember. This was taken at the Hollywood Charity Horse Show, during the horse reining competition. At the heart of the art of reining is balance between the horse and rider—and this shot exemplifies the perfect balance as we come to the end of a 30-foot sliding stop.*

Daryl Weisser

I've not appeared *in several animated films, includ-*
ing Over the Hedge *and* The Wild. *Here I'm not with*
Over the Hedge *costars Bruce Willis* (center) *and*
Gary Shandling (right) *at the premiere in Cannes.*
Author's Collection

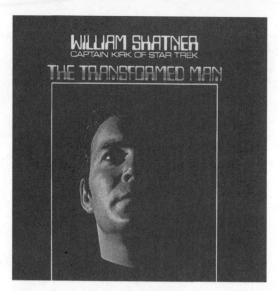

Only 38 years *after the release of my first album,* The Transformed Man, *I collaborated with the great Ben Folds on the critically acclaimed—for real—*Has Been. *Ben turned the poems I wrote into songs that I performed. Featured on the CD were Brad Paisley, Joe Jackson, Lemon Jelly, Aimee Mann, Henry Rollins, and Sebastian Steinberg.*
Author's Collection

Author's Collection

What makes Boston Legal *so enjoyable to do is the people with whom I work and the relationships between our characters. The friendship between Denny Crane and James Spader's Alan Shore has been acclaimed as one of the most profound, honest, and deeply emotional bonds between men in TV or movie history. It has taken both men to unusual places—for example, as seen on the next page, to jail. Or most memorably, to the office Halloween party, when we both showed up wearing pink flamingo costumes. Crane's relationship with the wonderful Candice Bergen's Shirley Schmidt* (above) *might best be summed up by the offer he made after she broke up with her boyfriend: "Whatever you need, Shirley—a shoulder, a hug, an erection—you can count on me."*

American Broadcasting Companies, Inc.

American Broadcasting Companies, Inc.

The Shatners Go to Africa. *Me (second from left) with my daughters Leslie, Lisabeth, and Melanie.*
Leslie Walker

My wife, *Elizabeth Shatner. No wonder I'm smiling.*
Jane Singer

SEVEN

Now, I know that a true autobiography is supposed to reveal to the reader those significant events from which the subject learned the important lessons that impacted his or her life. The takeaway lessons for the reader. Lessons far more important than "Don't take Esperanto as your second language in high school." And so I am very happy to be able to do so.

I have learned some very valuable lessons in my life, lessons that are indeed worth sharing. For example, at one point I was invited to participate in a televised poker tournament, *The World Poker Tour,* which was being taped at Trump's Taj Mahal Hotel & Casino in Atlantic City. I had never played competitive poker, truthfully I'd never quite understood what it was all about, so I agreed to do it.

I knew the basic rules of the game: twos, three of a kind, full house, straights, flushes

— that I knew, but that isn't playing poker. The true game of poker is a psychological contest, in which the weapon is bluffing and bidding. It is the delicate art of drawing your opponent into your net, or scaring him out of the game. It is the actor's game, where the ability to create an image is more important than the cards at play. That was the aspect of this tournament that really intrigued me.

They gave me a $5,000 stake and three professional poker players spent several hours teaching me how to play competitive poker on television. This event was going to last three days, they explained, and we want you to stay in the game as long as possible. So don't say very much because you'll give yourself away, watch the table to see who is bidding what and try to see patterns, and bet conservatively. Always bet conservatively. I repeated their advice; keep my mouth shut, watch who's betting what, and don't bet too much on one hand. I have never been a very skilled or lucky gambler. My objective was to last at least one full day; if I was careful, I thought, I might last two days before I was eliminated.

I began to play at a table of ten people. I did as I had been taught, kept my mouth shut, watched the table, and bet conservatively. I won a pot, maybe two of them. I was beginning to understand that any hand was only as good as the player who drew it. As I settled in there was one player who got my attention, a real loudmouth sitting to my left. What an ass, I thought. He was a fat, ugly, absurd man who obviously wasn't a very good player because he wasn't following the rules I'd been taught by my professionals.

Finally I drew a strong hand, a pair of kings. At first I bet very carefully, reluctantly even, trying to sucker other players into the pot. I was very careful not to bet too much too quickly, but gradually I began raising it. The fat-ass guy keeps seeing me and I realized, I got him. I got him! And I'm holding a pair of kings. He knew it too, he kept sighing and shaking his head and complaining, "Oh yeah, I bet you got me beat. I just know you got something under there." I knew he was testing me, but I smiled enigmatically and said nothing.

Finally only the two of us were left and a large pile of chips was sitting in the middle of the table. I stared at the pile. I had a pair of kings. I could double my money in one game, which would certainly be enough to keep me in the game till the second day. I had followed the rules and it had worked out well for me. But this was the time to express my personality, to demonstrate that I could play this game, to be bold. "Okay," I said, looking right into the eyes of fat ass, "I'm all in."

He let out a long, deflated breath, knowing he had no choice. But he was in too deep to fold. He shook his head, then reluctantly pushed all his chips to the center of the table.

The dealer turned over the last card, which to poker experts like myself is known as the last card. It was an ace. I've got a pair of kings, an ace doesn't do me any good. But I had a pair of kings. It was time to reveal our cards. I had a pair of kings.

And he had a pair of aces. He'd had nothing until the last card. He'd bet everything on the luck of the draw. That's why, as I discovered, he was the reigning world champion poker player, the top money winner on the circuit the previous year, and I was the eliminated-in-the-first-hour guy. I couldn't believe it; I said to my instructors, "I followed all the rules and he didn't follow any of them. He talked incessantly, he didn't pay attention to what was going on, and he bet everything on a single card. He played like an idiot, I played like the pro —

and I'm the one who's eliminated in an hour."

And so I had demonstrated two of the most important lessons which have made all the difference in my life: you can't win the jackpot if you're not in the game. And sometimes you just have to be lucky. Life is chaotic, chance plays a central role in everyone's life. Nobody knows how any decision you make is going to turn out. My career strategy had become just say yes to almost anything.

Want to make a record album? Yes. Want to appear on this quiz show? Yes. Want to star in *White Comanche*? Okay, sometimes decisions are not going to work out as well as you'd like. But you don't know when you make that decision. I remember someone asking me once, "Don't you worry about overexposure?"

To which I'd responded honestly, "Not as much as I worry about paying the mortgage."

Like our universe itself, *Star Trek* continued to expand throughout the television world, growing more popular and successful each year. With that success came recognition for the cast, but especially for myself and Leonard. For some reason I became strongly associated with real science and technology. Producers began hiring me to host specials, documentaries, and limited-episode nonfiction series about science and technology. I was even hired to do one of the very first commercials for a personal computer. It was strange. I'd played numerous doctors but no one expected me to give medical advice; I'd been a prosecutor and a defense attorney numerous times but no one asked me for legal advice; I'd been a homicidal maniac several times but no one ever confused me with a professional criminal. Yet for some reason I had become television's go-to host for anything to do with science or technology.

It had little to do with reality. As a student in Montreal I'd shown very little aptitude for those subjects. They just hadn't interested me. But even before I was hired by Gene Roddenberry I'd discovered the great science-fiction writers; I'd gone from reading the pulp magazines to all the great novels. And then I'd actually gotten to know several of these people, writers like Isaac Asimov and Theodore Sturgeon, while we were making *Star Trek*. I certainly understood why people would associate me with these subjects, but I also believed that on some level of the public's imagination it was not Shatner the actor hosting these shows, who most certainly would be an expert in all of these areas, it was Captain James T. Kirk.

So it was quite natural that, for example, when home computers first became available to the public, I would be hired as the spokesperson. At that time I was one of the very few people in the world who had any practical knowledge about computers, having worked with the plywood and cardboard props aboard the *Enterprise* for three seasons. "Why buy just a video game from Atari?" I asked viewers in what may be the first TV commercial ever done for a computer. "Invest in the wonderful computer of the 1980s for only three hundred dollars. The Commodore Vic-20. Unlike games it has a real computer keyboard. With the Commodore Vic-20 the whole family can learn computing at home — plays great games too! Under three hundred dollars, the wonder computer of the 1980s. The Commodore Vic-20!"

Honestly, I knew nothing about computers. I had seen the huge mainframes at NASA, but I'd certainly never used a computer at home. I didn't even know how to turn one on. This was long before the Internet existed, so computers were basically glorified calculators and word processors.

Mostly people used them to play video games like Pong. Legally, though, anyone endorsing a product is supposed to have some experience using it. So Commodore shipped two Vic-20s to my home, where they remained untouched in their boxes. My attorney insisted I take them out of the boxes and plug them in. That way no one could claim I didn't even know how to plug one in. So that was the entire range of my knowledge of computers: I knew how to plug one in.

The television shows and the movie documentaries I hosted or narrated literally went from the bottom of the world to the ends of the universe. They included the syndicated series *Secrets of the Deep* and *Inner Space,* both of which explored life in the deep oceans, and the syndicated special *Space Age,* which featured all kinds of futuristic gadgets like a home laser and the incredible — in 1973 — nineteen-thousand-dollar electronic typewriter. In 1976 I narrated the theatrically released documentary *Mysteries of the Gods,* based on Erich von Däniken's bestselling book *Chariots of the Gods,* which speculated that beings from outer space had visited Earth millions of years ago and influenced the Mayan civilization. *Universe* was an animated short documentary spon-

328

sored by NASA that explored the universe from subatomic particles to deep space, beginning with the Big Bang — and was nominated for an Academy Award as Best Short Documentary. We didn't win, though. *The Magic Planet,* which I narrated in 1983, was an early look at how changing weather patterns could affect the Earth's very fragile ecology.

I had become the entertainment-industry expert on science and outer space. I was *the* figure of authority. But the program in which I really became involved was the five-part, ten-hour miniseries for Ted Turner's TBS called *Voice of the Planet.* It was an unusual format; I played the fictional author William Hope Planter, who was talking to the spirit of the Earth through a computer located in a Buddhist monastery in the Himalayas, about the very real problems facing the planet in the future. Those problems ranged from overpopulation to a shortage of water.

I agreed to do this series when the producer, Michael Tobias, told me, "There's very little money involved, it's going to take a lot of your time, and it requires us to go around the world."

Go around the world? Several weeks later Marcy and I found ourselves at the Tengboche monastery in Nepal, looking up at Mt. Everest. Buddhists believe the Himalayas are the center of their spiritual world and the confluence of those mountains is in the valley. We had hiked in with a crew of five people and were camped in a small shed right next to an outhouse.

This was a truly awe-inspiring place. This monastery was on a ledge about fifteen thousand feet above sea level; there were no birds, no wildlife, very little vegetation. Just extraordinary snow-tipped mountains cutting into a radiant blue sky. The only sounds were the wind whistling through the valley and the mellifluous chanting of the fifty monks who lived there, the mmmm-sound of the universe disappearing into the silent valley. It was unlike any place I had ever been in my life.

Many years earlier, when I had been a teenaged counselor at a B'nai Brith camp, I had walked out of my bunk late at night and looked up. The sky was brilliant with stars and as I looked at those stars I was struck by an overwhelming feeling of insignificance. Suddenly I understood that in the whole of the universe I was meaningless to a degree I couldn't begin to fathom; smaller than molecules, atoms, quarks, smaller than my ability to imagine. I kept looking up —

and then I fell over backward.

That feeling of wanting to unite with the universe had stayed with me from that night. I'd searched for it. Several times in my life I'd had so-called Zen moments — when I was in perfect harmony with the horse I was riding, making love, or preparing mentally to shoot an arrow — but I'd never truly been one with the universe. I'd never had that mystical experience I'd read about. If I were ever going to reach that state, I realized, it would be at this monastery.

The first night we were there I went outside into the freezing air, wrapped in my sleeping bag. I sat down and stared into a sky of a billion stars and waited for the spirits of that valley to come to me. And I waited. Nothing happened; finally I was frozen and went back into the shed. Maybe the spirits would come the next night. The second night I did the same thing, and the third and the fourth, staring into the night, waiting for a moment of whatever I was waiting for. It. Finally, on our last night I sat outside again. I waited an hour, and then it struck me. Nothing! Absolutely nothing! I realized nothing was going to happen. Maybe my toes would get frostbitten, but nothing else. So I went back inside.

Later that night, as I lay in my warm sleeping bag, it suddenly occurred to me why I was in that valley. It is a truth that has never left me. I was there to understand that I didn't have to be sitting outside in the freezing cold night at a monastery in the Himalayas beneath Mt. Everest to recognize and appreciate the wonderment that exists in every object. It's with me all the time, wherever I am — even on the San Diego Freeway. It's in our skin, it's in our finger, it's in everything. All you have to do is pause and contemplate that thing, whatever it is, and allow yourself to be astounded at its existence, and you are on the verge of the Zen feeling of being at one with the universe.

We traveled around the world for *Voice of the Planet.* The budget was not large enough to afford stuntmen, so I took risks that in retrospect amaze me. I went ice climbing in the French Alps. I was dropped by helicopter on a plateau on Mt. Blanc. When Michael Tobias asked me to climb a vertical rock wall all I asked was that he get it in one take — although once I was properly roped I agreed to do it several times to get the right shot. It might well have been Jim Kirk who viewers imagined was climbing that wall — but if I fell I was going to break every bone in Bill Shatner's body. Through it all, though, one thought resonated in my mind: The star doesn't get hurt! The star doesn't get hurt!

This show received somewhat modest reviews, but I was extremely proud of it. I once said that it was a program I would be proud to pass along to my grandchildren. That's true, but more important, what I have passed along to those grandchildren is the love and appreciation for this Earth that I gained while making it. For me, it was an epiphany. I suddenly became aware of the way we were using up the Earth, and until very recently doing so without any concern. I became a committed environmentalist and have done my best since then to be responsible about my own use of our resources — although truthfully every once in a while I haven't been above giving Mother Nature a little pinch in her oil reserves.

My status as television's leading man of science and technology was assured in 1978 when I was invited to co-host the first televised Science-Fiction Movie Awards. It was just a simple awards show, not very different from the numerous awards shows broadcast each year, and ordinarily it would have been quickly forgotten. And it would have been, except for those fateful few words I said to producer Arnold Shapiro: "You know what, how about if I sing something?"

And thus a legend was born, a legend that will live in television history for what I think is going to be a long, long time. For it was on that show that I performed my unforgettable version of the Elton John and Bernie Taupin song "Rocket Man."

It has been said about my singing that I have great courage. But beginning with the album *The Transformed Man* I've tried to emphasize the poetry of the lyric by performing it dramatically rather than just singing along to some melody like all those other people, the Sinatras and the Streisands of the world. In fact, during this time I was touring with a one-man show in which I did dramatic readings from great science-fiction literature, accompanied by a complete philharmonic orchestra. For example, I would read an excerpt from an Arthur C. Clarke story while the orchestra played Stravinsky's *Firebird.* The live show was a tremendous success — at the Hollywood Bowl we drew eighteen thousand people, at Anaheim Stadium we had twenty-eight thousand people.

When I was asked to perform this song I thought I'd try something very unusual. I'd perform the song in its many layers, doing part of it like Sinatra might do it, another part of it emphasizing the rock-it, man, hip aspect of the song and, honestly, I've forgotten the third level. Lyricist Bernie Taupin actually introduced me at the Science-Fiction Awards Show. I was sitting on a stool on an otherwise bare stage, dressed impeccably in a tuxedo, smoking a cigarette. And I began talk-singing the story of the lonely rocket man on his way to Mars. ". . . I miss the earth so much, I miss my wife. It's lonely out in space. On such a timeless flight . . ." Eventually, using chroma-key video techniques, a second version of me appeared, a sadder version. And a few lines later a third Shatner appeared, a tired, disheveled, perhaps even dissolute man. And together the three Shatners finished the song. ". . . and I think it's gonna be a long, long time . . ."

The audience was stunned. People watched in shock and awe and then asked the question, Is he kidding? There is a very thick line between performing a song seriously and doing it in mock seriousness — doing it well enough to confuse the audience about that is the actor's art. Was I trying to make my performance humorous? Was it intended to be a parody of meaning-

335

ful singers with cigarettes? Or was I simply out of my mind?

As so many of the great science-fiction movies remind us, there are some things that mankind was never meant to discover. I will simply report that this remains the best-known performance of the song "Rocket Man" ever done.

For two decades stories about this performance have been passed down from father to son and rare bootleg copies of the video were passed around. Men boasted of owning a first-generation copy and invited women home to see it. Parodies of my performance have been done on several shows, including *Family Guy* and *Futurama.* But now several dozen versions of it can routinely be accessed on the Internet, particularly on YouTube — with more than a million people a year still mystified by it. And about that, I am not kidding.

The heroic characteristics exemplified by Captain James Kirk — among them honesty, integrity, compassion, and courage — were easily transferable, making me a desirable commercial spokesperson. At the beginning of my career it was well known that real actors simply did not do television commercials. Actors acted, spokesmen spoke, period. It was considered an act of artistic prostitution. Many stage actors would choose to starve rather than sell out, and a lot of them got the opportunity to do just that. I felt very much the same way, I was not for sale! Not that anyone was interested in buying, of course, but even if I had been offered a commercial I would have refused.

But in 1963 I co-starred with Paul Newman, Edward G. Robinson, Laurence Harvey, my friend Howard Da Silva, and Claire Bloom in *The Outrage,* Martin Ritt's westernized remake of Kurosawa's *Rashomon.* I played a disillusioned preacher who is told three different versions of a rape committed by a Mexican bandit played by Paul Newman. For me, the joy in making this film was the opportunity to work with Edward G. Robinson, whom I had long idolized as one of America's finest actors. One night he invited me to his home for dinner, and afterward took me out back where he had built a small round building that vaguely resembled New York's Guggenheim Museum. This was his art museum and inside was arguably the finest private collection of French impressionist works in the world. He was passionate about it. As he showed these paintings to me he referred to them as his "children."

Coincidently, a couple of days earlier I'd happened to see a coffee commercial he'd done. It had been jarring for me to see an actor of his stature doing a commercial, so I asked him about it. He looked at me, then pointed at a superlative painting by one of the masters. "That's why," he said.

After that I changed my whole attitude. If Edward G. Robinson, who'd made classic films like *Little Caesar, Key Largo,* and *The Cincinnati Kid,* could do television commercials, so could the person who made *Incubus.*

Among the first commercials I did was for Loblaw's, Canada's largest grocery chain. I'd walk down the produce aisle looking directly into the camera and say with the greatest sincerity I could fake, "At Loblaw's, more than the price is right." And then I would pause and pick up a big, round, juicy melon and examine it as if I'd never before seen such a big, round, juicy melon and say, with practiced surprise, "But, by gosh, that price is right."

I took this work very seriously. Whatever commercial I did I wanted it to be the best commercial ever done. I wanted people storming their local Loblaw's to buy melons. I wanted to sell more melons than anyone had sold before. When Marcy and I did a series of commercials for Promise margarine I wanted people bathing in margarine. When I did a local spot for a personal injury lawyer I wanted people hobbling over to their telephones as fast as they could limp to call that lawyer. I've done so many commercials for so many different products, most of them easily forgotten, but there is one classic advertising campaign that has become part of American pop culture, a job I got because of my unforgettable record album. But before I tell you the story of that unusual commercial campaign, let me interrupt with a brief anecdote.

The primary reason that most big stars don't do commercials is that they're worried about damaging their image. They've spent many years creating a positive impression in the minds of the audience about who they are, an impression that allows them to play and be accepted within a certain type of role, and they can't afford to risk it.

Early in my career, in Canada, I had done mostly light comedies. In fact, I'd become known as a light-comedy leading man. And I loved it. Believe me, there are few feelings for an actor more satisfying, more luxurious, than standing on stage bathing in waves of laughter. And when I came to New York I did comedy on Broadway. In one play, I remember, I got a nice laugh with a very simple expression. I was very proud of that laugh. Unfortunately, one day I didn't make that particular face — and I still got the laugh. Uh oh. And that's when I realized it wasn't me getting the laugh at all — it was another actor behind me doing whatever he was doing.

When I started working in television and the movies I was cast almost exclusively in dramas. So the recognition I earned came as a serious actor. There weren't a lot of laughs in *Judgment at Nuremberg,* for example. The audience got used to me as a Shatnerian actor. It was only much later in my career that once again I got the opportunity to do comedy. Shatner doing comedy? And when I discovered that I got laughs by poking fun at myself, I gleefully poked and prodded and pushed and pulled at myself. You see, ladies and gentlemen, I understood the psychology that enables people to find humor in the presentation of a somewhat rigid character remaining completely oblivious to the changing cultural scene around him. I got the joke. Actually, I created the joke — and I loved sharing it with the audience. We're all in this together! But still, I maintained some standards.

And then, with thirty million people listening, Howard Stern invited me to join him in the homo room.

Certainly one of the greatest fears of an actor is public humiliation. Oh please, whatever happens don't let me be embarrassed tonight. Being humiliated — being emotionally stripped naked in front of the world — is one of the worst things any human being can experience. To avoid humiliation people often refuse to take risks, and in response to it people — and even countries — have gone to war.

Every actor has their own way of dealing with it. I stopped reading reviews of my performances years ago, and I've rarely watched shows I had done so I wouldn't be upset by a director's edit that didn't come out my way. For many years the fear of being humiliated had prevented me from attending any *Star Trek* conventions. I spent several years thinking it was some kind of stupid game that people were playing, they were sharing a great joke, and if I took the show and my work seriously I would become part of that joke. I wasn't willing to risk that. Then I was told that fifteen thousand people were going to attend a convention in New York and I was offered a substantial amount of money.

I decided to attend the convention. I didn't prepare a speech, I was just going to answer questions. And then when I walked on stage and felt the massive love from that audience all my fears disappeared.

Several years later I was promoting my first *TekWar* book, the beginning of a new science-fiction series I'd created. I'd done a lot of radio interviews, all of them pretty much the same: please buy my book. And then I was scheduled to appear on *The Howard Stern Show*. I didn't really know who Howard Stern was, I think I listened to his show once before going on. What I didn't understand was that Howard had his own set of rules. He was limited only by what he could get past the FCC, so in those years he had very few constraints. What I did not realize was that he had planned terribly offensive things to do with me to see how far I would go. His program revolves around the humiliation of his guests to some degree — he likes to bust balloons of pomposity. He sought to jar me, to flummox me, and, I suppose, to humiliate me, by attacking my image.

The radio show and its audience were his turf. He was the bad boy, the street fighter; I came in as a married man, a father, with a reputation, an image, and a career to protect. After this brief interview I had to go back to the shows I was doing in a different world, so I was limited in my ability to fight back. "William Shatner's a little nervous," Howard began. "He's a big star and he doesn't want to embarrass himself."

That's when he invited me to join him in the homo room. "It's a better place to conduct the interview," he explained. "The only other guy we brought down here is like Dee Snider from Twisted Sister. He freaked out and tried to run out, but he handled it."

What do I do? He had challenged me to risk my professional image. Am I stupid enough and egotistical enough and curious enough to find out whether I can put the gloves on with him or not? If I agreed to join him in this fantasy I was risking offending many people who didn't understand Howard Stern, but if I refused I would be seen as an uptight visitor from another world, a man who took himself much too seriously. In front of thirty million listeners I was about to be humiliated.

I told Howard's sidekick, Robin, "If you hear screams for help . . ." and decided to go along with him on this fantasy trip. Meanwhile trying to remember I was there to promote my book and somehow I had to do that.

"The first order of business down here . . ." Howard explained, ". . . let's give each other girl's names first. Instead of Bill, you'll be Jill Shatner. You're Jill, all right?"

Who booked me on this show? All I wanted to do was promote my little book. It's a good read. Jill Shatner? The captain of the *Enterprise,* Jill Shatner? I realized that my only possible salvation was to play this game on his level. And then it became a game: can I amuse myself and amaze the audience? I did not let things like, oh . . . dignity hold me back. At that point Howard announced, "I'm going to sing a love song to Jill."

And I pointed out, "Gosh, I came here to plug a book."

"Don't worry," Howard told me. "You're going to plug the book."

"Yeah," I agreed cautiously, "but where are you going to put the book?"

Later, after we'd gone through several very raunchy but also very funny minutes — there are people who heard this who are still laughing about that ridiculous banana — Robin complimented me. "You're fitting right in down there."

I had to admit, "Fitting in isn't quite the expression I would use."

Rather than being humiliated, because I

choose not to try to defend my image, actually to defend any image of any kind, it turned out to be a very funny appearance. Because of that I've been invited back on the show several times. I was even given the honor of accepting the 2003–2004 Award for the Best Farting Moment for Will the Farter. In accepting the award I admitted it did have the sweet smell of success — and then I immediately began promoting my new album, *Has Been.*

So I wasn't above using Howard to promote my products, either. Eventually Howard and I actually became friends, although the fact that we've had dinner together has never stopped him from trying to humiliate me.

Believe me, after just one visit to Howard's homo room, you no longer have to worry that doing commercials is going to hurt your public image. So, for example, I had absolutely no hesitation when Kellogg's asked me to become the spokesperson for their All Bran cereal in Canada and the U.K. When I asked them why, of all the wonderfully talented, handsome, virile actors in the world they chose me to be their All Bran man, a representative explained, "Because you're a regular guy!"

Think about it.

Financially, the most desirable situation for an actor is to become the spokesperson for a company. To become so closely associated with one company that when people see you they almost automatically think of those commercials. For example, Lee Iacocca and Chrysler, Colonel Harlan Sanders and KFC, O. J. Simpson and Hertz, or what's his name, that tall guy, and Allstate Insurance. And me and Priceline.com.

Everybody knows about Priceline.com, the name-your-own-price-for-everything-from-airline-tickets-to-groceries Internet company. Well, at least they do now. But when the company was founded in the midst of the dot-com boom of the 1990s, it was just another one of the countless start-ups based on an original idea, desperately trying to attract attention.

My experience with computers was limited to — all together now — plugging it in. I didn't know what the Internet was. Apparently Priceline.com was looking for someone to do a series of radio commercials, someone, according to their chief marketing officer, who was "trustworthy, known for having futuristic ideas, and instantly identifiable across several generations." Once again, thank you, *Star Trek*. Their two choices were Bill Cosby and myself.

We met several times at my house. Finally I agreed to do the commercials in exchange for a substantial number of stock options in the company. At that point the stock had no value — but at least it wasn't uranium.

I did all the radio spots in one day. I was making a film in New Zealand and went into a studio in Wellington to record them. Priceline's executives were in a studio in Boston listening and making suggestions. I'd done numerous jobs like this, and then very quickly forgot all about them. I didn't think this one would be any different. Truthfully, I didn't even know what a dot-com company was. In fact, when I recorded the commercials I suggested they drop the words, "dot-com," to save a few seconds. Hey, who needs them, I wondered.

Um, Bill. That's the name of the company.

Oh. I thought "Priceline" was the name of the company.

Priceline-dot-com is the name of the company.

Well, what does that mean, dot-com?

It means Priceline is an Internet company.

So why don't we say that? Dot-com made no sense to me. But I did my job.

The commercials were successful, but radio and newspaper advertising has limited impact, so Priceline.com decided to advertise on television. It turned out that the copywriter on the account, Ernest Lupinacci, was a big fan of my 1968 album *The Transformed Man*. The "cult classic," as I like to refer to it. As he later told me, he'd also seen me on the Science-Fiction Movie Awards, and "the image was burned into my retina." Ernest Lupinacci deserves a tremendous amount of credit — especially for admitting that in public. Using that album for inspiration, he wrote a series of moody TV commercials in which I appeared as a sort of sorry lounge singer, talk-singing the money-saving praises of Priceline.com — in my own inimitable style — to the melodies of well-known songs of the 1960s and '70s.

Priceline.com offered me a large number of additional stock options to do the TV spots. Indeed, they were playing my song. I immediately suggested they double it, and they agreed. Two decades earlier people had ridiculed that album, suggesting that I sounded "in dire need of padded restraints," but because I had taken the risk and done *The Transformed Man* I was finally able to truly appreciate the meaning of the word "laughingstock." Because that's what I was being paid — laughing stock.

The commercials actually were very good.

In one of them, for example, I was very hip. "I wanted to chill but making all of my own travel arrangements was freaking me out, so I went to Priceline.com . . . You want some of this? You know what to do, dawg!"

In another one I was Pete Townsend-raucous, at the end of the spot grabbing a guitar from a band member and smashing it, declaring defiantly, "If saving money is wrong, I don't want to be right . . ."

"When the moon is in the Seventh House . . ." began the Priceline.com version of "Age of Aquarius," ". . . it's a whole new age of consumer power. With Priceline.com millions of beautiful people have named their own price and saved a load of bread . . ."

We did ten different spots. The reception was immediate and extraordinary. The objective was to bring attention to this new company, and it worked. Within a week I had been invited to appear on *Good Morning America,* CNN, *Entertainment Tonight,* Howard Stern, and several other shows to discuss the campaign. Jay Leno played two of the spots on the *Tonight Show.* Eventually the commercials were parodied on *Saturday Night Live* and even became an answer on *Jeopardy!* Slightly more than a year after they began running, Priceline.com was the second-most-recognized Internet company — behind only Amazon.com. More than half of all adults in the country had heard of it. The value of the stock eventually rose to $162. Wait, let me write it out, one hundred and sixty-two dollars per share. At that value Priceline.com was worth more than General Motors. The shares held by the owner of the company were worth approximately $12 billion. His ambition, he told me one night, was to build a university. Not endow a university, build it. On paper, and in my head, I was a rich man. No longer would I be Bill "I lost my life savings in uranium" Shatner; instead I had become Bill "the savvy dot-com millionaire" Shatner. Now who didn't know how to made a great investment? I would never have to worry about having eighteen hundred dollars in the bank again. In fact, I wasn't even certain the bank vault was large enough to hold all my money. I might have to buy a new bank!

However, there was one problem, just one slight problem. According to some ridiculous Federal Trade Commission rules people who held a certain type of insider stock weren't allowed to sell for an extended period of time. A lockup, it's called. And every single one of my $162 shares was locked up. I couldn't sell a single share. And as I watched helplessly, and with astonishment, the value of the stock fell to five dollars. Let me use the symbol, $5. Eventually it went down to pennies. Here's how bad it got: the company had given me the use of a car — they asked for it back. As it turned out, the uranium deal had been a lot less painful. In that deal I was rich for only a few hours.

Call me "Lost my life savings in uranium" Shatner. But don't call collect!

Actually, the stock did edge up and eventually I earned some money. But my association with Priceline.com has lasted more than a decade. All of this, of course, all of the wonderful opportunities I was being offered, was because of *Star Trek*. The continued identification with *Star Trek* was so strong, in fact, that when Priceline.com began offering customers the option of choosing a specific flight or hotel at a guaranteed price they did a series of commercials in which I was supposedly fired as their spokesperson. I was irate. "I'm the voice of Priceline.com," I said incredulously. "Who could possibly replace me?"

That's when Leonard Nimoy stuck his head in the door. "Hi, Bill," was all he had to say.

I've been doing Priceline.com commercials for more than a decade; meaning, I've been a corporate spokesperson longer than such great advertising icons as the Geico gecko and the Aflac duck! Mr. Clean has me beat, though.

The original *Star Trek* TV series, of course, turned out to be only the beginning. Just like me, for a long time Paramount didn't realize the value of the franchise. They knew that the audience for the syndicated series had continued growing, but they had absolutely no understanding of the real passion people had for it. For a long time they were very happy to continue exploiting what they already had, rather than spending any more money on it. Through the years there'd been all kinds of rumors that they were going to put the show back on the air or make a feature-length movie. I knew only what I read in the newspapers. Obviously I was hoping they went ahead with . . . with anything. They couldn't make *Star Trek* without Captain Kirk. In 1975 Roddenberry was hired to write the script for a low-budget feature. Roddenberry came up with a very unusual plot — the bad guy turned out to be God.

After that had been rejected the great science-fiction writer Harlan Ellison was asked to pitch his concept for the movie. Ellison's story had the *Enterprise* time-traveling back to prehistoric times to fight a race of evil reptiles, giant snakes. At about this time Erich von Däniken's book *Chariot of the Gods*, which claimed that alien visitors from outer space had visited the ancient Mayans — I'd narrated the movie version — was creating a sensation. Trying to exploit that, during a meeting at Paramount an executive asked Ellison if he could include some Mayans in his story.

Ellison explained patiently that in prehistoric times there were no Mayans.

Apparently that didn't bother the studio executive, who insisted, "Nobody'll know the difference."

While Paramount was slowly developing its low-budget *Star Trek*, *Star Wars* was released. It became an instant classic. But rather than taking advantage of this incredible new excitement about science fiction, the studio dropped the project. Instead, a year later, Paramount president Barry Diller and executives Michael Eisner and Jeffrey Katzenberg announced that the studio was going to form a fourth television network and *Star Trek: Phase II* was going to be its first original series. They ordered a two-hour

TV movie and thirteen episodes of the new series.

Now, I want you to think about this: what could possibly be a worse idea than making a movie with God as the bad guy? Here it is: the studio was involved in a lawsuit with Leonard over the merchandising revenue. As a result they decided to basically eliminate Spock from the new series. They offered Leonard a contract that guaranteed he would appear in a minimum of two episodes out of every eleven. They offered him a part-time job. It was ridiculous. *Star Trek* without Spock was like . . . was like, Priceline.com without Shatner. America would never stand for that. The United Federation of Planets would never stand for that. Leonard was furious and turned them down.

And then *Close Encounters of the Third Kind* was released. So much for Paramount's fourth network. Now it was simply a matter of producing a feature film as quickly as possible. The studio budgeted the film at $15 million and hired the great director Robert Wise to direct it. Wise had never seen an episode of *Star Trek,* but his wife was a big fan and told him the film wouldn't work without Spock. Eventually Paramount settled the lawsuit with Leonard and he

354

signed to do the picture.

For the animated series I'd been in great physical condition. I was drawn in absolutely perfect shape. In real life, though, I was actually in pretty poor shape. Marcy pointed out that I'd better start training. I began dieting, which meant basically eliminating food from my diet, and started jogging six or seven miles a day. Finally, when I got really desperate I went to a weight-loss center in the Malibu hills, a place that guaranteed you would lose twenty pounds in a week. There really is only one way you can lose that much weight that quickly, and generally it's illegal under the Geneva Convention. For a week all I did was hike, drink water, and eat carrot sticks; hike, drink water, and eat more carrot sticks. They didn't have single rooms in this place, and because I insisted on staying by myself they cleared out a storage closet for me. I put in a cot and slept there.

I can just imagine what the other people who were there that week must have said when they got home: poor Bill Shatner was there and he must really be doing badly. He had to sleep in a closet.

I lost twenty-five pounds that week. When I went home I was definitely in fighting shape — I could've killed somebody for a decent meal.

The $15 million budget eventually swelled to $45 million, and almost half of that was spent on special effects. The problem was the plot. Nothing happened, and it took more than two hours for it not to happen. The studio had spent all that money on special effects and they wanted the audience to see them. And see them. And see them. Warp speed never went so slowly. Gene Roddenberry wanted the *Enterprise* to be the star of the movie. So the film was replete with tedious shots of the *Enterprise* flying through space. There goes the *Enterprise.* Here comes the *Enterprise.* Whoops, there it goes again. Meanwhile, we never had a complete script. Every morning we'd be handed new pages. The result was the plot was too complex and the film was too talky.

I know Robert Wise was a wonderful director, just not for this film. He hadn't been a fan of the series, so he never understood its appeal. He was a very nice person, a master technician, but he didn't have a clue about *Star Trek.* What I admired most about him was that he never left the set. He sat in his director's chair and he watched whatever was going on. If it took two days to set up the lighting for a scene, he was there every minute directing the lighting crew. When they were decorating the set, he was there to tell them where to hang the photographs. The only time he left was for lunch and an occasional bathroom break.

Neither Leonard nor I could stand the picture. We were bound together by our mutual need to try to save this movie. It was just so ponderous, so serious. We had seen each other many times since the series had ended, but it was while making this film that we actually became friends. Good friends. We did everything we could to try to inject some humanity into it. Typically, in each episode after we'd destroyed the alien, we'd have a humorous wrap-up scene on the bridge. Our characters had an opportunity to play off each other. In the movie script I had a few lines thanking each member of the crew for coming out of retirement to save the universe. When we were rehearsing the scene Leonard ad-libbed a very clever line. I started by telling Dee Kelley, "I'll have you back to Earth shortly."

To which Dee replied, "Oh, Captain, you know, I might as well stay."

Then I turned to Leonard, and told him, "Mr. Spock, I'll take you back to Vulcan."

I don't remember the line that was written for him, but he said, "Captain, if Dr. McCoy is to remain onboard, my presence here will be essential." It was a great line, perfectly defining the relationship between Bones and Spock, and everyone laughed. But after the rehearsal Wise told us, "You know, the feeling is that the humor is inappropriate."

That was the problem with the script. It was just too absurdly serious.

The night the film opened I snuck into a theater in Westwood. The moment the theme music started the entire audience started cheering. They were screaming — and the picture hadn't even started yet. It was amazing. The audience had been waiting a long time for this film. Although it received generally poor reviews, it was a substantial commercial success.

Honestly, I don't remember precisely what I was thinking as I sat in that dark theater watching this movie. I might have been thinking about how incredibly fortunate I was to be at the center of this phenomenon. I might have been smiling as I remembered the decade of rumors and false starts we'd gone through to finally get to this theater. And I might well have been thinking, thank goodness, if this thing is successful I won't have to do any more quiz shows!

How can I describe all the quiz shows on which I appeared? What's another word for "every single quiz show ever done in the entire history of television"? Trust me, I'm going to tell you the truth about this or my name isn't William Shatner. I've got no secrets. I mean, can you think of any reason I shouldn't have done quiz shows? Who are the two men who created many of the greatest quiz shows in television history? Should I stop asking questions? What do you think the number one answer was when I asked that question?

The popularity that I'd gained from *Star Trek* made me a welcome guest on game shows. Mark Goodson and Bill Todman, who produced so many of those shows, really liked me. There were a lot of actors, the Robert De Niros of the industry, for whom doing a quiz show or a game show might have been considered a bit of comedown, but it hasn't been one for me at any time in my career — especially at that time. Game shows were fun and I enjoyed doing them. They provided great exposure — it was very good publicity for whatever project I was doing — but mostly for me. And finally, by any ordinary standards the money was good. Maybe not to the $10 million per picture actors, but to me. If I hadn't enjoyed doing these shows, well, I would have done them anyway. We would tape five shows in one day, and I could just hear my father telling me what to do. "Are you crazy? You're going to turn down a thousand dollars for one day's work? You know what I could have bought for a thousand dollars? And you call that work? Sitting there and playing a game? I'll tell you what work is!"

Among the game shows I did were *Hollywood Squares, The $20,000 Pyramid* and *The $25,000 Pyramid, Rhyme and Reason, Liar's Club, Tattletales, The Cross-Wits, To Tell the Truth;* I was the celebrity guest on the premiere episode of the *Blankety Blanks* show. That's not censorship, that was the name of the show, *Blankety Blanks.* On *The Storybook Squares,* the Saturday morning children's version of *Hollywood Squares,* I appeared dressed as Captain Kirk — that was okay, on the same show Paul Lynde was dressed as the evil queen from *Snow White.* I even rolled on *Celebrity Bowling.* I could continue but you get the idea: if they wanted me, I was there.

Here's one game that you can play along with me: *Masquerade Party.* On this show the celebrity guest came out dressed in a costume that hid his or her identify. Based on the costume the panel asked questions

360

until they figured out the identity of the guest. The mystery guest in this sentence is dressed as Cap'n Andy, the captain in Jerome Kern's classic *Show Boat,* and the set was the deck of a paddle-wheel steamer. Can you guess the identity of the guest? All right, here's the clue the mystery guest gave on the show, "We've got a lot of *stars* on our boat!"

Give up? Okay, it was me! As was very well known, I had played the role of the . . . captain of a starship! Now, I never said these shows were difficult, just fun.

A very good writer named Sean Kelly once approached me with the most unusual concept for a game show that never went into production. It was called *Land-A-Million,* and obviously he approached me because I had my private pilot's license. The way this show worked was I took off with the contestant in a small plane carrying a million dollars in cash. To qualify, the contestant could not have ever piloted a plane in his life. As soon as we got to five thousand feet I bailed out. And then, if the contestant was able to land that airplane he got to keep the money. I don't know what happened but this show never went into production.

Almost all of the game shows were taped all day Saturday in New York. So I'd get on the red-eye Friday night in L.A. and land at JFK at 6 a.m. I'd take a cab to the studio and be there by eight o'clock, nine o'clock at the latest. I'd hoped to sleep a few hours on the flight, but usually I failed, so I was tired before we started. We would shoot five shows in one day. In several of the theaters my dressing room was up several flights of stairs and I would have to change my wardrobe between each show. So I'd be rushing up and down four or five flights four or five times a day while I was already exhausted. The fact that I was enjoying myself would get me through the first three shows, but those last two were difficult. There were times I just got really giddy. On *The $20,000 Pyramid,* for example, the celebrity would say several words or names or events that fit into a specific group or category to try to get the contestant to identify that group or category. For example, I might say Vincent van Gogh, Mr. Spock, and Evander Holyfield to lead the contestant to the desired answer: people with strange ears. Or I might say *Land of No Return, Dead of Night,* and *The Fright* to get the correct answer, movies William Shatner never should have made.

One Saturday Leonard and I taped five shows against each other. My partner and I were winning the fourth show and were playing the bonus round, in which she was going for the $20,000 prize. I don't know about other celebrities, but when I was playing these games I really wanted to win, I really wanted to be entertaining, but mostly I really didn't want to look like an idiot. The contestant and I were sitting in the winner's circle. My task was to give her enough examples to lead her to the correct answer for $20,000, which was "Things that are blessed." I wanted to see this nice woman win all that money. I was thinking quickly, things that are blessed, things that are blessed. Okay, I got one. And I gave her my first clue, "You're blessed!"

That woman probably didn't need all that money anyway. I couldn't believe what I'd done. I'd told her the answer. I'd cost her the bonus. So I did the only thing possible considering the incredibly stupid mistake I'd just made, I went berserk. I started screaming. Laughing hysterically, or perhaps manically. I picked up my chair and heaved it out of the winner's circle. There was one rule: you can't use the answer in the question. One rule, and I broke it.

And just in case I didn't feel stupid enough, they began the next show by running the tape again — as an example of what not to do!

I liked playing the *Pyramid.* It was a challenging show. Once they didn't have a good opening for the show so Mark Goodson asked me to go out and have some fun — be both the contestant and the person giving the clues. Well, I took it seriously. Strangest thing that ever happened to me. The board with the answer on it was behind the contestant so the interrogator could see it. I started playing against myself — I sat in the interrogator's chair where I could see the answer and I gave the clues, then I raced around and sat in the contestant's chair. I got so involved in playing the game that by the time I sat down in the contestant's chair I'd actually forgotten the correct answer. I'm telling the truth. I completely lost sight of the fact that I knew the answer. It was a great opening spot, and they used it for several years.

Naturally I had some game show disappointments; I never made it to the center square on *Hollywood Squares;* in fact, contestants most often referred to me as "William Shatner to block." On *Celebrity Bowling* I believe Hugh O'Brian and I were beaten by Robert Culp and Marty Allen, although Marcy and I did well on *Tattletales.*

Many years later I made the transition

from permanent celebrity guest to host of two game shows. But before I tell you about that I've just gotten some very exciting news: I now have 53,038 friends on my MySpace page! For someone who had so few real friends growing up, that's incredible — 53,038 friends. They include laura, my bmf Big Chris, Che Guevara, old Hairball, The Dark Prince of Rainbows, the great Sid Caesar.com, and Flatface IV. I certainly hope all my new friends aren't going to be angry when I don't invite them to my home for one of my *Monday Night Football* parties. And I'm not sending out birthday cards either!

Okay, hosting game shows. I've hosted two of them. The Food Network bought syndication rights to a Japanese cooking show, *The Iron Chef,* and translated it into English. It became a big hit so the UPN network bought the rights to the concept and hired me to host *Iron Chef USA.* Obviously it was not a traditional question-and-answer show, but it did have contestants, or challengers. Basically, four elite chefs comprised the Gourmet Academy and on each episode their cooking superiority is challenged by other chefs. The combatants are given a secret ingredient and, on our show, had one hour to prepare five different dishes —

which are then judged by four celebrity judges.

On one show the secret ingredient was crab. We gave the chefs live crabs and they had to create five crab dishes. A young chef made a . . . ready for this? A crab sorbet. Okay, perhaps it doesn't sound too appetizing but when you actually tasted it, it was worse. It was fishy and crabby. So he was eliminated right away. One of the other contestants made a pasta dish with crab, and was eliminated when a celebrity judge decided, "This spaghetti isn't like my mother makes. I don't like it."

Wait a minute, I thought, is it fair to judge food that way? As chairman I wasn't permitted to criticize one of the judges, but I thought, what kind of frame of reference is that? It's not like my mother makes? Well, of course it isn't, that's not your mother. That's a renowned chef. Maybe you'd prefer a piece of toast with some jam on it? Personally, I'd love that. But would you rather have an egg soufflé with a bit of caviar on top? I wouldn't, that sounds awful, I want my buttered toast for breakfast.

That was going through my mind as I was chairing the show. Several weeks later I was reading an article about the great chefs of the world. One of them has a small restaurant outside Barcelona. At this restaurant he gives his customers what amounts to basically one spoonful of a dish so they can truly understand its taste, and then they go to the next dish. Apparently he bought a carload of tomatoes and an air machine that aerated the tomatoes and allowed him to get to the essence of the taste of a tomato. It was the pure taste of tomato. And as I read that I realized that the young chef had done exactly that, with his sorbet. He had given us the absolute essence of the taste of crab. I understood that this young chef and the master chef in Barcelona were tied together by their desire to bring their artistry to the consumer.

None of that helped the game show, though. After we'd done two or three episodes the network management changed and we were out of the kitchen.

Show Me the Money was a much more traditional game show. Contestants got money. Several years ago I appeared at ABC's Up Fronts, the promotional event held every year to promote the coming television season, representing *Boston Legal.* In the guise of my suave and sophisticated character, the brilliant litigator Denny Crane, I appeared onstage in a greatcoat, top hat, and cane, accompanied by a line of dancing girls. I proceeded to dance my way into the hearts of those in attendance. But unbeknownst to me, in the audience was the president of Endemol, the company that produces Howie Mandel's *Deal or No Deal,* and several other quiz shows. He had a concept for a new big-money quiz show that was quite different from *Deal;* for example, instead of twenty-five beautiful girls holding briefcases worth a certain amount of money, this show had thirteen gorgeous dancing girls in little cages holding scrolls worth a certain amount of money.

Basically, it was a game of greed. That's why it was called *Show Me the Money,* the classic battle cry from the Tom Cruise movie, *Jerry Maguire.* As long ago as *The $64,000 Question* in the 1950s contestants have had to answer the emotional question: take the money and go home or keep playing and risk what you've won. That's the question that gets viewers shouting at the set. Since Monty Hall introduced the three doors of *Let's Make a Deal* — which eliminated the question-and-answer segment of the game and made it purely about greed — that has been the central theme of so many really good game shows. *Deal or No Deal* is a show about greed, that's it, how greedy is the contestant going to be and when are they going to stop. That's the fascination of the show. The contestant comes on the show with nothing and gets a good sum of money and suddenly the greed factor kicks in. You think, is he crazy? They want to buy a farm. They have enough money to buy the farm — and now they want more than the farm. Howie Mandel is a master at milking that greed; somehow he managed to introduce humanity into a show about greed. That's what I intended to do, explore the humanity of that greed. I really wanted to ask the intriguing question: How much money is enough?

Admittedly, the rules were a bit confusing. The player picked question A, B, or C and I read the question that was picked but if after hearing it the player chose not to answer it he or she could pick a second letter which he or she also could choose not to answer after I read it, but the player had to answer the third question — but before I revealed if that answer was correct the player selected one of the thirteen gorgeous girls and music started playing and the gorgeous girl started dancing because she was picked and I danced because she was dancing. Have you ever seen me dance? Anyway, the dancer unrolled the scroll she was holding which revealed a certain amount of money and if the answer to the question was correct the contestant had that amount added to his collection but if incorrect it was subtracted from that pot. We continued playing until the player gave six correct answers and won all the money in the pot or had six incorrect answers in which case the player went home with their memories.

That's clear so far, right? Now, one of the gorgeous girls was holding a scroll that did not indicate an amount of money; instead this was the . . . "killerrrrr card!" If the player answered the regular question incorrectly he or she then had to answer the "killerrrrr card" question, and if they got it wrong the game ended and they went home with nothing. And then the gorgeous girls danced. But they changed that rule after our first episode so they didn't have to miss the regular question and then they . . .

You get the idea, right? Tell a few jokes, give away some money, watch the gorgeous girls dance. I had a lot of fun with it. My job was simple: if the player was comfortable, if he were just soaring along and confident, I was to make him uneasy; but if he were uneasy and nervous, I was to make him comfortable. Additionally, all the cues for music and dancing were up to me. I'd say, "Let's celebrate," and the music started playing and the gorgeous girls started dancing, or "Let's not celebrate" and the gorgeous girls did not dance.

I suggested they put a comedy writer or two in the booth to feed me lines I could ad-lib. No, they decided, that will only get in the way of your rhythm. They were right, the key to the game was the contestant. My job was to find a way for the audience to identify emotionally with the player, to bring out his or her personality. If they rooted for him or her, the game would work.

There were several problems with our show that turned out to be basically unsolvable — unless they changed the rules, in which case it was another show. The biggest failing was that the player didn't have the option of taking his winnings and leaving, he had to play the game to the end point. We had eliminated the greed factor, the player had to continue. Second, the rules were too complicated. The best game shows or quiz shows are the simplest. Too much was happening, and then the gorgeous girls danced. Personally, it was much harder to do than I had anticipated. We were taping over the weekend. Theoretically you should be able to tape an hour show in an hour. So if we were taping two shows it would take — with all the changes that had to be done

— three hours, four hours.

Oh, more nice news. I just made a new friend on MySpace. Welcome to my page, the Mad Mountain Man of Montana.

So, taping: because this was a new show and everything was computerized, all my cues and the questions had to be programmed into the teleprompter. It took twelve hours to do two shows. We ended up working all weekend and I was on my feet much of that time. Man can only dance so long. By Monday morning when I went to work on *Boston Legal,* I was exhausted.

When the show was canceled after a brief run people were very sympathetic. Everyone acted as if there had been a death in my career. It even occurred to me that perhaps we should sit shiva for the show, and then we could have my characters from *The Shiva Club* come and tell some jokes and cheer up everyone — then sell the rights as a special.

But honestly, I was not unhappy it was canceled. Much earlier in my career when a show was canceled or finished its run, I always experienced some anxiety as the actor's what's-next-is-my-career-over factor kicked in. Obviously I don't feel that way anymore. I can always get a gig singing at science-fiction award shows.

When we were making *Star Trek* Leonard

in particular was concerned about being typecast. As he remembers, "People were actually asking me, 'What are you going to do when this is over?' I wondered if I was missing something. I guess I should have been worried, but I wasn't. I wanted the credit for creating this character." Well, as it turned out neither Leonard nor I were typecast, it was much deeper than that. We were branded forever as Kirk and Spock and certainly for me that turned out to be wonderful. But after making the original series, the animated series, and the first motion picture, and after all the different kind of work I'd done, I wondered if I would ever escape that association. I'd made several failed attempts, including *Barbary Coast,* but in the collective mind of the audience I was the captain of the *Enterprise.* Finally, though, it was time to turn the page on Captain James T. Kirk.

EIGHT

"T.J. Hooker is the name, but you don't have to lose any sleep wondering what the T.J. is for. As far as you're concerned my name is . . . Sergeant . . ." That was my opening line in the pilot movie we shot for the police series *T.J. Hooker.* In this establishing scene Hooker is addressing a squad of future police officers about to get on-the-street training. "There's a war going on out there on our streets," he continued. "People are scared and they have a right to be. The body count is high . . . Street-savvy hoods have no fear. Not of the courts, not of prison.

"When a bust does stick, we house them, give them color TVs, and their wives visit on weekends. If that makes sense to you, then you and I are about to have a problem 'cause I'm your instructor here and I lovvvvve to weed out airheads and marshmallows."

Later in that show Hooker tells his recruits, "I've seen the past. And it works," which pretty much describes the character I played for five years — which was actually much longer than I played James T. Kirk on television. Hooker was a veteran cop who'd quit the detective squad to get back on the streets after his partner was killed. He was a Vietnam vet, a former Green Beret, a divorced father whose wife had left him — even though she still loves him — because she couldn't accept his dedication to the badge, explaining, "When I divorced you I should have named the department as co-respondent."

In response he began drinking. "There I was with no wife, no kids, I needed a friend and I found one."

When I brought T.J. Hooker to life I focused on the one word that I thought best described him: angry. Angry about the laws that made his job tougher. Angry about the Miranda rights for suspects. Angry about all the rules instituted by do-gooders who didn't understand life on the streets. He had to comply, but he was angry about it. Hooker was a conservative cop placed in a liberal setting, and at its best we were able to successfully represent that conflict. Had I met Hooker I would have liked him; he had a good heart, strong ethics, and even when he disagreed with the law he always upheld it.

The way *Hooker* came about was unusual. Most series are in development for several years before they get rejected. Even if a pilot gets made, only a few of them ever get on the air. But in the early 1980s legendary producers Aaron Spelling and Leonard Goldberg were ending their partnership and still had a guaranteed commitment for one more show from ABC. They hired a top TV writer-director, Rick Husky, to create the show and write the pilot. It took him only a few weeks, he remembers. The biggest problem he had was coming up with a name for the character. He was a Civil War buff so he called him Hooker after General Hooker. He couldn't come up with a first name that felt right, so he called him T.J. because "It was better than no first name." Only much later did I become Thomas Jefferson Hooker.

Within a couple of months we were making the pilot. That's how fast it happened. Initially the show wasn't supposed to be *T.J. Hooker.* It was an ensemble show called *The Protectors,* featuring a grizzled police sergeant and the group of eight young cops he's training. According to Rick Husky, it was supposed to be *Dallas,* with cops. Each week another one of those cops would be featured. One of the reasons I took the part, in fact, was because I wouldn't have all the pressure of starring in a series. Most weeks I'd just be a supporting player. But the response to my character was so strong they dropped that premise and focused on Hooker. They did not, however, raise my salary.

The show was an immediate hit. *The New York Times* called Hooker "the kind of character who would have been unthinkable for television just a couple of years ago . . . T.J. Hooker is a fascinating creation." But I knew we'd struck a chord even without reading that review. We used to film on the streets of Los Angeles, we'd have all our production trailers parked in a row, and before the show went on the air people would stop to watch and they'd point me out and I'd hear them say, "Oh, there's Captain Kirk." The night after the show went on the air, literally the night after, I heard people saying, "Oh, look, there's T.J. Hooker."

Hooker was an interesting character. He was a tough, conservative Los Angeles cop forced to deal with the new rules of a changing society, things like Miranda laws and understanding the root causes of crime, and didn't like it at all. When he joined the force the rules had been pretty straightforward; the good guys take the bad guy into the back of the station until he confesses. Instead, as he says sadly, "There's a war going on out there in the streets and, from where I stand, the bad guys are winning."

You know how much fun it is to play a character like this? What made Hooker's character so interesting to me was that he remembered the old rules of law enforcement: of course I understand you robbed that bank because you have no self-esteem. Boom, taste my nightstick. Yes, I know your addiction is a disease and you couldn't help mugging that person. Boom, say hello to my nightstick. But Hooker had to do his job under the new rules — and chafed at it like a stallion with a bit in his mouth.

And it wasn't just modern law enforcement, it was modern life. Hooker was always railing against "parents that don't care, kids that lack discipline," against gambling and a permissive society. As his partner Romano described him, "Hooker's just a little backward. He's not used to dealing with modern women."

I rarely had time to do any research for the parts I played. For Kirk, who was I going to talk to? For *Incubus,* I couldn't understand anybody. Well, perhaps I did research modern women. But before we started filming *Hooker* I did spend two days with LAPD officers from the North Hollywood station to try to get some ideas about their procedures. For example, a captain showed me how to pat down a perp. They made me lean against a wall at a forty-five-degree angle, arms outstretched, legs spread wide. Standing in that position, I asked, "What happens if I resist at this point?"

That's when the captain, standing behind me, rammed his knee into my crotch. He explained, "They may get a little loud, but by this time most of them cooperate."

Stars were twinkling in my eyes as another officer added, "His whole life is flashing before his eyes."

"Yeah," I squeaked, remembering suddenly why I didn't do research.

Eventually the cast included Adrian Zmed as my young hot-headed partner, James Darren as another veteran cop, and Heather Locklear played his partner, a female street cop who often worked underclothed . . . undercover. Actually, I think the most difficult problem faced by the writers each week was creating another plot that forced Heather Locklear to take off most of her clothes. Until I did this show I can honestly say I did not know how many criminals hung out at female mud-wrestling emporiums or how many stool pigeons insisted on meeting in the privacy of a strip club.

Heather Locklear joined the cast for the second season. The producers had decided to add a beautiful woman to the cast to attract a very specific demographic group: every man in the world. Rick Husky was looking out his office window one afternoon when this gorgeous blonde came out of Aaron Spelling's office and walked by. He immediately went into Spelling's office to find out who she was. "That's the girl I want for *Hooker*," he told Spelling.

Spelling shook his head. "No, you don't," Spelling said. "She can't act. We just had her on a *Matt Houston* and she just doesn't have it."

Rick Husky had seen her walking. He knew she had it. "That's who I want." Spelling tried to talk him out of it, but Husky insisted and Heather Locklear joined our cast. She was a sweet, nice, and beautiful young woman, who worked very hard to become a good actress. So good, in fact, and so popular that several months later Aaron Spelling added her to the cast of his new show *Dynasty*.

For several years she was working simultaneously in two hit series. That must have been some walk. Only once was there any kind of problem with Heather. On several shows Heather did not wear a bra. Finally, one of the top executives told Ken Koch, an associate producer who eventually directed several episodes, that he had to go down to the set and tell Heather that she was going to have to start wearing a bra. Koch had been in the army, when he got an order he followed it — although admittedly he'd never been given an order like this in the army. But he went to the set and took her aside to explain, "You know, in your profile shots, you're not looking like, you know, the Heather Locklear that everybody wants to see and the beautiful woman you really are."

I believe Heather was taken aback. And so she asked Ken in a soft voice, "Are you going to speak to Bill and Jimmy and have them stuff socks in their crotch so it makes them look like they've got big dicks?"

Ken admitted he hadn't thought about that. About a week later we were shooting the tag, the last scene after the bad guys have been caught, at Marina del Rey. When we finished we were all walking toward the camera. It was a good shot. When they cut

Heather kept walking, right up to Ken Koch, and she told him with a big smile, "You know, didn't Bill's dick look bigger?"

We had a really good cast and crew. I really bonded with both Adrian Zmed and Jimmy Darren. That was important, because we spent a lot of time locked up together in a cop car. Jimmy Darren, I remember, was afraid of birds. All types of birds. As I'm sure you'll appreciate, as soon as we found out about that we were all very sympathetic. The writers, for example, immediately started adding action scenes that took place on rooftops. We'd be running across the rooftops of Los Angeles in the middle of the summer. Nothing stopped Jimmy — except a pigeon. A single, unarmed . . . unwinged pigeon was enough to make him pause. As soon as he saw a pigeon he'd start to cower. He'd been jumping from rooftop to rooftop, tackling bad actors, doing whatever stunts were necessary, until he confronted . . . a pigeon.

Birds? Who could be afraid of birds? Now heights, that's a real fear. Hooker wasn't afraid of anything, Shatner hated heights. Even building roofs, so between Jimmy Darren and me those writers worked overtime to get us up on roofs.

Adrian Zmed had a lot of talent. In addition to being a good actor, he could sing and dance. He also had a terrific sense of humor. Many of our shows ended with me chasing the bad guy by myself and bringing him down, then seconds later Adrian would come running up to me. I'd tell him, "Get an ambulance, Junior."

So one night we were filming this climactic scene and I chased the perp down an alley and brought him down. Heeerrrrrrrrre comes Adrian. Breathlessly, I told him, "Get an ambulance, Junior."

Adrian looked at me and shook his head. "Why don't you get your own damn ambulance," he said, then turned around and walked out of the shot.

Well. That certainly was interesting. I was truly surprised. There was absolute silence on the set — until Ken Koch started laughing and then I realized I'd been set up. And started laughing.

Each episode adhered to a pretty strict formula: really bad guys, beautiful women, and plenty of action. Our criminals were always total "skels," or as Hooker described them, maggots, scavengers, vermin, creeps and scum, slimy, unctuous killers and rapists, really unpleasant human beings, men so completely lacking any redeeming qualities that in one episode they actually cut off the head of a teddy bear belonging to a teenaged prostitute trying to go straight — so whatever Hooker had to do to get them off the streets was acceptable. Each week Hooker faced some sort of dilemma: Should I inform on a cop who froze at the last minute to save a pregnant woman? Did a female cop I trained get shot and lose her leg because I didn't train her well enough? There was always some sort of humorous by-play between Adrian and myself that continued through the whole episode; Adrian gets a brand-new computer to pick the winners of horse races, Adrian is going to show me how to use modern sales techniques to sell my daughter's organization cookies. At some point in many episodes I ended up at Valley Hospital. Usually a colorful informer provided information that led me to the bad guy, anybody from a Rasta conga player to a blind news dealer to a friendly pawnshop owner. On the path to justice I always encountered a beautiful woman, from the prostitute with a heart of fifty-dollar bills, to my ex-wife, to a beach filled with bikini-clad girls, to the daughter of the victim, to the female cop who invited me to her place to "show him her calculator." To gain more information either Heather had to take off some clothes or

Adrian and I had to visit a place where women were taking off some clothes. There was always a lot of action, we tried to include three action sequences in each episode, and almost always ended with a chase scene. And we concluded with a humorous tag: the horse I picked by guessing number four beat the horse selected by his computer, my daughter wins the award for selling the most cookies — which I sold to all the people in the precinct who were going to show me how to sell cookies.

I once asked a detective who'd seen the show if he thought it accurately reflected reality. He smiled and said, "You guys can cram more police work into an hour than I do in a year . . . Some days I go all day without a call." Well, that wouldn't make a very interesting show, Hooker and Romano sitting in their police car eating donuts. What do you want to do today, Vince? I don't know, Hooker, what do you want to do? *T.J. Hooker* was an action show. There was at least one chase scene in every episode, either I chased a bad guy on foot or in our car or both. On foot I'd somehow manage to keep pace with the bad guy. Even though I was wearing my uniform and carrying all my equipment, inevitably I'd have to jump over a chain-link fence or a brick wall or climb a ladder onto a roof, roll over the hood of a car, then make a leaping tackle, after which the perp and I would roll down a slope or near the edge of the roof, but almost always I caught him and cuffed him. And without losing my breath. In the car, it seemed like every time Adrian and I got a call to rush to a location where a crime was taking place we happened to be going in the opposite direction, because we always ended up doing a squealing U-turn in the middle of the block. Generally our criminals were terrible drivers; for special effects we drove cars off buildings, we drove them into lakes, we drove them through fires, and we crashed them, so clearly there was a budgetary reason our perps drove terribly beat-up cars. Every few shows we had a tremendous explosion; we blew up a lot of cars in five seasons, we blew up a yacht — once we even had a getaway car crash into a gasoline tanker to give us two great explosions. Unfortunately the special-effects people put a little too much gasoline in the tanker and it exploded in a cloud of flame that went right over the heads of the sound crew. Dangerous as can be — but it looked wonderful on film. After that the philosophy of the special-effects people became, why use only one gallon of gas when you can blow up ten!

We probably had the highest body count on the network; at least one person got shot in every episode. People were constantly leaping between buildings and often falling off rooftops. On one show I put on a fireman's coat and raced into a burning building to save two kids; on another episode I grabbed onto the strut of a small plane taking off and held on as I became airborne.

I did many of my own stunts. I became extremely proficient with the SB24 side-handle nightstick. In fact, after watching me use it during one scene a crew member said, "Oh, now I understand why they refer to it as a billy club." Okay, maybe they didn't and I made that up. But it certainly could have happened. In more than thirty years my career had progressed from a sword to a stick. Actually, the movements were surprisingly similar. Both weapons were used to block blows, to attack, to fend off, and to bring down the enemy. A police instructor worked with me to get it right. I could twirl that stick and oww! Those memories hurt. Obviously I had to learn how to use it and as every officer knows you bang yourself up pretty good learning the correct way to use it.

In doing the show I gained tremendous

admiration for police officers. In most cases it's a difficult and thankless job. It is the thin blue line that keeps civilization from falling apart. That's why a bad cop is such a detriment not only to the police force, but to democracy. People working in law enforcement really liked this show. At times they would try to explain to me what the job was all about, what it meant to them, how tough it was. For whatever reason, they felt they could open up to me, that I would understand. Maybe they just wanted to make certain we got it right. But I've had several experienced police officers admit to me that on occasion they would see something going down and they would just get out of the way. They would drive off to avoid being involved, often because they didn't want to go after people breaking certain laws with which they didn't agree. One officer in particular told me about the dilemma he faced in breaking up drug deals. Was it worth risking his own life to save a drug dealer? They wanted me to truly appreciate the problems they faced every day on the streets.

I saw it myself very late one Friday night as I was being driven home from a downtown L.A. location. We were about to turn when I looked out my window and saw two men and a cop facing off. All three of them were in a crouch, the cop's hand near his gun. A cop and two bad guys, right out of a movie. Just frozen like that in my memory forever. The car turned the corner and I was out of there, never to discover what it was about or how it ended. But that scene so accurately described the job of a policeman for me.

Only once did I get to touch the reality of the job. I was wearing a uniform — obviously for me it was a costume — and crossing the street when a jeep that was stopped at a light got slammed from behind. The jeep suffered no damage, while the car that hit it had a crumpled hood. Both drivers jumped out of their cars. I saw what was about to happen and at best we were going to have a California traffic jam. I don't know what made me do it, but I decided to intervene. I . . .

. . . *Star Trek* handkerchiefs, towels, address books, cameras, welcome mats, picnic items including paper plates and cups, telephone calling cards, handheld electronic games, stereo headphones, laser disks, sunglasses, school supplies, flight log books, certificates, medallions . . .

. . . saw that the jeep had no damage so I forcefully told the driver, "There's been no damage to you. Get back in your car and move along. Go ahead." And he listened to me. I'm certain he didn't recognize me. I told the other driver, "It was your fault. You got a little damage. Come on, move your car, you're blocking traffic." He, too, got back in his car and did as I ordered. And just for an instant I'd felt the power of the uniform. It was an oddly educational experience.

Cops really liked me. It has always been fascinating to me how people assume an actor has the same philosophical beliefs as the character he or she is playing, and Hooker was no different. Many people assumed that in my private life I was the same reactionary person I portrayed. Throughout my career I've always tried to keep my philosophical and political beliefs to myself, partly because as a Canadian citizen I've felt like a guest in America and, being polite, I didn't feel it was my place to advocate loudly for my own beliefs. But I don't speak Esperanto, I've never conquered Mesopotamia, I've never beamed up, and I'm not Thomas Jefferson Hooker. That didn't stop police officers from believing that I felt like many of them did. Which led to an unusual situation.

A small group of cops visited the set one

day and asked if I had ever heard of Bo Gritz. I hadn't. Bo Gritz, it turned out, was widely known as a Vietnam veteran who believed the North Vietnamese continued to hold American POWs and had dedicated his life to finding them and rescuing them. He'd been there and come back. I read quite a bit about him and realized it was an amazing story. "I'd love to meet him," I told these officers.

About a week later I met Bo Gritz. The greatest American hero of the Vietnam War. He told me, "The only way I survived was to choose the path of death. Everybody else wanted to live. The people who wanted to live did things that got them killed. I said it doesn't matter if I live or die, if this is where I die, this is where I die. I choose. I'm a warrior."

Wow. He told me an elaborate story about putting together a Delta Force raiding party, swimming across the Mekong River, and crawling undetected into Vietnam.

Wow. Surveillance photographs had shown long shadows and short shadows in what was believed to be a prisoner-of-war camp. The short shadows would have been Asian — and the long shadows could have been American prisoners. He moved swiftly and with great daring through the jungles to get to the site. But when he finally reached it, there was nobody there. So he retraced his path and swam all the way back. "We know the MIAs are there, Bill," he told me, adding that he'd written it all down.

Wow. This is an unbelievable story, I thought. And as it turned out, I was right. I just didn't know it at the time. Instead I told him, "Bo, I want to tell this story. It's an important story."

He agreed with me, and told me he would be pleased if I told the story — as long as I paid him for it. I had a discretionary fund at Paramount that enabled me to buy the rights to stories I believed would make good movies. This was one of them. It had adventure and action and the most noble purpose imaginable — saving the lives of American POWs. We finally agreed on a $10,000 option. I gave him the check and asked for a copy of the manuscript. "I'll get the manuscript to you next week," he promised.

Oh. The check was cashed and Gritz disappeared. I never saw or heard from him again. However, several months later the media descended on me. It turned out that Gritz apparently had used the money I'd paid him, as well as $30,000 Clint Eastwood had paid him for the same rights, to pay for a secret mission to Laos to try to rescue

American prisoners. It had been a total disaster: He'd been arrested almost immediately after sneaking into Laos, when the guerilla leader he was supposed to meet showed up drunk and unarmed. Somehow reporters became convinced Clint Eastwood and I were funding secret missions — although Clint was paying a lot more than I was.

I never heard from Bo Gritz again. I was mortified by the entire situation. It certainly hadn't been my intention to get involved in anything this controversial. I just wanted to tell a heroic story — which turned out to be untrue. It was an awful situation, so many families whose husbands and sons had disappeared in Vietnam were given hope by Bo Gritz. I had no idea what was true or fantasy and I didn't want to raise the hopes of those families that the soldiers they loved were still alive somewhere. Eventually reporters pursued Clint Eastwood — did I mention he gave Gritz $30,000? — and left me alone. The last time I heard his name was in 1992, when he was running for president of the United States with the slogan "God, Guns, and Gritz." And no, I did not contribute to his campaign.

Like *Star Trek*, *T.J. Hooker* was a survivor. After four successful seasons on ABC and seventy-one episodes the show was canceled. At that time we still were getting a twenty-seven share, a number most shows running today never reach. Toward the end the producers did make a few minor changes. For example, they moved *Hooker* from Los Angeles to Chicago. They moved the entire show! And worse, they sent Hooker to Chicago without a winter coat. And rather than Adrian Zmed, they gave me a new partner, a black detective who dressed as a Rasta to go undercover. The concept was to exploit the then-popular *48 HRS.* pairing of Eddie Murphy and Nick Nolte in which I did a reverse *Beverly Hills Cop*. Rather than Murphy's Detroit detective in L.A., I was the L.A. cop in Chicago.

In very cold Chicago. Beyond-cold Chicago. I am a Canadian, I have lived through Canadian winters. I've skiied in races at forty-below temperatures. Take your finger out of your glove, you lose your finger. But it was never as cold as it was while filming *T.J. Hooker* on Lake Shore Drive in Chicago. You didn't just see your breath; you could take it right out of the air and put it in your pocket until it thawed out. The whole time we were shooting there I lived in fear of the words, "Let's try it one more time."

I mean, it was a completely different show,

with a new cast. It would have been like moving the survivors of *Lost* to a resort on *Fantasy Island.* "Da plane! Da plane! Uh-oh, dere goes da plane!"

Unfortunately, the seventy-one episodes we'd completed for NBC were not enough for the show to sell in syndication, so CBS bought the rights and scheduled it for late night. For that network I came back to Los Angeles and no one ever mentioned Chicago again. We did a stripped-down version of the show for CBS. Adrian had left the show, and we finished the series with a two-hour primetime movie entitled *Blood Sport* or, as I refer to it, *Hooker Goes Hawaiian.*

Apparently we'd cleaned up the streets of Los Angeles, because in this movie Hooker was sent to Hawaii to protect the life of an old college friend who had become a United States senator. In Hawaii, according to *The New York Times,* Hooker "runs into hanky-panky, hocus-pocus, the hula-hula and a hint of hari-kari." When I found myself lying on the edge of a cliff being hit over the head by a sword-wielding stuntman, blood pouring down my face, I knew that either Hooker or I was done. We did end up with ninety episodes, enabling the show to go into syndication, where it eventually disappeared.

Actually, I didn't have to get hit over the head with that sword to know that I wanted to direct — that realization had come much earlier. I'd worked with literally hundreds of directors in my career, including some of the greatest directors in the history of early television, but for me the best directors were those people who left me alone. I would always approach a role with my own thoughts and my own plan about how I wanted to create a character. Obviously they would stage the scene and tell me where to move, and if it made sense I'd move there. But too often in television young directors want to be *artistes,* they get an opportunity to direct an episode of *T.J. Hooker* and want to use it to build a career. So they try to reinvent the show, talking about subtext and motivation, creative lighting. Here was the motivation on *Hooker:* we had seven days to shoot an hour show within our budget.

It's the job of the actors who work there every week to protect the integrity of the program. Because I cared about the quality of the show I tested every new director. And if they didn't know what they were doing I would complain about it. That was my job. We had a young director one week who had drawn elaborate sketches of how he wanted the action to flow. He literally had planned the entire show beat to beat. This was the show that was going to earn him an Emmy, which would lead to an opportunity to direct a major motion picture. So I looked at his sketch and asked, "Just tell me one thing, why do you want to begin this scene with me walking out of the storage closet?"

Obviously the desire of the director to create art and the intention of the actor to get it done can lead to conflict on the set. Some directors believe the worst question an actor can ask is "Why?" Why do I move there? Why I do react like that? "Because I'm the director and that's what I want you to do" is not the correct answer.

There was little mystery to directing for me. I could say, "I want this camera right over there," or "Let's backlight this," or "You come running across the parking lot and leap onto the hood of the car and grab hold of the wipers and hold on," so obviously I had the necessary technical knowledge. And the producers of *T.J. Hooker* gave me that opportunity.

I had already completed one arduous directing assignment — I'd directed my wife, Marcy, in a production of *Cat on a Hot Tin Roof.* My friends, if you can successfully direct your wife in a highly dramatic role, you certainly can direct a TV show. Eventually I directed eight episodes of *Hooker,* as well as the opening-credit sequence that we used for most of the series, and Leonard Nimoy directed one. That was the price he demanded to appear in an episode. That, plus money.

Two years after the series ended I was directing my first major motion picture, the $30 million *Star Trek V: The Final Frontier.* Gene Roddenberry and Paramount executives had seen the episodes of *Hooker* that I'd directed and were so impressed by my ability to articulate an atmosphere within the confines of the capabilities of modern filmology that they realized I was the perfect choice — actually the only choice — to direct the fifth and most intellectually challenging film in the *Star Trek* saga.

And if you believe that you also believe I saw an alien in the desert. That is not exactly the way it happened. In the original TV series I was signed to be the star, and Leonard was a co-star. I was paid a higher salary. But eventually Leonard's Spock became so popular that we were both given a Favored Nations clause, meaning whatever I got he got, and whatever he got, I got. If I got a raise, he got the same raise; if he got a cold, I got it. At the time I didn't think it was totally fair, but I accepted the reality of the business. And then, as we were making the third film in this series of very successful movies, Leonard decided he would act in it only if he were allowed to direct it. The concept of a *Star Trek* film without Spock was as ridiculous as a *Star Trek* film without Captain Kirk. Who would want to see that?

I'm not certain that the studio realized when they agreed to let Leonard direct the third film, *The Search for Spock,* that they were also committing to allowing me to direct the next *Star Trek* movie.

During the years we were making *Hooker,* *Star Trek* had become one of the most successful movie franchises in history. The first film, *Star Trek: The Motion Picture,* had grossed more than $100 million and, when the merchandising revenue was added, it was one of the most lucrative films in history. Apparently Paramount learned a very important lesson from that first film: *Star Trek* fans were so loyal they didn't have to spend a lot of money to make a lot of money. In fact, the less they spent the more they could make. So Paramount cut the budget for the second film drastically and hired the very talented Nicholas Meyer to write and direct it. What he tried to do was bring some additional humanity — and humor — to the crew. As he said, "I tried through irreverence to make them a little more human and a little less wooden. I didn't insist that Captain Kirk go to the bathroom, but did *Star Trek* have to be so sanctified?"

Wooden? I thought that was another chapter of my life? Bathroom? Truthfully, I don't remember seeing a restroom aboard the *Enterprise.* Consider it immaculate elimination.

Whatever Nick Meyer did, it worked: *Star Trek II: The Wrath of Khan* opened with the largest weekend gross in movie history. By this time Captain James T. Kirk and Mr. Spock had taken their place among America's legendary fictional characters. And probably among Vulcans, too. They were certainly better known than any of the real astronauts. I think I probably resisted completely embracing Jim Kirk for a long time. Like Leonard, I hadn't wanted to be identified as him for the rest of my life, but that had ended a long while earlier. I had come to realize all the wonderful things being Captain Kirk had done for my life — and, in fact, continued to do. I remember once we were shooting in the desert and had a very early call. I told the wardrobe girl, "Give me my uniform and I'll put it on at the house so I don't have to come any earlier for wardrobe. I'll just wear it to the set." So at 4 a.m. I was racing across the desert to our location. I was way over the speed limit, figuring there wasn't another car on the road in the entire state. It turned out there was one other car — and he had lights and a siren. Yes, Officer, good morning.

Being Hooker, I knew that when you were stopped by a police officer the proper way to respond is to follow his orders, show the officer that you aren't being belligerent, and acknowledge that the officer is the boss — make sure he knows you know it. And if that doesn't work, then it's okay to beg.

So I got out of my car dressed in my uniform, ready to be amenable. The officer was actually wearing dark glasses in the middle of the night, so I couldn't see his eyes. But he looked me up and down and sort of frowned and asked, "So where are you going so fast at four o'clock in the morning?"

I told him the truth. "To my spaceship."

He sighed and said, "Okay, go ahead and live long and prosper." Then he turned around and sent me on my way.

When Paramount began discussing the third film, Leonard negotiated a deal similar to the one he'd made to appear on *Hooker:*

he agreed to appear in the movie only if he directed it. The studio readily agreed, but truthfully I didn't know how to respond. It was sort of like your brother becoming your father. Or your wife becoming your . . . the captain of your spaceship. It just upset the delicate balance that two actors in leading roles — who had forged a close friendship — had successfully managed to work out over many years. In other words, it wasn't fair!

When I read the first draft of the script I didn't like it. Spock appeared only briefly, and my role was relatively small. I just didn't believe Trekkies would accept a story in which neither Kirk nor Spock dominated the action. I invited Leonard and our producer, Harve Bennett, up to my house to discuss the script. Remember that meeting, Leonard? "It was tense, very tense."

Thank you, Leonard. It was tense, very tense. As we went through the script I asked for certain changes. I was very protective of Kirk. Mostly, though, I wanted to get some sense of how Leonard and I were going to work together. Leonard told me, "What's good for you, Bill, is good for *Star Trek*. My intention is to make a damn good *Star Trek* movie, and to do that I need you to come off well."

Oh, I get it. Clearly we were on the same 120 script pages. But it turned out that everybody was somewhat concerned about how Leonard and I would get along. Early in production I had a scene in which I received the devastating news that my son had been killed by a Klingon raiding party. It was a tremendously emotional scene, and initially I didn't quite know what I was going to do. To help me focus Leonard asked everyone not essential to the filming to leave the set. And as soon as they were gone I shouted at him, "I'm not going to do it your way."

"The hell you're not," he shouted right back at me. "You're goddamn well going to do it the way I tell you. So go stand over there and shut up. Come on, you're just the actor and I am the director of this motion picture."

I suspect the phrase "just the actor" gave it away. Everybody started laughing at that remark — no actor is "just the actor" — and any lingering tension that existed on the production disappeared. Once again the picture did very well, extremely very well, so Paramount immediately began planning the fourth movie. Originally, this was the film that I was supposed to . . .

Hold it, do you hear that? Shhhh, just

listen. Hear it? No, you probably don't, not unless you have tinnitus, which I do. And which Leonard also has. This was something else that both of us got from *Star Trek.* During one of the episodes Leonard and I were standing too close to a large explosion. It is the kind of thing that happens often on sets, most of the time with no problem. But afterward my ears started ringing, as did Leonard's, and both of us years later developed a medical condition called tinnitus, a constant sound that you hear that never goes away. For some people it can be a ringing tone. For others, like me, it's more like the hiss of a TV set that's not tuned to any channel. Millions of people suffer from it; it can be caused by anything from an explosion, continued exposure to a loud sound — many World War II airmen and rock musicians have it, for example — it can be a reaction to a medicine or caused by one of many illnesses or it simply can be a function of age. Millions of people live with it without much problem, but for more than seven million people it's debilitating. It makes it impossible to lead a normal life. There is no simple cure. And in extreme cases it can even lead to suicide. I developed one of those extreme cases.

There are parts of the world in which tinnitus is said to be the voice of God. In remote parts of China it is considered a sign of great wisdom. In rural Turkey it is considered good luck. But not in the San Fernando Valley. There it's considered a real problem. And it was driving me crazy.

I had a loud sound in my ear and it would never go away. I consulted several doctors, I had all kinds of tests. I kept thinking, this has got to stop, but it didn't. I've gone through several different programs; the one that worked for me is called habituation. This is a machine that produces what is called white noise, a sound you can't hear normally. For some reason if they can reproduce the sound you're hearing in your head on this device the sound waves are canceled out. I remember the moment they reached my level: imagine being trapped in a mine and rescuers break through and you can see the sunlight! That's what it felt like to me. I was given my life back. I wore a device similar to a hearing aid which continually piped white noise into both ears. After several months my brain got accustomed to the sound and I was able to wean myself off it.

There are doctors who tell patients they can cure them with an operation. I suppose on occasion an operation can work, but generally it doesn't. The majority of people eventually simply get accustomed to the sound and are no longer consciously aware of it — unless they think about it or some guy writes about it in his autobiography.

I know how devastating it can be waiting to get used to it. It can take months. I've done volunteer work with the American Tinnitus Association, which does research and is a very good resource. At one point they gave me a list of potential contributors and asked me to call them. Many of the people I called responded in the same way: Who is this, really? No, you can't be you. Really?

How do you prove you're yourself on the phone? I certainly wasn't going to offer to sing a chorus of "Rocket Man." I remember having a long conversation with one man who was having difficulty adjusting to tinnitus. It was destroying his life, he said. It was inescapable. Eventually he volunteered to contribute $45,000. He asked me to call him again a week later.

I did, and this time a woman answered. When I asked for this man she explained, "I'm sorry, but he committed suicide two days ago." Committed suicide? It was devastating. I'd had suicidal thoughts myself. But as I tell people suffering from this condition, time is the best treatment. They will become habituated. I have, they will. Please, listen.

So. As I was writing, I was supposed to direct the fourth *Star Trek* film, *The Voyage Home.* But because I had obligations to *T.J. Hooker,* I couldn't do it. Leonard also directed this one. As we had occasionally in the past, in *Star Trek IV* we went back in time. A deadly probe was approaching the Earth, sending out strange signals. These high-pitched beeps turned out to be an attempt to communicate with whales, which had long been extinct. So we were assigned to return to Earth of the 1980s to capture two whales and bring them home to the future. Spock, of course, was completely out of his century and had great difficulty dealing with the illogic he found in 1980s San Francisco. Once, for example, after he'd attracted too much attention with his odd behavior I explained, "Oh him? He's harmless. Part of the free speech movement at Berkeley in the sixties. I think he did a little too much LDS."

In another scene my love interest, Dr. Gillian Taylor, asked Spock, "Are you sure you won't change your mind?"

To which he replied logically, "Is there something wrong with the one I have?"

Chekov had a similar problem. An FBI agent interrogating him asked, "Name?"

"My name?" Chekov asked.

The agent replied sarcastically, "No, *my* name."

Chekov was stumped. "I do not know your name."

"You play games with me, mister," the agent threatened, "and you're through."

Chekov smiled. "I am? May I go now?"

The film cost $25 million to make and earned almost $150 million. It was by far the highest-grossing *Star Trek* film — which certainly made it a difficult movie to follow. And it was my turn.

I began by settling on a concept: the crew of the *Enterprise* goes in search of God. And instead we find the devil. I wanted Kirk and Spock and Bones to go to hell. Filmically. I wanted to explore the whole philosophical question of God and the devil and man's relationship to their worship, a subject that had fascinated me for a long time. And here I was being given a clean slate. What do you want to do, Shatner? God and *Star Trek*. That's a jaw dropper. I had it all worked out in my mind, McCoy falls into the grip of the devil. Spock and Kirk go to hell and are able to get out through the tunnel of Hades and are running for the safety of the

Enterprise when we hear McCoy calling for our help. And we have to turn back out of love for our partner. That was my idea: Kirk and Spock explore Dante's *Inferno*. I could visualize us crossing the burning River Styx, pursued by living gargoyles, fleeing into the depths of collapsing cities. The thought of creating hell on film was incredibly exciting to me. Heaven and hell, love and hate, God and the devil, that was the movie I wanted to make. I wrote a three-page outline and submitted it to Paramount. And they loved it. Yes, this is damn good. This is what we want to do.

It had to be approved by Roddenberry. He turned it down. I tried to do a God story, he said. It's not going to work. You alienate everybody. Nobody knows what God is, everybody has a different concept of God. Yes, the studio agreed with him, this is what we don't want to do.

No God story? I couldn't believe it. I wanted to do a God story. Then someone suggested, what if an alien thinks he's the devil? Maybe that would work. Yes, the studio agreed, if an alien thinks he's the devil we can do it.

Roddenberry agreed, as long as it was an alien and not really the devil.

I had my story. We go in search of God

and find an alien who claims to be the devil and we believe he's the devil but he's not the devil. That would work. What I realized only after the movie was completed and I'd made the first of many compromises was that I'd already destroyed my concept. It was no longer God and the devil; it's a psycho alien who is a devil worshipper. Every step of the way in making a movie there are compromises and this was my first one. But at least I had my basic plot.

And then I created my Big Bang ending. Now this was really going to be spectacular. Kirk was going to be running up a mountain to escape and the alien-devil's minions were going to come out of Hades in pursuit. What a concept! I knew they couldn't simply come out of the ground — they would be thrust out like rocks from a volcano. Yes! Smoke and fire streaming out of their mouths. I could see it. I described it to the special-effects people. They loved it. Smoke and fire! Everybody loved it. "How many rock people can I have?" I asked.

"We'll get you ten," they said.

Unbelievable! That's better than the Furies. They're smoking and flames are shooting out of their mouths and they're chasing Kirk. They're four-legged animals. I drew up some sketches of these rock men

410

exploding. This finale was going to be bigger and better than anything ever seen on *Star Trek.* So I've got a great beginning, a strong story, and a great ending. I know I can fill in the rest. And I'm going to direct it. This is going to be the start of the next phase of my career.

I was enthralled with the entire process of directing a $30 million major motion picture. On a film set the director isn't God — he's the one who tells God to run across the parking lot, leap onto the hood, and grab hold of the wipers and hold on.

Until we actually began filming I don't think I ever imagined how different it is directing a television program and a motion picture. When I directed *Hooker,* for example, I had to move in close; if I widened my frame more of the background was included, meaning it had to be lit or cleared, all the traffic had to be stopped, people on foot had to be held back. It meant getting permits and releases, staying away from identifiable product signs. Instead, we'll put the camera right here and do a close-up.

Let me give you an example: imagine a very simple scene. Romeo says to Juliet, "I love you." Juliet looks at him angrily and replies, "Oh please. Do you think I'm a fool?" Good dialogue. If we were shooting it

411

for television we'd put Romeo and Juliet a few feet apart, get a two-shot of the quarreling lovers together, and then shoot close-ups of each of them separately. Simple and quick.

But the director of a big-budget film would do it very differently. "To symbolize the distance between them let's go to Switzerland and put each of them on the summit of a mountain in the Alps. We'll shoot it peak-to-peak at sunset. Let's make it 70mm. And let's get Brad Pitt and Angelina Jolie. Then we'll hire John Williams to do the original music." And the producers are in awe of his brilliance. The Alps! Why didn't we think of that? And they will move five hundred people to Switzerland to get that shot. For a director the sense of power in incredible. Whatever you conceive in your imagination, whatever you dream, five hundred people are ready to make it happen.

Unfortunately, that was not my experience on this film. The plot was somewhat complex: it takes place in Stardate 8454.130. Kirk is on vacation, climbing El Capitan mountain in Yosemite when the *Enterprise* is dispatched on an emergency mission to rescue hostages on a desolate planet. The kidnapper is a Vulcan, Spock's half-brother, who is using the hostages to lure a starship to Nimbus III so he can use it to cross the Great Barrier — the final frontier — and reach the mythical planet Sha Ka Ree, which is inhabited by a God-like entity. Perhaps it even is God. Kirk agrees to travel there with him, and on that planet they encounter this entity. Eventually Kirk battles this alien — this is the battle with the rock men from hell — which is destroyed with the help of a Klingon commander who followed the *Enterprise* there to kill Kirk.

A week before we started shooting I still hadn't seen the rock men suits. This was my big ending, the whole film was building to that scene, I wanted to see them. Don't worry, I was told, they're coming. And then I got a cost breakdown. They were going to cost $350,000 a suit. Three-point-five million dollars for ten suits? We didn't have $3.5 million for anything. The producers told me we had to cut the budget. Okay, can I have five suits? I could make it work with five. Okay, five suits.

We started shooting. A week passed, two weeks, I still hadn't seen the suit. But I'm excited about it, it's going to be great. Fire is going to come out of it. It's going to be amazing. It's almost ready, I'm told. Great, when? Next week. Trust me. More weeks pass, we're shooting in the Arizona desert and we've got to shoot that final scene soon. I've planned it out, I see it in my head. It's going to be amazing. And then they told me that, essentially, we could afford only one suit.

One suit? One fucking rock man suit? Well, I had no options. I decided I'd shoot it up close, far away, in different locations, and then we'd use movie magic to make it appear as if it were an army of devils. Okay, one. When am I going to see it? On the 17th, they promised.

But we were scheduled to shoot the scene on the 18th. They guaranteed I'd have it on the 17th, and it would be great. It'll breathe smoke and fire. It'll be amazing. Amazing!

On the 17th I returned from our location and the special-effects people were waiting for me. They were smiling. "It's done and it's fantastic. George is wearing the suit. You want to see it?"

The sun was setting behind George as he appeared. It was awful, terrible. It looked like a monster from the 1930s Flash Gordon serials. I held my temper, maybe the fire and smoke will save it. I took a deep breath and asked, "Where's the smoke?"

And then a thin wisp of smoke curled into

the air from behind a rock. I looked behind the rock and two special-effects men were crouched there smoking cigarettes and blowing smoke into a tube. I was just about speechless. We'd started with $3.5 million for ten suits and we're down to one $350,000 suit with two men blowing smoke into a tube.

I took a few steps back and if I squinted and sort of looked at it from the corner of my eyes and if the lighting wasn't great it did look as if it might be oozing out of the rock. Okay, all right, I stayed calm, somehow I'd make it work. I was a director! And directors always make it work. "How does the fire work?" I asked.

"Well, the fire's a problem," they admitted. "We tried it and it burned the stuntman's face. So we'll put it in the CGI. We'll create it on the computer. We'll just create it in editing. He'll open his mouth and flames will come shooting out. It'll be great. Trust us."

There was nothing I could do. I thought I was getting Romeo and Juliet on mountaintops in the Alps, instead I was getting ALF in a playground. If I obscured him in a lot of smoke, and if we shot in dim light, maybe, just maybe I could get away with it. So the next night we all went up to the location on the side of a mountain and got everything set up. Finally, we were ready to shoot the climactic scene. Cue the stuntman. He appears and . . . and there's no smoke! "Cut! Cut! Where's the smoke? I need smoke!"

They looked at me sheepishly. "Well, we're blowing the smoke through the tube, but the breeze is dissipating the smoke." The breeze? They hadn't planned for the breeze? We're in the desert and the desert cools at night and creates a breeze. Since the beginning of time there's been a breeze at night in the desert. Instead of a fire-breathing smoking devil, I had a ridiculous-looking guy in a leather outfit. It was useless. I didn't have an ending. Not only didn't I have an ending, I didn't have my God. At one point the alien-devil sends out a shaft of light that we're supposed to believe is God. So what does God look like? Initially I intended to use a stylized Jesus Christ–like figure but then Roddenberry made his salient point: God is different for everybody. So we also needed God.

We were going to have George Lucas's Industrial Light and Magic create God for us. George Lucas! Just imagine George Lucas's vision of God. And ILM did extraordinary work, it was the most creative company in the entertainment industry. I was absolutely thrilled. Maybe they could save me.

Unfortunately, they were busy working on two major pictures — and they probably were a little too expensive. So we found this guy in Hoboken, New Jersey. I'm totally serious. This was a man who'd done some impressive work on television commercials. Five of us flew to New York and met with him in his house. His wife was a five-star cook and made us a wonderful dinner. Believe me, her potatoes were the best potatoes I'd ever eaten. It's worth going to Hoboken to eat these potatoes; believe me, no one has ever made potatoes . . .

Afterward he took us into his studio and created God in a tank of oil. It was a mixture of various oils swirling in a large oil lamp–like device. "If we shoot it tight," he explained, "we can get an image . . ."

We were all so seduced by this great meal and perhaps some wine that we offered him the assignment. Maybe we didn't have Industrial Light and Magic, but we did have this guy in New Jersey whose wife was a great cook.

What we should have done was use her potatoes. If we had mashed them just right it would have looked more like God than the images he created for us.

We just didn't have the budget to put the movie I saw in my mind on film. In the opening scene in Yosemite, for example, I was supposed to be climbing a sheer cliff. I had a camera on a plateau, looking straight down three thousand feet as I climbed up. I was wearing a safety harness so it wasn't dangerous, and as long as I didn't look down I was okay. The problem we encountered was that because the camera films in two dimensions it was impossible to get a sense of the true height. In fact it looked like it was about six feet down. I needed to drop some rocks so the camera could follow them all the way down to give the audience a sense of the actual height, but climbers in Yosemite are prohibited from throwing stones down. I solved that by having some rubber rocks made. As I climbed up, I was going to dislodge them and the camera would track them all the way to the bottom. Unfortunately, these rubber rocks had to weigh almost nothing so they would not pose any danger to people below. In fact, they were so light that when I touched them they floated away in the breeze. I had a large pile of floating rocks. And, obviously, completely useless.

We never did find an appropriate ending.

After we'd finished shooting I had to search through all the footage to find something, anything, that I could use to construct the final scene. Somehow we managed to put something together, but it was a poor compromise. From the beginning to the end the entire film was a compromise. As a result *Star Trek V: The Final Frontier* just wasn't that good. I wasn't terribly dissatisfied with it, there were some very good moments in it. The quality of a science-fiction film depends almost completely on the story and its special effects. In this film the tacky special effects actually hurt the story. Most of the reviews were disappointing, but the *New York Times* review was complimentary: "Scene for scene Mr. Shatner's direction is smooth and sharply focused." The film grossed $70 million, more than double what it cost to make; so it was profitable even if it wasn't an artistic success.

The night we opened was one of the most glorious evenings of my life. I sat in the back of a sold-out theater watching the glow from the screen highlighting people's heads. And they sat there entranced by my work. It was a magic trick. I'd created it out of an idea, a thought. An idea that eventually employed hundreds of people and entertained millions. My idea, my dream. And in the sense of taking a simple thought and transforming it into a complex product it was an overwhelming experience.

I loved directing, and I certainly wasn't soured on the process. In the future I just had to be leaner and smarter. The lesson I'd learned was that the company runs on the strength and personality of the director. I had been too timid. Early on we'd spent a considerable amount of time trying to visualize God. I needed creative help but nobody came up with any ideas. The producer, rather then being helpful, took out on me whatever frustrations he was having dealing with the studio. Rather than being supportive, he was destructive. For example, I had recently seen *The Wizard of Oz* and in desperation I suggested that the face of God appear in a whirlwind. In front of the entire crew the producer snarled, "For Christ's sake. I bet you saw *The Wizard of Oz.*"

Of course I had to admit it. But I was furious. For no reason, except perhaps his own ego, he had humiliated me in front of the cast and crew. If he didn't show me respect, why would any of them? What I should have said to him was, "How dare you talk to me that way. If you don't like the idea, that's one thing. You come up with something better." But I didn't have the strength of character to stand up to him. I was so intent on getting this movie made and not ruffling any feathers that I stood there and accepted his abuse.

Half of directing is politics and in my first attempt that was the aspect I'd failed. If I was going to be successful as a director, I'd learned, I had to take complete charge. And so, several years later, when I wrote and directed and starred in the feature film *Groom Lake,* I had almost complete control.

Do me a favor, please, don't tell that to anybody. Let's just keep it between us.

This was a film I wanted to make in the worst way, and that's exactly what happened. This was a wonderful story of love and life. A dying young woman travels with her husband to Groom Lake, which is another name for Area 51, the super-secret military installation ninety miles north of Las Vegas. Investigators into UFOs and alien visitations have long maintained that the U.S. government base there is the center of our investigation into extraterrestrial activities — and that at least one alien was captured and lived there. The young couple go there to try to find some evidence that there is life beyond what we know, and that someday, in some form, they will be together again.

It was a movie about the mysteries of life and death, a film with an ambiguous but hopeful conclusion. I had a very difficult time finding the money I needed to make it. But finally a man named Charles Band, who had produced numerous C-movies, including *Bimbo Movie Bash, Teenage Space Vampires, Femalien, Beach Babes from Beyond,* and *Horrorvision,* offered to make it as a low-budget film. I guess he figured that my name attached to a science-fiction film would be enough to recoup a small investment. I initially had it budgeted at $1.5 million. If I had to squeeze everything I probably could have made it for a million. But at half a million dollars it's almost impossible.

One advantage we did have was that because I was involved we were given permission to shoot inside the biosphere just north of Tucson, Arizona. Outside it was a weird and strange-looking building — perfect for my needs — and inside it was even more bizarre. We had permission to use it so we rewrote the script around it.

I didn't know how I was going to make this film for only half a million dollars. But rather than being discouraged, I looked at it as a challenge. I was going to get this film done and it was going to be good. The beautiful story and the extraordinary performances I would get from my actors would cover up what we lacked in production values. But what I didn't know when we started was that Charlie Band was telling the executive producer he actually intended to get it made for $250,000. The producer was caught between Band telling him not to spend any money and me trying to make a decent movie. He pulled all kinds of shenanigans to try to stop us from wasting money on things like film stock and actors. When we were scheduled to shoot at night, for example, the cable from the generator had to be laid in the daylight. No cables, no lights, so you can't shoot. It turned out he'd forgotten to order the cable. Whatever we wanted to do, he was prepared with a reason we couldn't do it: there's no film stock. We can't get actors. There's no money. There was no food for the company. Finally I ended up using my own credit card. We ended up paying the extras in pizza.

It was insane. It made Roger Corman look like a spendthrift.

Several key scenes had to be shot from the air. After a lot of screaming the producer finally agreed to rent a small two-person helicopter for four hours. We couldn't even afford a camera mount for the helicopter, a basic piece of equipment. The cameraman was going to rope himself in and hold the camera in his hands. We had to shoot every scene we needed in those four hours. That was okay, we could do it if I planned every minute. In preparation I lined up a series of shots on local roads several miles apart. We'd use two units: while the cameraman was shooting with the first unit the second unit would move into place. When he was working with the second unit the first unit would race to the next setup. If everything went perfectly, we could get all the shots we needed. It required a tremendous amount of organization but it could be done.

Do you think there was any chance at all of everything going perfectly? The first shot was scheduled for 4:30 a.m. — an hour before sunrise. At 4:30 we were standing on the road, waiting for the helicopter. And waiting. It was coming from about fifty miles away and it was late. And I began to wonder if we were waiting in the right place. And as people do in that situation I began to doubt myself: I think I'm the right place? But maybe it was around the bend? What did I tell him? The first glow of the sunrise appeared over the horizon. Shit, where's that helicopter? I saw a bright light hovering in the distance. It was the helicopter and he was in the wrong place. Or we were in the wrong place. It didn't matter who was right, the only thing that mattered was getting the shot. I shouted to my assistant, get him on the radio right now!

She smiled. Radio? He doesn't have a radio with him.

I was thinking very quickly. How am I going to save the shot? Okay, I shouted to everyone, pack up and roll. Right now! We got into our cars and drove like maniacs on this unlit back road — only later did we learn that these were the roads used by drug smugglers and we were under constant observation — driving toward the helicopter. But as fast as we drove we didn't seem to be getting any closer.

I'm not quite certain when I realized we were chasing the North Star. That spot of light that I thought was the helicopter's running lights was actually a very bright star. We could have driven forever and never gotten there — it was a thousand light-years away. I guess I wasn't surprised that no one in the crew told the director that he was pursuing a star. Believe me, if I was acting in this film rather than paying for a lot of it, I would have been laughing at me. Turn around, I screamed, and we went racing back to our original site.

Somehow we managed to get most of the shots we needed. This was the most memorable — and expensive — shoot of my career. We shot in Bisbee, Arizona, and stayed in a haunted hotel. It was while making this movie that Elizabeth and I went night riding with the Border Patrol and an illegal immigrant recognized Captain Kirk. From the beginning to the end of the production we had nothing but problems, many of which Elizabeth was able to solve. When *Groom Lake* was finished it had some nice moments, including several fine performances by some very good actors. But, honestly, it didn't tie together smoothly. Again, it was my fault; I was just so blinded by my desire to make this film that I agreed to conditions that really made it impossible. No, we don't need film, we'll just take a lot of still pictures and string them together. It made a little money in rentals and plays occasionally on the Sci-Fi Channel, so with the tax write-offs I probably broke even on my investment.

Actually, as a result of that film the Sci-Fi Channel asked me to come up with an original idea and direct a film for them. "Come up with an alien-of-the-week that we haven't done," an executive suggested. They had done three pterodactyls, four dinosaurs, and seven Frankensteins. I presented several ideas to them but the one they sparked to was a great ball of intelligent fire from another solar system that survived by consuming planets. This *Alien Fire* had consumed Venus, it had consumed Mars, and it was on its way toward Earth!

I was going to direct it during a hiatus period from *Boston Legal.* We had a budget of about $1.5 million. Unfortunately, the producers cut short the hiatus and I didn't have the time to direct it. Actually, maybe it was good fortune. The making of *Alien Fire* did not go well. It rained. It rained all the time — and this is a story about fire. *Alien Smoke* just doesn't sound as threatening as *Alien Fire.* Once again this film depended on the quality of the special effects, and with all the other problems during the production they had only two hundred thousand dollars left to produce all the special effects. Not enough, not nearly enough. How about *Alien Embers?*

It was during this period that I suddenly, and certainly unexpectedly to me, became more popular than ever before in my career. I became . . . ready for this . . . Shatman. After becoming Captain Kirk I received a lot of attention, particularly from Trekkies, but this was different. In public, people began expressing real affection toward me. They would often tell me how much they enjoyed my work and even thank me for entertaining them. I can't begin to explain how gratifying that has been, nor can I explain why it's happened. At first I would go into the denial mode, figuring they can't possibly mean me! What had I done to deserve it? Say a few words on film? I didn't believe I'd done enough to warrant the affection that I felt — and still feel — when I go out.

It's funny how it happened. Seriously. There have been a lot of articles written that claim the public embraced me because I finally learned how to laugh at myself, that I finally showed my sense of humor to the audience. If it's true, it wasn't a career decision, it's because I was offered a job. My career in comedy began when I appeared in *Airplane II: The Sequel,* playing the role created in the original movie by Kareem Abdul-Jabbar. The kind of commander who orders a profile on anyone who watched *The Sound of Music* more than four times. It was in that film that I first began poking fun at my serious image. But here's the truth about that: I was acting funny. I'm an actor, this was a comedy, my lines were funny, and the audience responded to it. John Lithgow, who like me almost exclusively played serious roles before finding success in comedy, explained accurately, "Once you're funny people no longer think of you as quite the serious actor they're used to seeing."

A few years later I appeared on *Saturday Night Live* and, once again, I think the audience was surprised I could be funny at my own expense. I parodied Kirk and Hooker. Well, if I hadn't been funny it would have been a tragedy — and *SNL* is a comedy show. When I agreed to host the show I knew I would be poking fun at my somewhat somber image, that's the foundation of that show. But rather than resisting, I embraced the opportunity to be funny. For me, it is our sense of humor, our ability to laugh even when life can be so bleak, that separates us from all other living things. Have you ever seen a flower laugh? There are no great turtle comedians. Laughing hyenas do not get the joke. But humans laugh at all types of humor: bathroom humor, ironic humor, witty humor, slapstick, silliness, and knock-knock jokes. Name the different types of laughter that are available to us and that's what life is all about. Looking back on my life and all the things that have happpened, success and failure, marriages and divorces, broke and less broke, it finally had become clear to me that it was all funny.

Except perhaps *The Transformed Man,* although there are people who claim my comic career began with that album. So none of this was new to me. I'd learned that the audiences at *Star Trek* conventions most enjoyed the funny stories we'd tell about working on that series.

After that *SNL* appearance I began to get offered more humorous parts. Bill Cosby saw me act, thought I was funny, and asked me to appear on *The Cosby Show.* And when John Lithgow needed someone to create the role of his boss, the heroic Big Giant Head, on *3rd Rock from the Sun,* he immediately thought of me. I mean, let's be honest, who better to portray the Big Giant Head than myself? And the audience embraced me as the Head man.

Once I started doing more comedy my career — and my life — seemed to move in a very different direction. And ironically, some of it wasn't at all funny.

NINE

The door of the dining room snapped open. A lovely blond android, clad in just about nothing, came stumbling out. There was blood splashed across her face and breasts. She bumped into Jake, caught hold of his arm, crying out, "They killed him! They murdered poor Zacky!"

Shoving the mechanical woman aside, Jake carefully crossed the threshold.

The large dining room's interior offered a simulated moonlit terrace with a long formal dining table set up on the mosaic tiles. A large rectangle had been seared out of the far wall with a disintegrator cannon and the real night showed through. A chill wind was blowing into the room, carrying rain with it.

Another nearly naked female android was still seated at the table. Most of her left side had been sliced away with a laz-gun and her inner works were spilled out and dangling.

A third android, this one in the image of a naked young boy of . . .

Let me introduce you to Jake Cardigan, the futuristic detective hero of the *TekWar* series that I created, which eventually became nine books, twenty-four comic books, four movies, a TV series, sets of trading cards, and a computer game. These few paragraphs are from the third book in the series, *TekLab,* written with the very talented Ron Goulart.

An acting career is extraordinarily difficult to sustain over a long period of time. In most professions the experience people gain enables them to become even more productive as they get older. Actors just get older. The audience slots actors into certain types determined by the roles that first brought them success, from leading man in action films to a character actor in serious dramas. But as they grow older and change physically they also have to change type. Nobody wanted to see John Wayne gather a posse to save the Old Actor's Home. But often the audience won't accept them in that new type. There is a word used to describe that: unemployment. So as I started getting older and began wondering how much longer my acting career would survive — let's be honest, I could only survive as a heroic, handsome leading man for three or four decades — I started focusing on the off-camera areas of the movie and television business, including directing, producing, and more writing than I'd done in the past.

All of which explains how I got into professional wrestling.

TekWar was one of the first projects I developed. While I was directing *Star Trek V* the Teamsters Union went on strike, forcing us to shut down production for three months. I didn't know what to do with myself. I get nervous when I don't have something scheduled in the next half hour, so just imagine what I felt like facing three completely unscheduled months. There's nothing more frightening to an actor than a future with nothing scheduled. So I began working on a novel: *T.J. Hooker* meets *The Fugitive* in the *Star Trek* future. I started by giving my character a past. He's in the cooler, but the cooler is actually a deep-freeze in space. He had to have an objective, so he was wrongly convicted of a crime and his wife and child left him to be with the man who gave false evidence against him.

I'd been living in the world of science fiction for more than two decades, and this was my first opportunity to create something entirely new. There were bits and pieces I'd been thinking about for years, with brand-new ideas tossed into the future. *TekWar* was set in the twenty-second century.

My main character, Jake Cardigan, was released from his cryogenic state when the wealthy owner of a private detective agency needed his help. Cardigan became a private detective, not only pursuing the enemies of the future, but also intent on proving his innocence by finding his wife and child and the people who framed him. The most fun about writing science fiction is that anything is possible. You want to cure a disease: "The diseases of the twentieth century had been wiped out." There, it's done, there is no disease in your environment. Snow in Los Angeles? "An artificial snow was falling across Greater Los Angeles, part of the seasonal special effects." The universe is your imagination.

In my universe ex-cop Jake Cardigan had been convicted of murdering his partners while under the influence of an extraordinary drug, Tek. At night I often leave the television on as I fall into sleep, and in that state there is a diffusion between reality and whatever is on television. Tek had a similar effect; for the user it made fantasies seem real while reality seemed like a dream state. Tek users lived in their fantasies and would do almost anything to stay in that pleasurable state and, most dangerously, when the drug wore off, return to it.

So that was the basis of my stories, the adventures of a hard-boiled private detective two hundred years in the future. The novels were very successful and created a lot of interest in the property. But I discovered that I'd made a mistake setting these stories so far in the future. I didn't realize how expensive the future was going to be. Futuristic sets and props and costumes made it too expensive for TV. Fortunately, Marvel Comics approached me to turn *Tek-War* into a comic-book series. We sold them the rights — but insisted that they set the stories only fifty years in the future. Marvel changed the name to *Tek World* and eventually published twenty-four Epic Comics.

By setting the stories only fifty years in the future we could use existing buildings as our backgrounds. Suddenly several companies who wanted to buy the rights. Universal in particular had watched Paramount make a fortune with *Star Trek* and wanted to own part of the future. So eventually I

435

made a deal with them for a series of movies to be broadcast on the USA network. I directed the pilot.

I'll bet you're beginning to wonder how this leads to my career in professional wrestling. Here's a hint: Regis Philbin.

Our budget for three movies was less than the budget for a Movie of the Week shot in Los Angeles. So we had to do everything possible to save money. I did, for example, create the most inexpensive elaborate computer in history. The computer was central to our plots. We needed a computer that actually could exist a half-century from now that we could use throughout the series. It was a central reference point so it had to look spectacular — and it had to cost about the same as a laptop. What I imagined was a highly complex three-dimensional computer that would project its own image 360 degrees around the operator — a holographic computer. It would be there, it would produce images, but the audience wouldn't see it. The computer operator would reach behind him and manipulate an invisible switch, then turn and reach over there, just as if he was surrounded by a huge console. This was a truly amazing computer. Unlike games, it has a real computer keybo . . . Well, actually that was the Commodore Vic-20, this computer didn't have a real computer keyboard. But to make the operator's gestures look plausible, I brought in a dance choreographer and a sign language expert to work with him on his movements.

We had to figure out some way to demonstrate the extraordinary power of Tek. What would people look like in the middle of a fantasy they believed to be true? In one scene Cardigan's son was supposed to be drugged. I was working with an inexperienced child actor and I needed him to show complete euphoria. Finally I suggested, "I want you to look as if you're seeing the sunrise for the first time." Go ahead, try it yourself — and you're Tekked!

Greg Evigan, who had starred in *B.J. and the Bear,* played Cardigan. Greg was terrific in it. I played his boss. We shot wherever we found a viable location. Viable meaning free. For one scene, in fact, we needed a location where homeless people would sleep — and our location manager discovered the worst place I've been in my life. It was an enormous abandoned warehouse complex, a huge open room with cement walls and a cement floor. All the windows were smashed, enabling sunlight to stream in. Almost every foot of floor space was covered with cardboard pallets, large cardboard boxes that had been broken apart and spread open so the homeless could use them as bunks. Every disgusting thing you can imagine littered the floor. The stench was suffocating. As I walked through the place I could feel the filth right through the soles of my running shoes, I could almost feel the bacteria eating through them. When I left that place we just had to throw them away.

"This is fabulous," I said excitedly when I saw it. It was so awful I couldn't wait to shoot there. The decay was so visual. The light was perfect. It was a perfect location. We shot all over Toronto. That city has a large number of abandoned sugar silos — we built sets inside one of them and it became our prison. We found an abandoned five-floor oil-cracking plant. Our character was supposed to be larger than life, a man with magical powers, so I put him on the fifth-floor balcony, then suddenly he appeared on the third-floor balcony, then he was standing on the ground. It was definitely movie magic. We completed the first film on time and only slightly over budget.

Before the first film was broadcast the USA Network wanted me to do publicity for it. Publicity? Shatner? Promote something on TV? Could I possibly overcome

438

my shyness and appear on television? Let me think about it for a second. Okay, I'd love to do it. During my career I've appeared on almost every possible TV show to promote my projects. You've got a crystal set? How many rooms of your house do you reach? I'll be there. Regis and Kathie Lee, Sally Jesse Raphael, Dennis Miller, John Tesh, Pat Sajak, Sonya, Merv Griffin, Jay Leno, Max Headroom, David Letterman, Conan O'Brien, I've done them all. To promote *TekWar* I did Regis and Pat Sajak, Dennis Miller, all the usual shows. And then the USA Network told me with great excitement that they were able to book me on their most popular show . . .

Hmm, I wondered, now what would be the most popular show on the USA Network?

"We're putting you on the WWF! It's the perfect target audience for the movie." And that is how I became involved in professional wrestling and eventually went to the WWF Hall of Fame. The way it was planned I would appear on their show, stand near the ring, and tell viewers, "Stay tuned after wrestling for my new movie!"

I thought it was a great idea. I'd never attended a professional wrestling match but I'd looked at it on television. I knew what it was all about and I thought it was a lot of fun. It was wrestling; people got hit over the head with chairs, eyes got gouged out, nobody got hurt. But it occurred to me if I was going to fly all the way to Texas I wanted to do more than stand next to the ring. "Can we do something better than that?" I asked. "Can I get in the ring?"

What is wrong with me? Where do these ideas come from? "Sure," they said with great joy. "If you want to get in the ring that'd be great."

Now I was excited. I could see the possibilities. This is what happens when my enthusiasm takes control of my brain. Usually I end up convincing someone to try the sushi, rarely does it involve my medical insurance. "Well, what do you think about me wrestling?"

Two weeks later I was in the men's room of the Freeman Coliseum in San Antonio, Texas, with the legendary wrestler and broadcaster Jerry "The King" Lawler, working out moves for the ring. An hour later the two of us were in the ring — promoting *TekWar* — and Lawler started with me. With me! He may be the King, but I was the Shatman! After he poked me, I pushed him into the ropes and he said, "I know these idiots look like they're from another planet,

440

but there's nobody with pointed ears gonna come out and save you!"

"These are not idiots," I immediately responded. "This is our audience. These are the people who watch *TekWar*!" There. Finally, when the King persisted, I picked him up and tossed him over my shoulder. The crowd went wild.

I loved it, just loved it. So I decided to make a second appearance. That was when I became Bret "Hit Man" Hart's manager. The "Hit Man" was my man. I appeared with him the following week to promote *TekWar* — but also to promote his upcoming match on USA with Double J, Jeff Jarrett. "I got his back," I snarled.

When "Heartbreak Kid" Shawn Michaels asked me, "Mr. Shatner, who's gonna be watching your back?" I laughed at that question.

And then I warned him, "I took care of Lawler last week. I've got something to tell Roadie . . ." — Roadie was Michaels's partner — ". . . Don't touch Bret Hart. Roadkill, that's what your name will be, not Roadie!"

It was great fun and quickly done. It was quickly forgotten. I thought. But fifteen years later I got a call from Jerry Lawler. Apparently he hadn't forgotten. He was being inducted into the WWF Hall of Fame, he explained. Would I come to Detroit to introduce him?

Coincidently I was flying to Toronto that weekend, so I agreed. They had written a nice speech for me and it was a great pleasure being there with Vince McMahon and a group of legendary wrestlers. There were about three thousand people there and when I was introduced I walked out on stage — and about five hundred of them started booing me. Booing! Me! Booing the Shatman! Some people started screaming, "Get off the stage." I spoke as loudly and as rapidly as I could and got off. They were booing me. Later it was explained to me that this was a wrestling audience and they didn't want to hear from some phony actor, they wanted to hear from some real fake wrestlers. Now, if I had thought about it, I would have told them that yes, maybe I was just another Hollywood phony, maybe I was willing to make things up to please an audience, but I was there because I so deeply loved wrestling. That would have won them over. And if it hadn't I would have tossed Lawler over my shoulder.

In all the years of my career, with all the fascinating places I'd traveled to and all the shows I'd done, there was still one thing I had never learned how to do. I didn't know how to not work. The curse of the actor's life. I am absolutely fascinated as I look over my shoulder at my past — and Jerry Lawler — at how the simplest decisions I've made have had the most complex reactions. A career is a series of connected events. So when I turned down an offer I wasn't simply rejecting a job and a paycheck, I was completely eliminating the possibility that it might lead to something else. When you turn down an opportunity to work you're also turning down an experience, maybe even an adventure, and a universe of possibilities. *The Transformed Man* led to Price line.com. Saying yes to possibilities has been the core of my career.

Let me give you a perfect example. In addition to acting and producing and directing and writing and doing commercials and appearing at conventions I also worked quite often as a host or narrator of some kind of special. I had become . . . the voice of authority! I hosted *Heroes and Sidekicks,* which celebrated motion-picture heroes. *The Love Boat Fall Preview Party* celebrated love on a boat. On *The Search for Houdini* famous magicians attempted to re-create some of Houdini's most famous illusions — and in a live séance at the end of the show we tried to contact him. Obviously he was out that night, as he didn't call back. I hosted the *Dick Clark Bloopers Show,* Don Rickles's bloopers show *Foul-Ups, Bleeps & Blunders, An Evening at the Improv, The Best of Us Awards Show, TV's Funniest Game Show Moments, The Horror Film Awards, MTV Movie Awards.* I had gotten quite good at standing in front of a camera and reading lines with great sincerity. So when producer Arnold Shapiro called and asked me to host a series of three specials he was doing about people calling 911 for help, I immediately agreed.

Arnold Shapiro and I had first worked together for a couple of days more than a decade earlier, when he'd produced the *Science-Fiction Awards* on which I'd performed the classic "Rocket Man." A few years after that he'd produced a tribute to the Air Force on its fortieth anniversary called *Top Flight* — and had hired me to host it because I was known for piloting a rather impressive spacecraft.

We also worked on *Rescue 911* which had started with a terrible crime. Late on December 14, 1988, in Arlington, Texas, an eighteen-year-old thief armed with a knife broke into an apartment. There was some speculation that he was on drugs, but obviously he intended to rob the place. A man

444

and his two children, a fourteen-year-old boy and a nine-year-old girl, were asleep inside the apartment. The man woke up and confronted the thief, who attacked him with the knife. The kids woke up and the nine-year-old had the presence of mind to dial 911 for help. She started screaming into the phone, "This man's attacking my dad! He's got a knife!" Suddenly there was an explosion — the fourteen-year-old had grabbed his father's shotgun and fired once, killing the thief. The entire 911 call was recorded; the girl screaming, the shotgun being fired, and finally the police arriving. Journalist Charles Osgood got hold of the chilling tape and ran it on his radio show, *The Osgood File.*

The president of CBS's Entertainment Division, Kim LeMasters, heard Osgood's show while driving to work. He wondered if similar tapes existed, maybe even enough of them to fill an hour of television. Norman Powell, then the head of CBS Productions, hired Shapiro to produce two or three specials based on 911 calls. Documentary specials needed a celebrity host to do promotion and attract an audience. Kim Le-Masters had a great idea for that host, suggesting, "What about Leonard Nimoy?"

"And as soon as he said that," Shapiro

once told me, "I thought, no, what about Bill Shatner? He'd played T.J. Hooker, a police officer, and police officers participate in rescues. It worked for me."

Coincidently, ABC was developing almost the exact same show, to be hosted by Pernell Roberts. So we were in a great race to get on the air first. We beat them by two weeks and got a very good rating — they broadcast their show against *60 Minutes* and got a very bad number. No one could rescue the ABC show.

Star Trek changed lives, *Rescue 911* saved them. We know we saved at least 350 lives, but the true figure may well be thousands. After both of our specials had won their time period CBS decided to turn the show into a full series. Now, please pause here with me for a moment as I savor a delectable situation. I want you to pretend you're a CBS executive, sitting in your office, leaning back in your comfortable chair with your feet up on your desk and looking out the window, feeling very good about the amazing ratings these two specials received and confident about the prospects for the new series. What's this? A knock on the door. An assistant walks into your office with a troubled look on his face. "Guess what?" he says reluctantly. "Somehow we neglected to sign Shatner to a deal for a series."

The actor wins! The actor wins! Remember how ABC did not renegotiate my contract when *T.J. Hooker* was changed from an ensemble to the show in which I worked in almost every scene? Now it was my turn. This was one of the very few times in my career that I had the advantage over the producer — and we milked that advantage. As producer Arnold Shapiro describes it, "Needless to say the deal that we made was very favorable to him. In fact, to that time there probably never had been another deal like that in television."

Rescue 911 was on the air for seven and a half years. What set this show apart from the reality shows currently on the air was that our stories were real. We didn't create reality. We made approximately 185 episodes. At one time it was on the air on CBS every Tuesday night — as well as in sixty countries. For almost three years we were one of television's top twelve shows. It was a series dedicated to the men and women who saved the lives of strangers, often at the risk of their own lives, ranging from emergency medical technicians to good samaritans. Each episode was an hour long, consisting of between three and five pretty amazing stories. We used existing footage and when necessary our own re-creations, and whenever possible when we did re-creations we used the actual people involved in the event. As host, I introduced the show — "True stories of dark despair and unexpected heroes on . . . *Rescue 911*" — and each segment — "On October 3, 1985, Michigan state trooper David Ayer was only an hour away from the end of his shift. But on this day David would not be able to serve out his time uneventfully. Instead he was forced to watch as a freak accident on a road outside Northville, Michigan, changed the lives it touched . . . forever." "Children's curiosity can drive them to the heights of achievement. But it can also push them beyond the boundaries of what is safe, as Rene Durschell discovered on June 23rd, 1995, at her home in Boynton Beach, Florida." — and then I did the closing. We actually filmed my stand-ups on Sundays. Every other Sunday we'd set up at an EMT center — in Glendale, Manhattan Beach, everywhere — and shoot several shows. I did a lot of walking and talking with police cars, fire trucks, or ambulances in the background, depending on the type of story we were telling. With the number of different takes we did and the time it took to set up, we were there most of the day. And pretty much every Friday I'd be in a Hollywood sound studio doing voice-over narration. That was my job, show up and read my lines every Friday and every other Sunday. It took a full-time staff of about seventy-five people to do the show, yet somehow the audience perceived *Rescue 911* to be my show.

We told an extraordinary range of amazing stories on the show. An Idaho hunter mistakes a couple for a bear and shoots them. A police officer leaps onto runaway boxcars that are pushing an automobile down the tracks. Children lost in the mountains. Divers trapped underwater. A toddler falls into a hole. A teen touches a hot power line with a pool pole. People shot and stabbed by intruders. A truck's brakes fail and he plummets forty feet into a swamp. A young boy trapped under ice for forty-five minutes. A plane whose landing gear won't deploy. A unconscious skydiver. A seven-year-old girl helps deliver her mother's baby. A ten-year-old boy performs the Heimlich maneuver to save his choking brother. A duck gets its head stuck in the plastic rings from a six-pack of soda. A good samaritan dives into a river to try to save two women trapped in a submerged car. A woman is trapped in her smoke-filled home when her TV set explodes. A pregnant deer is hit by a car. A woman has to drop eight babies from the window of her burning apartment. Explosions, fires, floods, shootings, stabbings, runaway cars and trucks and trains, falls and accidents with tools, and heart attacks and difficult births — and almost always, nobody died. Perhaps most amazing was that almost all of the stories we told had a hap . . . satisfactory ending. Only when we told a cautionary tale did people die — the teenager who inhaled cleaning fluid to get high and couldn't be saved. People who took absurd risks. A litany of dangerous acts that we wanted to warn our viewers not to do. In truth, a high percentage of the calls answered by these medical technicians do end in a death, but we concentrated on their successes. The reality of television programming is that people don't die on Tuesday-night reality shows.

We saved at least 350 lives. That's not an estimate, that was based on letters we received from viewers telling us that because of a story they saw on *Rescue 911* they either were able to save someone else's life or their life had been saved. We never anticipated that happening. This was a prime-time program on CBS; our primary objective was to save our jobs. So when we started getting these letters we were astounded. And very, very pleased.

The first letter we received came from a family in St. Louis. On a very cold Tuesday in November 1988, they were moving into a new apartment. The apartment was freezing and they had great difficulty figuring out how to keep their furnace lit. The husband had spent the day transporting boxes from their old apartment as his wife and their four children unpacked. But as the day progressed she felt progressively sicker. Finally she told him, "You need to take me to the Emergency Room right now. I think I'm dying."

The Emergency Room was crowded and as her problem was not visibly life threatening this couple was told to wait. As they waited they watched a TV in the waiting room, which happened to be tuned to CBS. The second story we did that night was about a woman who suddenly and for no apparent reason got very sick. Coincidently this couple had been having problems with their furnace too, and her husband had been smart enough to call the gas company. A technician rushed to their house and discovered a potentially lethal carbon monoxide leak.

The couple in that waiting room was stunned. The story had accurately described her symptoms. In a voice on the edge of panic she asked her husband, "You think that's what could be wrong with me?" Both of them realized instantly that their four children were asleep in that new apartment. The husband raced home — by the time he got there three of their children were unconscious. The fire department rushed them all to the hospital where their lives were saved. As the doctor who saved them said, "In another half hour one or more of these kids could have died from carbon monoxide poisoning."

It was miraculous. Nobody really expects CBS to save lives. But that was just the beginning. The *St. Louis Post-Dispatch* did an article about it, which got picked up and was reprinted around the country. And then we began receiving letters from people who had saved someone's life by applying the Heimlich maneuver, which they had seen demonstrated on our show, or by using CPR as we'd shown it, or by picking up an extension cord that had been hidden under a heavy piece of furniture and discovering it was badly frayed. When we first went on the air I was told that slightly less than 50 percent of communities even had a 911 system — by the time we went off the air the nation was well on the way to almost 100 percent coverage. After we did several stories in which the person calling 911 couldn't correctly identify the location from which they were calling, many communities switched to a more sophisticated emergency system in which the address came up automatically. Eventually we had documented more than 350 situations in which information from *Rescue 911* had saved lives. Undoubtedly there were many more.

Our stories came from police and fire departments, 911 dispatch centers, hospitals, newspapers, and viewers. It was impossible to meet these people, to do this show, without developing a tremendous sense of appreciation for what they do on a daily basis as well as satisfaction with the entire system. It works. When someone needs help, the system gets help there literally in minutes. It may well be the one government agency that delivers what it was established to deliver. Of course, there were many stories we couldn't tell. One man, for example, managed to get his tongue stuck to the door on his freezer compartment and couldn't get free. We had several stories about naked people who had somehow managed to become wedged into the space between their toilets and the wall and couldn't get free. Several thieves got caught in chimneys, and I remember a pair of burglars who robbed a store then had to call 911 because the doors were locked and they couldn't get out. We didn't tell the true story about a local fire department that was called to help a squirrel whose head had gotten caught in a hole in a tree. And we definitely could not tell the story about the couple who liked to play sex games.

I was told by our producers that this was indeed a true story: apparently a man dressed in a Batman costume had tied his willing partner to the bed. The man in the Batman costume then climbed up on a bureau. The plan was that he was going to leap onto the bed — Batman arrives to save the day! Unfortunately, when Batman jumped into the air he hit his head on a beam and plummeted straight to the ground, unconscious. Somehow the woman managed to call 911, and the firemen who rushed to the scene found the naked woman still tied to the bed and Batman lying unconscious on the floor.

Now, had we done that rescue the re-creation certainly would have been interest-ing. Perhaps you'd like to write my introduc-tory narration: "For Jane and John Doe it started as just another boring evening at home; as usual he was dressed in his Batman outfit while she lay naked, tied to the bed . . ."

Another story which we could not use on the show was my personal encounter with an EMT. Just before *Rescue 911* went on the air I'd bought a horse farm in Kentucky. I had always wanted to own a brand-new pickup truck with those big tires and a rifle hanging in the rack on the back of the cab. I don't know why, perhaps I'd seen too many Marlboro commercials. The horse farm provided the rationale for me to buy me a rip-snorting new pickup, although I never did get that old rifle. One night just after I'd gotten the truck I was driving alone at night on a dark side road, really just having fun with my new pickup, when . . . boom! I hit something. It was the most awful feeling. Many years earlier, when my father had been teaching me to drive in Montreal, a dog had run into the street and I'd hit it. I'd slammed on the brakes but the car slid on leaves and I'd hit the dog. I looked in the rearview mirror and the dog was obviously dead. I wanted to stop but my father had insisted, "Keep going. There's nothing we can do."

I'd felt guilty for years afterward. And

now, once again, I'd hit something in the road. This time I wasn't going to leave. A dark lump was lying in the road, still moving. A squirrel, I thought. But as I approached this animal I realized it was a skunk. Oh my God, I thought, I've killed a skunk. And as I got within a few feet the tail came up and it squirted me. That was its dying wish: skunk juice all over me. I was bathed in skunk juice and I didn't know what to do. I certainly couldn't get back in my new pickup which I loved so much, the smell would permeate the seats. I'd never be able to get rid of it.

I started thinking. All the way back to that summer I'd lived in the back of my truck while doing summer stock. I'd had my dog with me, a beloved Doberman. We would go everywhere together. When I was performing he'd sit in an aisle and watch the show. A wonderful dog. But one night he'd apparently had an encounter with a skunk and carried the evidence with him into the tent theater. The odor was just terrible and the audience couldn't take it. One of the stagehands solved the problem by pouring several cans of tomato juice over my dog. Apparently the acid in tomato juice neutralizes the stink of the skunk. So standing there on that dark Kentucky road I realized what

I needed to do.

I'd passed a gas station a mile or so down the road. They might have cans of tomato juice there. I ran to that store and shouted my needs to the clerk. He tossed over several cans which I proceeded to pour over my head and my clothes. Within minutes the terrible smell began dissipating and I started walking down the road to my truck. If necessary I would get rid of my clothes before climbing into the cab. Several cars passed but I wouldn't dare ask for a ride. Then about ten minutes later I heard the wail of sirens coming from somewhere down the road. Soon I could see the flashing lights of what turned out to be a police car and an EMT ambulance racing toward me. I stopped walking to watch them pass, but instead they squealed to a halt in front of me. A police officer leaped out of his car, yelling, "Are you okay? What happened?"

The EMT personnel was right behind him. "Oh no," he said, then started laughing hysterically. As it turned out, tomato juice is not as effective as I had believed. "Shatner," he added — obviously I was not the first person to have had this problem — "you stink."

Apparently the driver of one of the cars that passed me had stopped down the road

457

to call 911 — there was a guy on the side of the road bleeding very badly from what appeared to be a head wound, he'd told them. They'd raced to save me. A part of me was gratified that the system had worked so well — but a much bigger part was embarrassed. "You get any calls tonight?" the wife of the EMT driver would undoubtedly ask him when he got home.

"Just one," he could respond honestly. "We saved Bill Shatner from dumping any more cans of tomato juice over his head!"

It was almost impossible to work on *Rescue 911* without wondering over and over how you would have responded to these situations. What would I have done in that emergency? Twice in my life I've faced that kind of crisis. And unfortunately, only once did it work out well.

Marcy and I were walking on a Malibu beach on an overcast, windy day in September 1983. There were very few people on the beach, but we walked past a father and his son playing in the surf at the shoreline. When we came back twenty minutes later the father was in the water up to his shoulders, but at first I didn't see his boy. Then I saw him, much farther out, struggling. I realized that the father was trying to get to his son, but the surf was too strong for him.

Somebody had to go in and save that kid.

Marcy and I were the only people close by. There were no options.

I don't remember what I was wearing, but it wasn't much. I'm a strong swimmer, so I put my face in the water and started fighting through the waves. It was a rough surf, and by the time I reached him I was totally out of breath. I knew that seawater would support a person who isn't moving too much — but if you panic and start thrashing around you'll go right under. I was out of breath, the waves were breaking into me, and this boy had his arms wrapped around my neck. I was on the edge of panic. And I suddenly realized I was going to die. I didn't have time to be afraid, I was too busy fighting for survival.

Meanwhile, Marcy was running up and down the beach, desperately searching for someone who could help me. Nobody could. Finally she remembered someone we knew with a house on the beach who could help. She raced to his house.

I was holding on to the boy, trying to keep his head above water while fighting my way to shore. But I wasn't making much progress. A strong element of self-preservation kicked in. I don't know how I did, but by the time the strong swimmer had gotten to us I'd made it closer to shore. I did save that kid's life and I felt . . . I felt unbelievably good and exhausted. I don't think the man ever knew that his son had been saved by an actor who played a hero on television.

The second time was a lot more personal. It was the night several years later when my wife Nerine drowned in our swimming pool.

Marcy and I were married for seventeen years. I think if a young actor were to ask me for advice about relationships I would probably respond, whatever you do, don't marry an actor. Of course, Marcy probably would respond exactly the same way. Marriage is the most complicated of all relationships, made considerably more difficult when both people are dealing consistently with professional acceptance and rejection.

Marcy was a wonderful person, a terrific stepmother to my three girls. As an actress, she had talent, she had class and style, but she didn't have luck. And the reality that her career never seemed to take off always bothered her. We worked together quite a few times, she was killed in *Kingdom of the Spiders,* she stood in a long line in *Airplane II,* she played a crew member in *Star Trek: The Motion Picture,* we appeared on game shows together, and I had directed her in a good production of *Cat on a Hit Tin Roof*. We built a home and a family and that horse-breeding ranch in Kentucky together. We were good together for a long time. We liked so many of the same things; for us a perfect day would be to go to two or three movies, eat unbuttered popcorn with beer or Perrier — and then finish the night by going out for sushi.

But her career was an extension of mine and that did not make her happy. She spent a lot of time searching for that elusive balance between being a mother and wife and being a successful actress. The fact that she never found it to her satisfaction made her unhappy.

The failure of our marriage certainly wasn't her fault. Where divorce is concerned, it takes two to tangle. And I played my part, I certainly played my part. The humanistic philosophy to which I faithfully adhered at that time might be accurately summed as: it seemed like a good idea at the time. Look, I've always taken responsibility for my actions. The reality of some marriages is that over time a husband and a wife grow apart. Their needs and desires change. Marcy realized that; in fact, she once told a reporter, "Life took us apart and it was time to move on."

Our marriage ended long before it was legally over. Few marriages end because of one event; rather, it's an accumulation of things culminating in one incident that may even be very minor. What? You didn't turn the light out? You know how much that cost? That's ridiculous, I'm done. It's not the light or the electric bill, that's just the evidence of a lack of caring in many areas.

Our divorce was relatively amicable — although several years later we did have a serious legal fight over my sperm. That's a joke, readers! A joke! Remember last chapter when I started my career in comedy? The truth is that it wasn't physically my sperm, it was the sperm of several champion horses I owned. As part of our divorce settlement I agreed to give her "fresh-cooled" semen from our champion saddlebred horses, which is extremely valuable to horse breed-ers. There was a mistake made one season, which was eventually rectified by lawyers.

I've never been very good at being alone. I've had a lot of casual relationships: one-night stands, two-week stands, six-month layabouts. With cars, Italian food, and women, when I find something that excites me I become passionate about it. But almost always I've lived with the hope of a long-term relationship.

I met Nerine Kidd when I was in Toronto directing an episode of the television show *Kung Fu*. Ironically, as it would turn out, we met in the bar of a hotel. It was the place where movie folks who were shooting there would meet at the end of the day. I was there meeting an old friend of mine, and we were laughing maybe too loudly and I looked over his shoulder and saw her. I can close my eyes and still see her. I was struck instantly by her beauty and this marvelous sort of fuck-you attitude, this arrogance, that was so much a part of her. She had strawberry-blond hair and freckled pale Irish skin, the brightest blue eyes you've ever seen, and a spectacular figure, and, I was to soon find out, street-smart intelligence and a wonderful sense of humor.

We spoke briefly that night. But I remember thinking, I've got to meet this girl again. Just about every night after we finished shooting I would go to that bar to look for her. It was almost a full week before I saw her again and we just fell into each other's arms.

The first days of a relationship are a gift that lives forever in memory. You always remember the smiles and the laughter and the moments of discovery. Nerine and I went to the Ontario Fair with a male friend of hers. One of the amusements was a bungee cord jump built for two. Let's go! she said.

"I'm not going up there," I told her. I rationalized that I had done enough exciting things in my life. I didn't need to make myself sick to prove to her that I could do dangerous things. I remember standing below watching her flying through the air, screaming with absolute delight, being free.

There was some chinaware for sale at one of the booths and we looked at it together. We stood there comparing our tastes; we'd known each other a few hours and both of us knew we were picking out dishes for our future house. We were together for more than seven years.

I had met the girl of my dreams. I fell in love with her and believed she was everything I'd spent my life looking for in a woman. She had the beauty and brains and a joy for living that I had rarely seen before. And she also had one other thing that I didn't learn about for quite some time: she was an alcoholic.

Nerine was in Toronto visiting friends, actually she was living in a rented house in Santa Monica. She was a model, but at that time was working only occasionally. For so long we had so much fun together. Once, for example, we were celebrating a friend's birthday on a yacht in St. Tropez. We had dinner at a hotel and when we finished I looked out at the boat floating at anchor and said, "I think I'm going to swim out to the boat."

Please, don't ask. I don't know why, either.

Nerine was right with me. "Well, if you're going to do that, I am too."

We jumped in the water without any fear and managed to get about a third of the way there before we had to climb into the tender. Maybe that describes her best, she had no fear. Whatever I did, she kept up with me.

We were together six years before we began talking about getting married. For much of that time she was able to hide her alcoholism. Unless she had been drinking very heavily she didn't show it on the surface. What happened was that her attitude would change, when she drank she would get a little meaner. I'd think, wow, that's too bad. It didn't occur to me that it was caused by alcohol. I thought she just had a mean streak. I didn't like it, but because I loved her I accepted it: nobody is perfect.

I tried to be understanding because she came from a difficult background. She was from south Boston, she was my Irish rose. There was a history of alcoholism in her family. What I did not know then is that to a large degree alcoholism is genetic. Having that gene means only that an individual has a propensity for it, but then so many other things become factors in whether or not the disease ever manifests itself.

But I didn't know anything at all about alcoholism then. I'd played an alcoholic in several movies, but really I'd just been playing a cliché. In the TV movie *Perilous Voyage* I'd been the happy drunk, the back-slapping good-time guy who just goes into a corner and passes out. In *The Third Walker,* another TV movie, I was sort of a creepy, somewhat crazy drunk. But I had no idea what a real addiction was; there had never been an alcoholic or any addiction in my family. In fact, I always believed that if you really wanted to change your behavior it was just a matter of willpower. I was a smoker, for example, and during the second season of *Star Trek* I happened to be in a limo with three other actors and each of us had a motive for giving up smoking. Mine was that one morning I went to kiss my girls and they turned away from me, telling me, "Oh Daddy, you smell."

So I stopped cold turkey. It was very difficult. At times I was desperate because the nicotine wasn't out of my system. Leonard remembers a day when I finished a scene and walked away and started screaming, "I want a cigarette! I need a cigarette." But I beat it and it seemed obvious to me that if I could beat an addiction, then anyone who sincerely wanted to beat a demon could do it too.

I didn't know what I was talking about.

We were together six years before we began thinking about marriage. We certainly were a couple in every other way. But one day she said to me, "Bill, we should get married," and I understood that she was telling me she needed the permanence of that particular commitment. I agreed. It wasn't a difficult decision. I was in love with her.

But it was around that time, maybe a little earlier, that her alcoholism first began to get out of control. I didn't know then that before we'd met she had been through rehab. The details of that were always sketchy, but apparently it was because of cocaine. Okay, but there were a lot of people in the entertainment business who had successfully fought that particular addiction. It wasn't unusual and certainly nothing about which I was going to make a judgment.

We were making preparations for our wed-

ding when she was caught driving drunk —
and almost killed my daughter. She had
picked up my daughter from a spa in Palm
Springs and, apparently, as she drove home
she would stop at gas stations, go into the
ladies' room, and down a small bottle of
whatever she was drinking. She was exiting
the freeway and for no obvious reason suddenly slammed on the brakes. If there had
been another car behind her it would have
slammed into her car at a freeway speed.
What kind of insanity, what kind of mental
illness, allows someone to do that? To drive
drunk with a young person in her car? After
that she swore to me that she was done with
drinking, that she could control it and
would never drink again. I didn't just want
to believe her, I did believe her. Of course
she would stop drinking, she would do it
for me, for us. See, that's all it took to solve
this problem. So we set another date for six
months later.

Five months later she was again arrested
for driving while under the influence of
alcohol. "We can't get married under these
circumstances. You promised me that if we
got married you'd stop drinking. How can I
marry you now?"

She turned to me with her bright blue eyes
and said to me in the voice only lovers

know, "Don't do this to me, Bill."

Don't do this to *me,* she said, and she said it with such frankness and honesty that my heart just went out to her. It was a plea, it was a cry. I just couldn't resist her. But by now, at least, I had some help. We had been to a dinner party with several other couples at Leonard and Susan Nimoy's. At that party she was, as Leonard later described it, "erratic in her behavior." I thought she had hidden it well, but apparently it had been obvious to everyone. Leonard recognized the symptoms immediately. The next day he called me and said, "Bill, you know she's an alcoholic?"

"Yes," I said. "But I love her."

"You're in for a rough ride, then."

I didn't understand what Leonard was saying to me. I didn't have the vocabulary. I was so certain that by loving her enough I could cure her. I know it's a romantic concept, but I'd seen it work. I'd seen children flower and animals respond to love. I'd experienced the joy that love could bring to a life, happiness almost beyond description, and it was inconceivable to me that there could be something stronger than complete love. Particularly something so dark and destructive. I believed without any reservation that love heals. So what I thought Leonard was saying to me was that I had to love her that way, I had to surround her with the love and support that she needed to beat this.

That wasn't at all what he was saying. What he said was simple and clear and came from the depth of his own experience. "Bill, you know she's an alcoholic?"

I decided to marry her, perhaps believing that she would rely on me rather than alcohol to provide whatever it was she was looking for. I still believe that marrying Nerine at that time was the greatest sacrifice I could have made for her. I married against the advice of my family and friends, against my own good sense. But I thought it might be the only chance we had. That she would recognize how strongly I believed in her and would make a sacrifice of her own; she would risk giving up alcohol for me. She was my fantasy and I was going to heal her. During our wedding ceremony I read her a poem I'd written, pledging my love to her, and in return she said, "I pledge my sobriety to you." We had a beautiful celebration in Pasadena with our family and friends. Leonard was my best man. "It's wonderful that we're all here tonight to celebrate the coming together of these two wonderful people," he said, toasting us. "And Bill has asked me to take advantage of this wonderful opportunity. He doesn't want to let this opportunity go by without telling about his latest book, which is available in most of your local . . ."

Nerine and I danced the night away. I just didn't want to let her go. She took down her hair that some Hollywood makeup person had done, scrubbed off the makeup that a Hollywood makeup artist had applied, and there she was in her natural beauty. She was sober, and to that point it was the happiest day of my life. Imagine being able to point to one day and know it was the happiest day of your life. It was truly amazing. And finally we put all the presents people had brought into our car and drove home. We climbed into bed and I was ecstatic. Ecstatic, that's the only way to describe it.

I woke up about eight o'clock the next morning and she was drunk. Later we discovered that she had hidden bottles of vodka all over the house, in places we would have never dreamed of looking. There were small bottles at the bottom of the clothes hamper, in a small drawer hidden below my athletic socks. Places I would never imagine looking.

I tried to understand her addiction. If I

said anything about it she would immediately become defensive, she'd respond by becoming furious with me. "I'm not drunk," she'd say in a slurred voice. "What makes you think I'm drunk?"

"Because you're slobbering."

"I'm not slobbering," she'd insist, slobbering. She used all the clichéd phrases. I remember her telling me, "Alcohol is my only friend," which I took as an accusation that I had let her down. Once, when she was drunk, she looked at me sadly and asked, "Why, Bill. Why?"

I thought she was saying, Why am I drinking? When she was sober the next day I asked her if she remembered asking that question. She didn't. I asked her, "Why do you think you asked, why? It was a profound question, what do you think you meant by it?"

She sighed. "I was probably asking you why you didn't understand why I drink."

I tried so hard to talk to her. "You're killing us," I told her. "Why can't you stop? I love you. What do you need? We've got love. We've got our home. We've got our future together. Why are you getting drunk?"

"I'm not drunk."

The situation got steadily worse. We had to install an alcohol monitor in the car, a device that makes it impossible to start a car with alcohol on your breath, so she couldn't drive drunk. We were terrified she was going to kill herself, or someone else.

Two or three months after our marriage I just couldn't take it anymore. Finally I told her, "Nerine, I'm going to get a divorce."

"You can't use that word," she said. "You should never use that word."

"You promised me you would be sober and you haven't stopped drinking. I'm starting divorce proceedings." People who have not dealt with the addiction of someone they love deeply can't really understand the compromises you make to love that person, the lies that you tell yourself, the insults that you have to accept. But I didn't know what else to do. I didn't know how to get through to her. We separated for a brief period during which she pleaded with me for another chance. This time, she swore, this time. I was facing decisions unlike anything I'd ever had to deal with in my life. Did I really believe in the healing powers of love or was that just something I said because it sounded good? Finally I told her, "You go to rehab and I'll stop the divorce."

She agreed. I thought we'd won. When she came home we spent a quiet evening together, talking hopefully about the future.

She was committed to sobriety, she told me. The next morning I went to play tennis with some friends. "Come with me," I said. "Everybody'd like to see you." Instead she stayed home, and by that afternoon she was drunk.

Nerine was in rehab for thirty days three different times. I understand now that the concept that a person can change their life in thirty days of rehab is nonsensical. A person can't change the driving forces in their life in a month. Perhaps it could be done in a year, but certainly it takes a minimum of six months to let your body heal.

Twice she almost drank herself to death. Once, when we rushed her to St. John's Hospital in Santa Monica, her blood-alcohol reading was 3.9 — legally 0.08 is considered drunk. She couldn't stand, she was as pale as death. Four days later I brought her home. "You almost died," I said. And there was such an arrogant, quizzical smile on her face, similar to the expression I'd seen so many years earlier when she jumped off the platform on the bungee cord ride. It occurred to me at that moment she wanted to see how close she could come to death. I asked her, "Do you want to die?"

"No," she said. "I don't want to die. I

don't want to die. I'm stopping." Within a day she was drinking again.

The second time she was literally missing for three days. No one had any idea where she was. I was totally frantic. Finally someone called from a charity home in downtown Los Angeles, a flophouse really, telling me that "a woman who said she was Mrs. Shatner" was there. The people in that home welcomed her and saved her life.

I was so frustrated, so angry. We were so close to a wonderful life together but we just couldn't get there. She was everything I had ever wanted; she was a princess, she had such majesty about her. And then to see her drunk, to see our life together being shattered. I would sit in our house and cry. I remember sitting in a chair one morning, my hands over my eyes, sobbing softly. She had been drunk the night before and I'd finally begun to understand that my dreams of our life together were never going to become reality. She came down the stairs and looked at me and asked, "Why are you crying?"

"Don't you know?"

"No." She had no memory of the night before. I remembered every ugly detail, I remembered the impact and she remembered nothing. I just couldn't solve the mystery of alcoholism, why our love wasn't strong enough to overcome her need for alcohol.

Leonard and Susan were incredibly supportive. Leonard tried to help, he knew from his own experience what she was fighting, and he tried so hard. Leonard felt blessed that he had been able to stop drinking. We talked about his alcoholism, and he remembered being with Susan one night shortly after they were married and she asked him if he was happy. He was, he told her, he didn't remember ever being happier. "Then why are you still drinking?" she asked.

That was the day he got serious about stopping. And Leonard has always been extremely proud of the fact that he never had another drink. So he knew what Nerine was going through and he got involved. It was one of the most noble acts of friendship I'd ever experienced, although I'm certain he would insist he did it for Nerine, not for me. He took her to Alcoholics Anonymous meetings, he spent time just talking to her, he offered advice and suggestions to me. Leonard told me once that she didn't want to stop, she had no intention of quitting. And until she reached that point, there was little I could do.

The horror began when she went into rehab for the third time. As always, I was so hopeful that this time would be different. This time it would work, she'd stop drinking and we'd be happy forever after. About a week before she started we were at the horse farm in Lexington, Kentucky. It was a beautiful July night and we went out for a moonlight motorcycle ride. I stopped and we just stood there, listening to the rustle of the wind. It was a beautiful, sensual moment. "What will it take to get you to stop?" I asked.

"If you're with me twenty-four hours a day," she said. "If you're there, I won't drink. That'll stop me."

"Then I'll be with you twenty-four hours a day," I promised.

She had been in rehab for only a few days when the director called. "I'm sorry," she said. "You have to come and get Nerine. She's drunk. We want her out of here now."

I had finally understood that our marriage couldn't work and I was helpless to do anything about it. Once again, we began talking about a divorce. This time I was serious about it, I thought. She was drinking every day and there was nothing I could do to stop her. Finally I called the director of the rehab facility and begged her to take

Nerine back. She was very reluctant, but finally I convinced her. She said, reluctantly, "Okay, Bill. Get her sober for one day and we'll take her back."

One day is such a short period of time, but for Nerine it seemed impossibly long. One Monday morning I asked a friend of mine, a New York psychiatrist who had been working with addicts for years, to help me. She wanted to hold an intervention. "I'll come out and you get some of her family and friends together and we'll confront her." Nerine's family couldn't help, they had their own issues. So I got some friends together. We were going to hold the intervention on Tuesday and after that she would go back into rehab. Hope is resilient.

After setting up the intervention I called the rehab center. "I'll have her there tomorrow," I said. Sober.

I had planned to visit my grandchildren in Orange County that afternoon. Nerine had been drunk the night before, but had been sober in the morning. There were two people to help at the house, so I knew she wouldn't be there alone. I decided to go. As I was backing out of the driveway she stopped me. "Where you going?"

When I told her she asked to go with me. "I can't," I said. "Nerine, you've been drunk so many times in front of the kids that they're fearful and I don't want to go through that scene. I'll be back in the evening." Then I added, more from habit than anything else, "Please don't drink."

As I put the car back into reverse she said softly, "Please don't leave me, Bill."

"I'll be back later," I said and kept going. I spoke with her several times during the day. By eight-thirty that night I was in the car driving home. My daughter Melanie called me on my cell phone. "I can't raise Nerine on her cell," she said. "Can you call her on the landline?" I tried calling the house several times, but there was no answer. When I got home about nine-thirty the house was quiet. We had three wonderful, loving Dobermans and they were attached to her — but they were in the kitchen. If she had been home they would have been with her. I called her name several times, walking around the house. When I got no response I just assumed she'd gone out. But I checked the garage and all the cars were there. I began to get a very strange feeling.

The phone rang. My first thought was that it was her, calling to tell me where she was, asking me to pick her up. It was her AA sponsor. "I don't know where she is," I told her. "I can't find her."

Her sponsor asked, "Have you checked the pool?"

A chill went down my back, but I quickly dismissed it. "No. The gate was closed and the dogs were downstairs."

"Check it," she insisted. I put her on hold and went outside. The pool area was dark, although part of it was dimly illuminated by lights from the second level. "Nerine?" There was no one around the pool. I looked into the pool, and in the darkness I saw a dark shape in the deep end. I wasn't certain, it could have been a shadow — or it could have been . . . It had to be a shadow. It couldn't be my wife. I took several steps backward to try to avoid the horror in front of me. I turned my back on the pool as I picked up the phone. This wasn't possible. How could this be happening? "She's in the pool."

"Call nine-one-one."

"Help me. Call nine-one-one." I hung up on her and called the number I knew so very well. Nine-one-one. "Oh my God," I said. "My poor wife is at the bottom of the pool."

The dispatcher spoke evenly, just as I'd heard so many times on the show. "OK. Did you get her out of the pool yet, sir?"

"No. Not yet."

"I want you to take her out of the pool right now."

I put down the phone and dived into the pool. I had enough breath for one deep dive. One of her arms was floating above her and I grabbed her by that arm and lifted her, pulling her toward the shallow end. As I did that I remember screaming, "What have you done! What have you done!" As I did that I looked up into the sky — and a helicopter was hovering over my house. I may have realized that it was a news copter, which had been monitoring the 911 calls.

I laid her down on the side of the pool. Her skin was blue. Her strawberry-blond hair was still curled. I remember every second. I put my finger in her throat to try to breathe life into her, and I heard a click. Later a policeman suggested that was her neck breaking, but it wasn't. Something was caught in her throat. This was my nightmare. This was grotesquery. I couldn't believe this was really happening.

Until that moment I had never truly experienced horror in my life. But this was horror. Oddly, I had never seen a dead body. I'd seen countless thousands of actors play dead, but death . . . She was dead. There was nothing I could do to save her. She was dead. The emergency responders arrived within minutes. I had to go down and open the gate for them, but I was confused, I didn't want to leave her body alone. This time there would be no happy ending. My daughters came quickly. Reporters and news crews gathered outside the front gate. Everything was happening so quickly. I was in shock, in complete and absolute shock. This didn't happen to me and the people I loved. This was the type of event I read about in the newspapers, it wasn't about me.

My memory is that I spoke with the police that night. At least I think it was that night. "This is an accident," the commanding officer told me. They had seen this scenario before. What appeared to have happened is that she had been drinking outside by the pool — they found a broken bottle — slipped and hit her head, and blacked out. An autopsy eventually found that her blood-alcohol level was 0.28, more than three times the amount considered intoxicated, as well as that there were traces of Valium in her system. But this officer did say to me, "I have to tell you, if there was any hint of foul play, you're the first suspect."

Maybe he didn't actually use the word "suspect," but that certainly was his inference. It sounded like dialogue from . . . from *Hooker*. It was absurd. Who could possibly think any such thing? "What are you talking about?" I said. "I mean, this is the woman I loved more than my life. I wouldn't hurt her."

I remember lying in bed that night. The police had left, the coroner had come, my children started taking turns staying with me. I remember my head pounding, I remember feeling that my head was moving in time with my heartbeat. The shock and the grief were overwhelming, and along with that came the knowledge and the fear that I was alone again.

Very early the next morning I walked down the long driveway to make a statement to the mob of reporters. Apparently they'd stayed there all night. I picked up the day's newspaper that was left in the drive and I told them, "My beautiful wife is dead. Her laughter, her tears, and her joy will remain with me the rest of my life."

After the O. J. Simpson debacle I suppose I should have known what was going to happen. I hadn't, though. It was so clear what had happened that night; there didn't seem any room for doubt or for questions. But that didn't stop people or the media from asking those terrible questions. Did Shatner kill his wife? A day after I'd made my statement about loving her forever someone sent a note to the police, "Anybody who is innocent doesn't stop and pick up a newspaper."

It dawned on me then that people were watching me to see how I acted. It was insane. Exactly how do you act when the woman you love has died and people are wondering if you had anything to do with her death? The fact that people could even think this way was stunning to me. Everybody reacts to horror in their own way. It's one thing to have someone you love who has been sick or struggling die, but this? There's no way of preparing for a cataclysmic event like this. The feelings I had were vaguely similar to the pain I'd experienced as a little boy, when I'd come home from school one day and found my dog lying in the street. My mother had left the door open and my dog had run outside and been killed by a car. I had completely forgotten that until once again I was experiencing that intense grief. I remember, I'd picked up my dog and carried him home. We had a brick stairway in front of the house and my father had covered the area under those stairs with latticework. There was a little opening so you could get underneath the stairs. I took my dog's body and I opened the latticework and crawled in there. Sunlight streaming through the latticework formed rectangles that lit this hidden space. And I sat there holding the body of my dog and sobbing.

As a little boy I'd lost the thing I'd loved the most, and now it had happened again.

Within a few days of her death I learned that the *National Enquirer* was going to run a story asking, basically, "Did he or didn't he kill her?" All the facts had not yet been made public, and as disgusting as it is, people were wondering what had happened that night. I wanted to get the true story out as quickly as possible. We called the *Enquirer* and offered them a deal. "Don't run that story. Instead, we'll give you the exclusive story of what happened that night." In exchange they contributed $250,000 to what would eventually become the Nerine Shatner Foundation, which I intended to form to help addicted women. That was the only interview I did for months and I did it because they were going to run a tabloid story, so the fact that I was able to give this money to charity somehow made it seem sensible. Whether or not I would have done it given more time to think I don't know. Some of her friends didn't like me saying she was an alcoholic and have resented me ever since.

Other tabloids did run variations of that story. And people were trying to twist facts and create some kind of conspiracy scenario. There wasn't anything I could do about it. But to think that any sane person in this world would believe that I had anything to do with killing a human being, let alone contributing to the death of this woman that I loved so much, was beyond my comprehension. I just couldn't stop thinking about her standing next to my car that morning begging me, "Please don't leave me, Bill." I'd left. Twelve hours later she was dead. For anyone to even think, I'll bet he killed her, is the worst possible thought. It makes me so sad that anyone would think that way.

About a week after Nerine's death the police released a tape of my call to 911 for help. These were the kinds of tapes that we had used as the foundation of *Rescue 911* for seven and a half years. I heard the familiar anguish and desperation, except this time it was my voice on that tape. I had no expectation of privacy; as every celebrity knows, the price you pay for all the positive things written about you is the surrender of any claim to privacy. It's a deal and we all make it: once you use the media for public-ity you lose your right to complain about the media using your life to sell its product. But admittedly, hearing the worst moment of my life being used as a form of entertainment was extraordinarily painful.

Irresponsible people made accusations or tried to create suspicion. I guess the question asked most often was why did I call 911 before diving into the pool to try to save her? For a long time I'd wondered about that myself. Why didn't I dive right in? It took me years to fully understand, and even then it was only because of my fourth wife, Elizabeth. Every year on August 9 we would go up to the pool in the evening to try to understand what happened. The moon is in the same position, the lights are the same. On one of those August nights I stood there with Elizabeth looking at the pool and suddenly I knew. The water in the pool had been still. That's why I didn't immediately know she was there. There wasn't a ripple. Any movement in the pool agitates the water, it moves and continues moving long after it has been agitated. When I looked at the pool that night it was placid. Still. And somehow I had known that whether I dove in and rescued the body and then called 911, or called 911 and then rescued the body, it would have made no difference. Obviously it wasn't a conscious thought, but had there been any sign of life I know exactly what I would have done.

Other people talk about problems in our marriage. There was only one problem: alcohol.

I don't think you ever really get over an event like that. You deal with the grief, then as that passes you absorb the substance and it becomes part of you. For a while you think about it every day, and then a little less, and a little less, and then a word or a place triggers a memory. But we go on. No matter how awful, we go on. The only positive thing that came out of it was the Nerine Shatner Foundation. I was able to raise several hundred thousand dollars in her memory, which was used to finance the Nerine Shatner Friendly House, a place where women with addictions can go and be safe and try to recover. Nerine had often said that when she was finally sober she wanted to help other women fighting the same battles. Friendly House had taken her in when she needed a place, and in 2001 we were able to help them open a twenty-four-bed facility in Los Angeles. Several times since then I've had people tell me that the facility made a difference in their lives. I hope so.

Still, I can never think about Nerine or

talk about her without feeling pain, and I live with an appreciation for the woman she was and regret for the person she could have been had she not had this incredible flaw — and I will never believe it was her fault.

I had believed that the force of my love for her was enough to effect a cure, I couldn't imagine that it wasn't enough, but to my sorrow I learned that sometimes love is not enough.

I did write a song about Nerine that was part of my album, *Has Been.* It was called "What Have You Done?" It ended:

My love was supposed to protect her
It didn't
My love was supposed to heal her
It didn't
You had said don't leave me
And I begged you not to leave me
We did

TEN

My name is Lisbeth Shatner. I wanted to tell you a great story, another this-is-Dad-in-a-nutshell story. When Nerine was still alive he took the whole family on an amazing trip to Botswana. I know he got some sort of discount on the tickets, I believe he bought an African safari for two people at an auction, so he paid much less than the regular cost. Then he decided he should share this trip with his three daughters and their significant others. "That was the reason the company donated the trip," he pointed out. "They expect you to do that. I didn't want to let them down."

He wanted to go to Botswana because its government concluded a long time ago that keeping their animals alive and in their natural habitat is good business because it draws tourists. The terrain in Botswana goes from desert to savannah to rain forest to swampland. They have giant water-holes around which animals congregate. So it's an ideal place to see a lot of beautiful wild animals. But it also can be very dangerous. For some reason they don't attack humans in an open car; they don't recognize it as prey, so lions literally come right up to the front fender. But if you get out of the car you can die. They continually remind people not to get out of the car for any reason. People have gotten out of their car to take a picture and been killed. And the guides don't want anyone dying in their midst, as it definitely would be bad for business.

The same thing is true for the camps. We spent the nights in tents or thatched huts. These are only temporary structures. But we were reminded over and over, do not leave your hut at night. These animals are wild and they will eat you. One night I thought there was a lion outside my door and I thought, if I die I'm at least part of the natural cycle. I just hope it doesn't hurt too much. There were no locks on the door and apparently the animals don't know how to open doors. Nevertheless, I thought this will be the one that finally figures it out. The one thing I was really afraid of was bugs, because the bugs are not ordinary American-sized bugs. They were size of cockroaches and . . .

Thank you Lisbeth, I'll take it from here. Sorry, I was away from the page for a while. I was just looking at a book someone sent me, *The Encyclopedia Shatnerica.* It's an encyclopedia of my life until 1998. Full of information about me that I can't imagine people find interesting. For example, because of *Rescue 911* I appeared on the cover of the *National Safety Council's First Aid Handbook.* It includes my grandmother's recipe for *matzo kneidlach,* about which I'm quoted: "To prevent rising beyond your station, my grandmother put a *kneidel* in your stomach. It made it very difficult to rise at all." I don't remember saying that, but I can't imagine I would be misquoted about *matzo kneidlach.* It also has an entire entry entitled Los Angeles Pet Memorial Park and the fact that one of my favorite dogs, a Doberman pinscher named China, is buried there.

Actually there have been several books chronicling my life and my career. I don't read them, I was there for most of it. But it certainly is flattering. All of the attention and the affection I receive is unbelievably flattering. There is something quite . . .

quite . . . satisfying about hearing actor Ed Norton say in the movie *Fight Club* that of all the celebrities in history, of all the people who have ever lived, if he could fight just one of them, it would be "Shatner. I'd fight William Shatner." I can't really explain the reasons for it. Apparently I once said, "Possibly there are aspects to me which people see that I'm not aware of," and that's true. But I do appreciate it, and I enjoy it, and whatever it is I'm doing that engenders it I'm trying to do more of it.

Where were we? In Africa, Botswana, with Nerine and my daughters. So the guides emphasize not to go out of our huts at night because if you do the animals might kill you and eat you. As one of my daughters may have said, that's a whole new way of having a movie star for dinner. Now, on the night Lisbeth was writing about, the night she thought she heard a lion, we had all settled into our flimsy wooden huts with thatched roofs. At some point during the night I was awakened by an overpowering stench. And then I felt our hut move and heard a rustling on the thatched roof. I looked out the one window but it was completely black outside, there wasn't a star in the sky. And then I realized there was something standing in front of that window that blocked it, something

493

very big. I think it was about then that I figured out an elephant was standing there eating the roof of our hut. None of the guides had told us what to do when an elephant ate your roof, so I began frantically looking for the safety manual we'd been given hoping there might be something in there under "roof, elephants eating."

Just then Nerine woke up. I whispered some extremely important instructions to her, somehow imagining that elephants, who have the biggest ears of any living thing, wouldn't hear me say, "Don't go to the bathroom."

And then that thing about myself that I fear most kicked in: my ability to completely lose sight of the consequences of my actions. I suspect others might call it a complete lack of good sense or perhaps, for short, nuts. It's the thing that makes me want to ski hills beyond my ability. Or get behind the wheel of a race car and drive 160mph. Or skydive. Or do a stunt on top of a train. I thought, wow, a wild elephant, you certainly don't get to see a wild elephant up close very often.

I opened the door of the hut just in time to see the tail of the elephant disappearing into the bush. I thought, what a great adventure. Truthfully, I probably wouldn't have even considered following that elephant into the bush if I wasn't under the impression that, for the most part, I can communicate with animals. I hold this concept that I can communicate with them based on my love of animals; they can instinctively feel that I mean them no harm, and that I bring peace and love. And I bring my hands, which can stroke them and make them feel good. That's what was going on in my mind when I opened the door of the hut and told Nerine, excitedly, "I'm going to go out there."

I felt so alive. My whole being resonated with the incredible feeling that I was going to go visit with an elephant on a starlit moonless night in Africa. How amazing! And I was going to visit that elephant in my underwear. I took my flashlight and I started running after the elephant.

At that moment the classic Groucho joke, "I shot an elephant in my underwear last night. How he got into my underwear I'll never know," did not occur to me. I don't know what the elephant was thinking. I do know that my daughter Melanie was awake and saw what appeared to be lightning flashes in the camp, then realized it was someone running with a flashlight. "That's my dad," she told her husband, Joel.

"It couldn't be," Joel said. "We were told not to leave the huts."

"Trust me," she responded knowingly. "That's my dad."

I had lost sight of the elephant. I ended up running all the way to the river, thinking the elephant might have gone into the water. The elephant was not there, but a herd of hippopotami was bathing there. They paid no attention to me. That was fortunate, as I learned later that hippos are foul-tempered animals. Rather than peace and love they're more into kill and eat. So I turned around and went back to my hut.

The next morning our guide told us that there had been a lion in our camp during the night, and he showed us the paw marks right outside Lisbeth's door. Apparently two years earlier that same lion had killed one of the workers in the camp. While showing me those marks the guide told me, "If you had been out there when the female was there, there is no telling what she might have done." When the gamekeeper found out that I'd gone outside he was furious. But contrary to the way my daughters describe this, he never actually used the word "psychopath."

He did, however, radio ahead to our next camp to warn the guides there, we've got a

496

bad one. That was me.

We stayed in this camp for one more night. An elephant, probably the same one, came back in the night and started foraging right next to our hut. And while he was doing it he leaned against the wall — and the whole hut started leaning. I thought it was going to collapse. If that elephant had decided to sit down on our hut we were going to have to make a run for it.

We survived. And years later, after Nerine's death, my daughters basically moved into the house and kept me from chasing elephants in the night. And we survived.

Even during the worst of times I was able to escape into work. I put on my costume and said words written by someone else, and for a few moments at least I could escape the complications of my own life. When you show up on a set nobody is interested in your problems at home. They're dealing with their own issues. They want you to be there on time and prepared. I was able to work because half of my life has been spent masking my true feelings before the camera. Acting is getting away with it, putting on another face for the camera and internalizing my true feelings.

What was especially ironic was that several

years before Nerine's death I had to deal with the death of a wonderful part of myself. I had been James Tiberius Kirk for almost thirty years when Paramount called to ask if I was willing to play his death scene.

I was Jim Kirk, but I didn't own the rights to me. Paramount owned the character and could do anything they wanted to him. The decision had been made by the studio that after twenty-five years the original crew of the *Enterprise* had finished its five-year mission. The *Star Trek* movies had an average gross of about $80 million. The executives believed they might make more money with Captain Jean-Luc Picard and his *Next Generation* crew in command. They were determined to kill off Captain Kirk so the movie torch would be passed cleanly to Patrick Stewart's Picard. They explained their decision to me with the great sensitivity I had come to expect from the studio: Kirk was going down, baby! There was a *New Generation* in space. If I wanted to appear in the movie it would be to play his death scene. But whether I agreed to appear in the movie or not, Kirk was going to die.

They also asked Leonard to appear in the film, but after reading the script he felt that Spock was not being treated with sufficient respect; he declined and Spock's few lines were given to Scotty. After agreeing to put on my Kirk one last time I wondered how I was going to die. What would be the appropriate death for James T. Kirk? He certainly wasn't going to die of old age or get run over by a rocket. I knew it was going to be heroic. So I read the first draft with considerable expectation.

In the early drafts of the script Kirk took control of the *Enterprise* from Picard and flew it into combat against the Klingons — and died fighting for mankind at his station. Wow. That was certainly a noble way to go. But probably not exactly what Patrick Stewart had in mind. The later version that they decided to film had the mad scientist Dr. Tolian Soran, played by Malcolm McDowell, shooting him in the back with a phaser. That coward. Shot in the back?

So that's how Kirk dies, shot in the back. But the challenge became making it meaningful. As an actor I had died a hundred deaths. At first I'd played the cliché, my head would snap back and my eyes would close. But eventually I began to realize that's not the way people die. People die differently, for different reasons in different ways. They die calmly and they die in the midst of a panic. They die peacefully or fighting. And as I did not yet know, they die at the bottom of a swimming pool. As an actor, I had choices. So I began spending considerable time wondering how Jim Kirk should die.

Eventually I started focusing on an event that had happened about a year earlier. I had been riding a three-year-old saddlebred in the World Championships in Lexington. As I was coming back to the stable a golf cart was driving toward me. The golf cart spooked the horse, who reared into the air. As I started to roll off I made the mistake of grabbing hold of the reins, which pulled the horse toward me. I hit the ground and this large horse fell on the inside of my right leg, then rolled over on top of me. The horse got up, it was fine. People came running to help and I wanted to reassure them I was okay. I'm fine, I'm fine, I said. I tried to get up, and I couldn't. I'm fine. I tried to get up again. And failed again. And all the while continuing to insist I wasn't hurt.

I kept telling them I wasn't hurt even as they put me in the ambulance and rushed me to the Emergency Room. I didn't want to be hurt. I could move my arms and legs, so I wasn't crushed. I was sore but I wasn't in terrible pain. But sometimes a serious injury doesn't hurt. I refused to admit that I was hurt. I was okay, but for some reason

I couldn't stand up. It turned out that my leg was bruised badly from the groin to the knee and I'd torn some ligaments. Nothing that wouldn't heal over time. But I remember that feeling of trying to get up, of wanting to get up, and falling down. So I decided that was how Jim Kirk would die. I would try to get up and fall down. Try it again and fall down — and gradually lose my strength and die. I thought that would be an appropriate way to express the indomitable will of this man who refused to go willingly into the dark night.

Executive producer Rick Berman agreed. "Okay, that sounds dramatic. Let's do it that way."

The night before we actually did the scene I tried to imagine the feelings I would have. I began imagining my own death. This was the first time in my career I'd ever done anything like this. I tried to look at it technically rather than emotionally. I drew on my experiences; I remembered being knocked unconscious. I also remembered fainting from putting too much cold beer in an overheated body. As you lose consciousness there is a moment when everything slows down; that horse falling on top of me slowed down. You are completely aware of everything that's happening around you: oh my

God, that horse is falling on me. Oh my God, I'm tied into this kayak and I'm turning upside down and I can't get free and I can't breathe. Oh my God, I'm in a stunt plane and I'm supposed to land and I can't line up the runway. As you lose consciousness you first lose your peripheral vision, you get tunnel vision. You're aware of what's happening until the very last instant, until that last bit of being aware that you are no longer going to be aware. And then.

That was my plan. That was the way I was going to play it. I wanted Captain Kirk to look at death and have a moment and I knew what that moment would be: it would be everything he saw in the voyages of the *Enterprise*, every strange monster, every bit of human understanding in an instant — and at the end he would see this extraordinary thing that was nothing like he had ever seen before. But rather than being afraid of it, his reaction was: isn't this the most marvelous experience. How do I deal with it? I wanted to give Jim Kirk that moment of seeing whatever it is you see at death while he was still alive and reacting to it as I knew he would: oh my . . . isn't that interesting?

It was all technical. As I prepared I had to remind myself that this was just another performance. I was determined not to get overly emotional about the death of this character. And I was able to do that right up until I got up the next morning and realized Paramount was going to kill Captain Kirk.

Kill Kirk? What are they, out of their minds? How could they kill a franchise? Why did I agree to this?

Gradually I managed to calm down. It's science fiction, I reminded myself, they can bring me back when they want to. In the movies, I knew, a character is only as dead as his grosses. After the studio realized there was a demand for Kirk, they would find a way to resurrect him.

Patrick Stewart, Malcolm McDowell, and I did Kirk's death scene. Kirk's last words, spoken with awe and humor as he saw something that was never shown to the viewer, were "Oh . . . my . . ."

I went home that night with a great sense of satisfaction. I didn't feel it was the end of an era, just the end of a character. I was satisfied. Kirk had been given the noble end he deserved. And then I sat down and wrote a forty-page treatment for a story in which Kirk comes back from the dead.

I called it *The Return,* and a couple of days later presented it to the producer. As I explained, there was a very important reason to bring back Kirk. Eighty million dollars. "That's very interesting," he told me. "But I think we're going to go on with the *Next Generation.*"

Well. Kirk may have been dead in the movies, but there was no reason he had to be dead to the publishing industry. I sold my treatment to Simon & Schuster and *Star Trek: The Return* became a best-selling novel. Co-written with Garfield and Judith Reeves-Stevens, in my story, "the Borg and the Romulan Empire have joined forces against the Federation and the ultimate weapon is James T. Kirk, resurrected by alien science to destroy the Borg's most formidable weapon: Jean-Luc Picard." Actually, they reanimated my dead tissue and gave me back my *katra.* But what they really did was implant false memories that turned me against the Federation.

To my surprise, and admittedly my pleasure, when Paramount screened *Star Trek: Generations* test audiences hated the ending. They had too much invested in Kirk to see him die so simply. They wanted Kirk to have a spectacular death. So the writers created a new death for him. It cost Paramount $4 million to go back into the desert and film this new ending.

In this version Kirk dies saving an entire universe. Now *that's* an ending. In this ending Picard and Kirk are desperately trying to stop Soran from launching a missile into this universe's sun. I'm forced to leap from one side of a collapsed bridge to the other to get the device that enables me to uncloak the invisible missile, and Picard destroys it. And then the bridge collapses and Kirk falls to his death — but not before getting that last line, "Oh . . . my . . ."

Actually I had written some other lines for this scene. When I leaped onto the bridge I said to Picard, "Captain on the bridge," which was the way I had always announced my presence on the bridge of the *Enterprise*. And when the bridge collapsed on me I managed to say, "Bridge on the captain."

Those lines were cut out of the scene.

The only hesitation I had about making this film was the fact that once again I would be working with Walter Koenig and Jimmy Doohan, both of whom had taken every possible opportunity to say unpleasant things about me. I wasn't sure how they would react to me. In fact, both men were very professional on the set and we had no problems. In fact, after a couple of weeks of working together I was able to talk both men into posing with me for a photograph. After everything that had been written about our relationship, I figured a picture of us holding hands would really shock the entire Trekkie nation. But truthfully, I was glad that they agreed to pose for the photo. I thought, maybe they're mellowing a bit. And I continued to think that until Walter said to me as we posed, "Any picture of the three of us holding hands has got to be worth at least five hundred dollars at a convention. If we all sign it, fifteen hundred."

And so Kirk died, although since then he has continued to live long and has prospered in the series of *Star Trek* novels and, more recently, video games.

I'd been playing James T. Kirk for almost thirty years. But Kirk was done. And naturally with that reality I began to wonder if the greatest days of my career were done too. There would always be small roles for me, I knew that, and that I could always earn a reasonable living, but there does come a time when the phone rings less often. I did wonder if this was the beginning of the end of my career.

And after Nerine's death I began wondering if I was condemned to spend the rest of my life alone too. Obviously I had my daughters and their families, which happily included a growing number of grand-children, but they all had their own busy lives. My greatest fear was being back — emotionally — in that ribbed-bed, rat-infested room in Toronto. All alone.

As it turned out, rather than this being an ending, it was simply another beginning.

I went back to work about two months after Nerine's death. There is no such thing as "enough time," or "being ready" to work. I just couldn't sit around the house any-more. I'm an actor. I needed to act. Fortu-nately, the perfect role was offered to me, a role truly befitting the status I had earned in the entertainment industry. John Lithgow offered me the role of the Big Giant Head in his sitcom *3rd Rock from the Sun.*

When I started watching the show I re-alized what a master farceur John Lithgow is. *3rd Rock* is about the adventures of four aliens who have come to Earth on a mission to investigate life here and have taken hu-man bodies. I love farce — very broad, wide-open, full-throttle madcap comedy played absolutely straight — but I hadn't had the opportunity to do much of it since working in the theater in Canada. Great farce has all the meaning and depth of a soap bubble, it shimmers for an instant and then disappears. It really was precisely what I needed at that moment. Great farce means giving wit a swift kick in the pants — and it was the best possible work for me.

In this half hour the unit's superior officer, the Big Giant Head, was making his first inspection of the mission. He had never been to Earth before. Well, what fun to play that. My part was written extremely broadly. In an early scene I discovered I had these things called legs and kicked Lithgow in the pants! And it was so much fun I kicked him again. And then I got slapped in the face by a woman when I commented how much I liked "the round part at the end of her legs!" Kicks in the pants, slaps in the face, plot misunderstandings, and slapstick — I had to dump a large bowl of red punch over a prom queen wearing a white gown. What actor wouldn't want to dump a bowl of red punch over the head of a girl in a white prom gown? It was everything farce is supposed to be, even the lines were properly broadly absurd. For example, when the beautiful Kristen Johnston discovered the Big Giant Head had promoted her because of her sexy appearance, she complained, "When a woman with a body like this gets a promotion everybody questions it. But if it were a man with a body like this no one would ask a question!"

As Lithgow told me, no one in the cast knew what to expect from me. None of them had ever seen me playing broad comedy — although John claimed he had seen me singing "Rocket Man." He told me that a series of performers ranging from Dennis Rodman to Naomi Judd had guest-starred on the show. "Some people wanted to come in and join in the fun, some knew it was their job to be a foil, and there were some people who just didn't have a clue."

I know that when I showed up for rehearsals some members of the cast were a little dubious, wondering how serious I was going to be about protecting my image. At first we did have a bit of a problem — I was playing more broadly than they were. I was really into it, over-the-top into it, and my performance had to be modulated — so I only kicked Jane Curtin in the pants once!

What was truly nice is that the writers included several inside Shatner gags in the script. For example, knowing that Lithgow and I had played the same *Twilight Zone* character — the man on the plane who sees the monster at twenty thousand feet, in my opening scene Lithgow asked me if I'd had a good flight. "It was horrible," I said. "I looked out and saw something on the wing of the plane."

Lithgow's mouth fell open and he exclaimed, "The same thing happened to me!"

Later when I was trying to woo Jane Curtin I told her, "I'm a rocket man, you know." And then I asked her if I could help her jettison her pants. And in one of the final scenes which took place at a high school junior prom — did I mention that I got to dump a whole . . . oh, sorry — during this scene the police asked me if I had seen any kids with Lucy in the sky with diamonds.

I had a great time doing the show. And apparently it was so popular that they brought Big Giant Head back for several additional shows. To my great surprise and pleasure — and I'm not kidding here — I was nominated for an Emmy Award as the Outstanding Guest Actor in a Comedy Series. After working in television for forty years, even considering the great success of *Star Trek* and *Hooker* and *911,* this was the first time I'd been nominated for an Emmy. Yes, I had been nominated for other awards; I'd won a science-fiction Saturn as Best Actor for *Star Trek II: The Wrath of Khan* and I'd been nominated for several awards for TV's first interracial kiss — I'd kissed Nichelle Nichols in a 1968 episode — as well as a Razzie. I'd even been honored as the subject of an entire art show — about seventy-five artists created original pieces about me for an exhibition and book called *The Shatner Show* — with a portion of all proceeds donated to the Hollywood Horse Show. It is an astonishing collection, with pieces made from an extraordinary variety of materials — including a bust made of LEGOs and another one of clay, limestone, artificial ferns, and plumbing pieces. So I've seen myself in plastic and plumbing, but I'd never even been nominated for an Emmy. And at that point in my life, considering the events of the past year, just to be nominated was quite an honor and I truly appreciated it.

But I really wanted to win. I mean, I really wanted to win. I'm not going to pretend I was satisfied with the nomination. I wanted to take home that little sucker. So I very carefully looked over my competition. The other nominees for Outstanding Guest Actor in a Comedy Series were . . . imagine a drumroll here, please, but hold your applause . . . John Ritter! Charles Nelson Reilly! Woody Harrelson! And Mel Brooks! Mel Brooks? I was nominated for a comedy award against Mel Brooks? What chance did I have? That's sort of like being nominated for Best Appearance on Money against

Abraham Lincoln. I attended the awards but I didn't write an acceptance speech. Guess who won? Mel Brooks!

Whether it was *3rd Rock* or just my time, again, rather than my career coming to a gentle end as I feared, I began being offered better roles than I'd played in years. The Shatman was back! I was "hot." I was in demand! For example, I was given a full hour to peddle my wares on The Home Shopping Network during which I set sales records that have yet to be broken.

Okay, that I am kidding about. I have appeared on just about every television channel in history — I've even been an answer on *Jeopardy!* — but I have never been invited to appear on the Home Shopping Network. It would seem to me that Bill Shatner and the Home Shatner Net . . . Shopping Network would be a perfect match. Perhaps I might appear on there selling . . . this book. I could appear on HSN selling my autobiography, which claims I'd never appeared on HSN! The tabloids would love that story! It would be great publicity for HSN — and me.

But one of the roles I did accept was to play a beauty-pageant organizer in Sandra Bullock's movie *Miss Congeniality.* This is a comedy in which the awkward FBI agent

Bullock goes undercover as a Miss United States contestant. Obviously it was pure fiction, Sandra Bullock could never be awkward. And in addition to working with Sandra Bullock — and for her because she was the producer — this was the first time I'd worked with Candice Bergen. I'd always admired her work, among her other attributes I'd long admired. We had several scenes together. In a wonderfully dramatic moment, Candice looked up at me and stated so proudly, "I would much rather cancel the show than have my girls blown up."

To which I responded nobly, "Especially without their knowledge."

Supposedly some of the dialogue came from actual beauty-pageant contestants. It's possible. For example, the script called for me to ask one beautiful young woman, "Please describe your idea of a perfect date."

She thought about this, then said, "That's a tough one. I would say . . . April twenty-fifth, because it's not too hot, not too cold, all you need is a light jacket."

For me, it was oddly disconcerting to be working for a female producer. I like to think I'm one of the least sexist men in our universe, not that I ever actually think about it. Because if I did have to think about it, that would indicate I was sexist by nature but trying to make myself aware of it. But I don't, so it can't be. Honestly, I love women. I'd never knowingly worked for a female producer before, especially a producer who looked like Sandra Bullock. It was actually kind of scary for me, to be in a situation in which a woman had absolute power. Not that I'm sexist. And while Sandra Bullock was not the director, the director deferred to her. She was in complete charge of everything that happened on the set. I watched her working and thought, wow, that's an interesting person I'd like to get to know better. We have become nice acquaintances, even if we've never had the opportunity to become friends. But I have extended to her something I value very much — an invitation to come to my house and join a large group of friends to watch *Monday Night Football.*

And then we'll just see who's sexist!

Miss Congeniality was the first of the several large-budget major-movie-star films in which I appeared — but that didn't stop me from also appearing in considerably lower-budget films, particularly those that I thought would be fun. In *Shoot or Be Shot,* for example, I played the role of escaped mental patient Harvey Wilkes, who kidnaps an entire film crew in the desert and forces them to make the movie *Shoot or Be Shot.*

Several years later I did another project about making a movie — and this was arguably the greatest practical joke ever played on an entire town. It really is difficult to accurately describe what was happening in my career during this period. But, for no specific reason that I could determine, I had become a bigger star than ever before. I was appearing in movies and on television, I was Priceline.com's spokesperson, and I made many other commercials, I was writing books, creating and producing projects, even making my first new record album since 1968. I was having a great time doing it all. And almost daily people were approaching me with the most unusual and occasionally intriguing ideas.

One afternoon I was in the lobby at MTV waiting to start a pitch meeting. I had several good ideas I wanted to discuss with executives there. Two young men who had produced the successful reality show *The Joe Schmo Show* were also waiting there to pitch a project. With great enthusiasm they told me they had a concept for a wonderful show for which I would be perfect. Generally, when people have a project for which "Bill, I swear, this is perfect for you," what they really mean is that they don't have any money, Robin Williams's agent has turned it down, and they would like to attach my name to it to get financing.

But I always listen. You never know. Two days later they came to my office in Studio City and pitched their idea for the greatest practical joke in television history. It was a good old-fashioned hoax. I liked it, I liked it a lot. Remember, I'm the man who tried to convince my daughter Melanie that a giant pine tree had actually once been a bonsai. This was the idea: I would pretend to buy an economically depressed small town and proceed to try to save it by making all kinds of bizarre changes. The first thing I would do, for example, was change the name of the town to . . . Billville!

My initial reaction was, that's genius. And seconds later I pictured a poor single mother with her crippled child crying as she thanked me for saving the lives of everyone in the town by buying it.

And I would be playing a joke on them all. Ha ha ha, end of career. That would be beyond cruel. But we continued talking and eventually I suggested, "How about instead of buying a whole town, we fool a whole town!" And I knew exactly what town. The result was *Invasion Iowa*. We would bring a film crew into a small town on the pretext of making a movie, but in fact we would actually be doing a reality show, filming their reaction to a very bizarre Hollywood production. The whole production would be a hoax. It would be hysterical. What could possibly go wrong?

Eventually Spike TV bought the concept. Then Priceline.com agreed to support it in return for some mention. Actually a lot of mention. I would co-produce and direct. It was actually a substantial financial risk for both companies — if one person found out that the whole production was a practical joke and exposed it, the show would fall apart and their investment would be lost. In fact, when we pitched the show we didn't reveal to anyone that we intended to shoot in Riverside, Iowa, population 928, which for several years had promoted itself as "The future birthplace of Captain James T. Kirk." A plaque claiming that Kirk was "conceived at this point" used to hang *under* the pool table at Murphy's Bar and tourists could buy "Kirk Dirt" from the site of his birth for ten dollars.

Pulling off this massive joke required tremendous technical planning and on-the-scene improvisation. We had to somehow get a film crew into the town to shoot us shooting a movie, and make their presence believable. The story we finally came up with was that in addition to the film, we were shooting behind-the-scenes footage to be used on the DVD as bonus material, and our film crew was shooting that material. Our visible cast and crew, which consisted of about four actors, four or five technicians, and the promise that eventually Sean Connery was going to show up, plus our real technical crew, stayed in a motel about twenty minutes out of town. There was no script, just general situations and a lot of improvisation. We made it up as we went along, depending on the reactions of the real stars of our show — the citizens of Riverside. Our entire crew met early every morning to plan our day and then again at the end of the day to review our progress and discuss ideas for the following day.

This was going to be amazing! Hollywood meets Iowa! The city slickers meet the country bumpkins. We were going to have such fun with these people. They were going to believe that we were making this nutty movie entitled *Invasion Iowa* and we'd tape them doing unbelievably crazy things. We fooled a lot of people outside the town too; we hired publicity people to create a buzz about this film. The Associated Press ran a nice feature story, quoting me as describing it as "my baby," a baby "I've been dreaming of making for more than thirty years." Unfortunately, almost immediately we confronted a problem we hadn't anticipated. The citizens of Riverside were just too damn nice. The day we got there a large crowd turned out to welcome us to Riverside, and as a spokesman said warmly, "First of all, welcome home."

These people were so innocent. But perhaps the first wisp of a doubt that perhaps it wasn't such a great idea to surprise these people occurred when the mayor told me earnestly, "I felt fine after the initial heart attack. Honestly, I felt fine."

How do you set up people who welcome you to their town with homemade apple pie? How do you have laughs at the expense of people who invite you into their homes and offer you their trust? How do you lie to people who leave with the good wishes, "See you in church on Sunday."

This simple concept very quickly became complex. I began to wonder, what have I done? Within a few days members of the crew were developing friendships with these people. It was impossible not to. I mean, how could I lie to a wonderfully sweet elderly man named Don Rath, who graciously shared with me one of his most prized possessions, his good-luck raccoon penis?

We had to modify our original idea. We realized that we had to make ourselves the fools and focus on their good-natured re-action to our stupidity. *Invasion Iowa* be-came a spoof of Hollywood pomposity — a send-up of all the over-the-top foibles and eccentricities people read about in their newspapers. And guess who was the most eccentric? Here's a hint: it wasn't my "spiritual advisor" who accompanied me on the set. We hired half a dozen townspeople to work with us on the film and they became our subjects. We were watching them as they watched us make ever bigger fools of our-selves. These were the people the audience really got to know. One of them was our cue-card woman. In one scene, for example, I discovered the aliens had followed me to Earth and I had to scream a great echoing, "Noooooooooooooo!" That was the entire scene, one word. So naturally we wrote it on three cue cards. And we carefully in-structed our cue-card woman that the first cue card had to have exactly five O's. Then she had to hold up the second cue card, which contained precisely four O's. And the final card had three O's.

And this wonderful woman really counted my O's to make certain she got it right. Of course I couldn't get it right, I kept getting the length of my "no" confused. You actually could read her expression: These people are crazy, but they're probably harmless so I'll go along with them.

The film we supposedly were making, also called *Invasion Iowa,* was the quite confusing story of an alien who comes to Earth to find . . . well, it doesn't matter. There was no plot. But it did have some very funny lines. For example, I arrived on Earth buck naked. After first pretending to be from Nebraska, I told the young woman from Riverside we'd cast as our ingénue, "I know this sounds crazy, but I come from the future."

To which she responded, "I thought you came from Nebraska." We also gave her the classic science-fiction line, "I would much rather carry your seed than seed that would destroy the Earth."

Most of the real action for the TV show took place off the movie set as we put our cast and the townspeople in bizarre situations. For example, when our leading lady, Desi Lydic, went shopping at the local Kwik 'n E-Z, for example, we whispered to the store owner that "Gryffyn," the character she was playing on the show but not in the movie, was a kleptomaniac. We'll pay for everything she takes, we said, but please don't say anything about it. So this woman watched with growing incredulity as Desi went through the shop putting items like Remington gun oil and Travis Tritt's Bar-be-cue in a Jar in her purse.

Then we decided Desi was going to solicit advice from a group of women about a children's book she was writing. A small group of them gathered to hear her read from this manuscript. It was the story of a female penguin who was very unhappy because she had small "wings." Her wings were so small, in fact, that her sweater just drooped in front. Naturally, as she read this story we had a cast member dressed as a penguin making absurd remarks. Fortunately, in Desi's story, the penguin was able to get wing-enhancement surgery so her sweaters would be really tight and people would love her and she lived happily ever after. Ta-ta!

These women finally gathered the courage to suggest that her moral — plastic, surgically enhanced "wings" are the key to happiness — was probably not the best message to send to children. So Desi went right back to work and a few days later read from her newly rewritten children's book in which her penguin doesn't care that her wings are small and meets another female penguin with small wings who becomes her friend and they move in together and live happily ever after.

Naturally I was at the center of most of the absurdity. Right from the beginning I practically insisted that rather than wearing hats, the townspeople should wear Shats, sort of like berets. One night, we had decided that I should entertain these people with my stand-up comedy act, which consisted of jokes like, "One of my favorite places in town is the Kwik 'n E-Z. They named it after my first girlfriend. It's a good thing they didn't name it after my first wife, because then it would be the Fat 'n Ugly!"

I think the proper way to describe their response is dumbfounded, completely and absolutely dumbfounded. Those were the jokes, folks. They didn't get any better than that.

Part of our continuing story was my growingly acrimonious relationship with my large and often loud nephew, Tiny. Eventually, though, I revealed to one of the townspeople that Tiny wasn't really my nephew — he was my son! And when I revealed it to . . . dumbfounded townspeople, Tiny looked at me lovingly and said, "Dad, I want to have a catch!" And we proceeded to take out the baseball gloves and have a catch.

The citizens of Riverside were so unbelievably accommodating. When my aides suggested they change the name of the town to . . . Did you really think I was going to let loose of this idea? . . . Billville, they actually printed petitions and handed them out, then helped us make and hang a large sign reading, WELCOME TO BILLVILLE. They also went along with our producer, who whispered to them just before the townspeople vs. cast and crew softball game, "Bill doesn't like to make an out. So whatever you do, it's very important that you let him get on base. Otherwise he's going to be in a real bad mood for the rest of the day." So they did — and amazingly I then successfully stole second base and third base and then I stole home! Yeah, Shatner!

And no matter what we did, our new Priceline.com spokesperson was always somewhere in the background, wearing his Priceline.com shirt and hat, and occasionally I would point to him and he would immediately do a promo for Priceline, "Go to Priceline to save a lot of money." And when we thought Priceline had enough mentions, we made him the spokesperson for Bryl-creem.

When one of my assistants explained I'd always wanted to ride on a fire truck and fight a fire, a member of the Riverside Fire Department actually set fire to an old car. We raced to the fire and they let me man the hose! However, they were a little reluctant to go along with my suggestion that we tell everybody that I'd saved the lives of two people by pulling them out of the front seat.

Just about the only thing we suggested that they absolutely refused to do was smash the hundred-year-old extremely valuable stained-glass windows in the church. In fact, when we made that suggestion they were . . . dumbfounded. And even after we told them it was absolutely necessary to break just one window, a small one, when the aliens showed up, they refused.

There were times when we were afraid people were beginning to figure out that this whole thing was a hoax, particularly when one resident pointed out, "With William Shatner you never know what's going on. You don't know if he's just whacko!" But somehow we managed to keep the secret. Certainly the most difficult thing for us to do during the shoot was continue the deception. Each day it got more difficult to continue lying to these people. Sometimes at our meetings at night people would begin crying about the lies they had to tell. Personally, I began to dread the moment when we would have to reveal the truth. For some reason I had visions of the townspeople carrying torches as they came up the mountain toward Dr. Frankenstein's castle.

This was the first time since making *The Outrage* in a small Southern town more than three decades earlier that I started planning an escape route.

We couldn't quit, though. This was a comedy reality show and we had to continue the deception. And then, just when I thought the situation couldn't possibly become any more difficult, Don Rath, who had already bestowed upon me the honor of wiping my face with his good-luck raccoon penis, gave me his handmade mustache cup and asked me for a favor in return. "Come with me," he said.

Don Rath took me up to the town cemetery to visit the grave of his wife, who had died in 2001. There was Don with his walker and I standing in this sort of barren cemetery before his wife's tombstone. "Look, Mom, look who I brought up to see you."

If the citizens of Riverside, Iowa, had

known what we were doing and wanted to turn the joke back around on us, this is precisely the way they would have done it. The man was taking me to visit his wife's grave. And as he spoke he began crying. Oh my goodness, I knew exactly how he felt. Exactly. As it would be forever, Nerine's death was never further than a thought out of my mind and my soul was deeply wounded. The real emotion of that moment was so strong that Don and I hugged and I started crying. No reality show in the history of television has ever been more real.

That was not the funny part. Trust me.

Eventually the time came to reveal the truth. Coincidently it was April first. We invited the key townspeople to a dinner-picnic. It was left to me to tell them the truth. Oy, this was tough. We had absolutely no idea how any of them were going to react. There was every chance it was going to get ugly. There is no movie, I said, my heart thumping wildly. This whole thing is a reality TV show. That was met with the longest silence I'd ever experienced in my life. Finally, someone said, "You dirty dogs." And other people started laughing.

This group of people loved it — with one exception. This man was a farmer, a big, powerful guy with tremendous dignity. I wanted him not to be angry — and he was fucking angry. "You mean you played us the fool all along . . ." His body language was far worse than his words — he was turned halfway away from me and his arms were locked in front of him. We had learned what each of our principals wanted — one man had dreamed his whole life of going to Hawaii, we sent him and his family to Hawaii. A woman needed money for her efforts to adopt her grandson, we helped finance her successful effort. Our ingénue desperately wanted to bring her horse to Riverside but couldn't afford it, we paid to board the horse for a year. Another cast member wanted to see Paris, we gave him a trip there. Each person received either gifts or cash worth several thousand dollars. But when we reached our farmer, he had left. He didn't want anything to do with us.

I felt awful. Just dreadful. That night we were meeting with the entire town to reveal our secret to them. The local members of our cast had kept our secret. And as they arrived they were greeted by their neighbors with a red carpet and cheers. And at the end of the line was the farmer — with a big smile on his face. As we found out, he'd gone home and discussed it with his family, who convinced him our prank was harmless and fun. The citizens of Riverside took the joke good-naturedly — particularly when we told them we would be contributing one hundred thousand dollars to the town treasury. In addition, our crew and actors raised an additional thirteen thousand dollars which was used to buy books for the elementary school.

Spike TV eventually ran the show as a miniseries and it received very good reviews. Several reviewers specifically pointed out my success at self-parody, writing that finally I'd "got it." Of course, that just proves once again that my acting skills had not dulled — I was not doing self-parody. That was . . . William Shatner!

The movie death of Jim Kirk turned out to be a new beginning to my career, but I believed completely that Nerine's death was the end of my married life. And perhaps it also meant that I would never again have an intense loving relationship with a woman. If there was one thing I had proved, it's that marriage just didn't work for me. And as difficult as it was for me to deal with that particular reality, it was pretty obvious that I was doing something wrong.

And honestly, for a long time after Nerine's death I had little interest in women. The concept of dating at that point in my life did not seem very appealing to me. To fill some of the enormous loneliness I was feeling in those months I found considerable solace just being with my horses. In the early 1980s we were filming an episode of *T.J. Hooker* where we needed a police car with its siren whining to race through a horse barn. We ended up in a barn where saddlebreds were stabled. I had been involved in a minor way in a quarter horse breeding operation, but as I stood in the barn that day looking at these magnificent animals I was . . . I was stunned. It was an enchanted moment. Looking across a crowded barn I fell in love with saddlebreds. One look and I was smitten. Saddlebreds are works of art. These horses are bred to be beautiful and to move beautifully. These horses are an esthetic delight and the pleasure they give your eyes is magnified by the grace of their movement.

Well, that day I had discovered a new passion. These were obviously the most magnificently proud beasts on earth. I thought it was impossible to look at them and not want to fill fields with them. There was one in particular that just mesmerized me. I asked the owner its price and when he named it, I said flatly, "I'll buy him."

The next day I flew home to Los Angeles.

I called a trainer I knew and asked him to handle all the details for me. He called me a short time later. "You know that horse you bought two days ago for X dollars?" Yeah? I said all excitedly. "Well, now the price is two-X dollars."

Welcome to the horse breeding business, Bill.

Actually, raising the price was illegal. In that business the price you name is the price. Period. But I was so naïve I decided I probably hadn't heard them correctly. I was so in lust with this horse that I was willing to pay almost anything. And so I did.

I was taken for a ride — literally and figuratively. But that was the beginning of what has grown to be a substantial horse breeding business. A very expensive horse breeding business. Eventually I bought a ranch in Lexington, Kentucky, Belle Reve Farm, an eighty-seven-acre spread. At various times I've owned as many as sixty horses. But of all the horses I've owned, the most magnificent of them all was Sultan's Great Day. A two-time World Champion in his category, Sultan's Great Day was all black, and when he ran he looked like a silhouette in motion. Just looking at him made it clear his choice would have been to be running free in the woods; he did not easily accept being domesticated. I rode him at his leisure. We put him out to stud and his offspring have won almost one hundred World Grand Championships and Reserves in all the major saddlebred divisions. I admired him, loved him, and respected him. He was a great thrill to own.

But by 2004 he was done. It was time to end his life. I wanted to be there when the vet put him down so I flew to the ranch. And then, on a warm spring afternoon, the two of us went for a final walk in the pasture. I led him into a shady dell and then stood there, content to watch him graze. Wanting to stop time, really. I was anticipating, and dreading, the moment when the vet would arrive to give him his final shots. All of a sudden, from across the field, three horses came running toward us. Great Day raised his head and then, in an instant, became the stallion of old, the great protector of the herd. His instincts took hold and on his feeble rear legs he reared high, proud, pawing the air with bandaged front feet, neighing his defiance. The other horses rightly turned tail, and ran.

He was a champion. A champion.

Great Day settled back down, defiant and proud. As someone remarked later, he went into the next world feeling like a stud horse.

Probably the least expensive aspect of owning horses is the initial cost of the horse. It's everything that comes after; the housing and feeding and training of that animal. The cost of medical attention and the proper equipment. If it's a competition horse there is the cost of getting to the competition; the trucks and the feed and the care. And then there are the people who actually run the operation, the good people as well as those who quit and those who cheat. And then, if you choose, there are even more esoteric ways of spending your money — for example, consulting an animal psychic.

While I was growing up in Montreal, I'm certain I never thought that someday I would be successful enough to consult an animal psychic. There is one woman I know who channels dogs.

Fish who talk is a concept I have for an animated undersea movie. A woman who channels dogs is a person I've paid to find out what my dog is thinking. I don't actually remember how I found her. But what happens is she focuses on an animal and sits at a computer and goes into a trance and types the animal's thoughts. This is for real, this is not seeing aliens in the desert again. Often she doesn't actually see the dog or its environment, but she told someone I know that their dog was barking like crazy because someone had taken away its plaid blanket a month ago — and sure enough, the owners had thrown out that dog's ripped plaid blanket.

I consulted this psychic when a dog I loved very much got sick. This was Kirk, a champion Doberman who was dying from what is known as wobblers, a condition in which vertebrae come loose and impact on the central nervous system. When this dog started to show the first signs of wobblers I was desperate, hoping that I could save his life. So I went to see this woman whose expertise is talking to race horses before a race to build up their confidence.

She lived in Southern California. I put the dog in the car and we drove to her house. When we got there she had a psychic conversation with my dog. Truthfully, at no point did I think of Leonard doing a mind-meld. "He says he's got a headache," she told me. "He's been dropped on his head. Have you shipped him anywhere lately?"

Several weeks earlier we had shipped him to Seattle to breed.

"He says they dropped his crate. He'll be fine, but you need to take him to an acupuncturist."

I believed every word she said. I mean,

how could she have known that he'd recently been on a trip unless he told her? That is the extraordinary power of hope. And it is how I ended up taking him to the animal acupuncturist twice a week. And for about an hour after each visit he would be fine, as if his pain had gone away. But it quickly came back and my dog died within the time frame predicted by the vet.

Actually, there are several well-known animal psychics. A friend of mine once discovered one of them in a stable, standing directly in front of his horse. "Excuse me," he said politely. "But you're making this horse nervous."

"I'm sorry," she said, "I talk to horses. Tell me, what kind of horse is this?"

He smiled. "Ask the horse."

I'm passionate about horses and dogs. The presence of animals in my life has made a great difference. No matter what else was going on, they were always there for me and even in the worst circumstances provided great comfort.

And eventually — and certainly unexpectedly — it was my horses that brought me the most surprising happiness of my life.

ELEVEN

One of the most beautiful shows we did on *Rescue 911* was the story of a young woman who had been killed in an auto accident. Although we rarely told stories in which people died, while this young person was on life support her parents had made the agonizing decision to donate her organs to several people. We invited those recipients whose lives she had changed forever to appear on the show.

That was not the case when I sold my kidney stone on eBay. I was on the *Boston Legal* set in the fall of 2005 when I suddenly felt this incredible pain in my back and fainted. They were afraid it was a heart attack and rushed me to the hospital. As it turned out I was passing a kidney stone, which was only slightly more painful than taking a knife and sticking it into your side. Once it passes, it's done, no aftereffects. The story got some minor coverage, people thought it was amusing. I thought it really hurt a lot.

Soon afterward we got a call from an online casino who wanted to buy it. Because it is an offshore business this casino is not permitted to promote gambling in the United States, so they advertise their presence with stunts that will get the name of the casino in the newspapers. These were the same people who had bought a decade-old half-eaten grilled cheese sandwich with the image of the Virgin Mary on it for twenty-eight thousand dollars — and then sent it on a national tour. They were calling to ask if I would donate my kidney stone. Donate? Donate? Who gives away their kidney stone? What is its value, I asked. Is there a black market in kidney stones?

The casino told me this donation would generate a tremendous amount of publicity. Right, publicity for them. Finally they offered to pay for it. I decided to donate whatever they paid to Habitat for Humanity. There was only one problem: I didn't have my kidney stone. The last time I'd known where it was, was when I was in the hospital. At that point it had been right inside my kidney. I contacted the hospital. I would not be party to selling a fake kidney stone. The hospital was not certain they still had it. I was really hoping we weren't going to have a legal battle over ownership; from what I have been able to determine the Supreme Court has never ruled on who owns a kidney stone after it has left someone's body. It's still very much unsettled law.

On the other hand, I didn't know exactly how the casino could determine if the kidney stone I gave them was the kidney stone in question — although when it was in my body it felt more like a kidney rock. We decided they probably could do a DNA test. But when the hospital claimed they found it, I believed them. Who lies about a kidney stone? The casino offered fifteen thousand dollars. An insult, I felt, for a kidney stone of my quality. Didn't they know where that kidney stone had been? And it also did not seem very much for the amount of publicity they could reasonably expect to gain from it.

So I decided to determine its actual market value on eBay! One of a kind, I hope. I told all bidders, "If you subjected it to extreme heat it might turn out to be a diamond."

Finally the casino folded — raising its offer to seventy-five thousand dollars, which I accepted and donated.

Some months after Nerine's death it finally occurred to me that in all probability I would never be married again. That was very depressing. While I believed I would never again love someone as deeply as I had loved Nerine, I was just so lonely. So in my mind I began making a list of those things I wanted in a woman. I created my fantasy woman: obviously she had to be single. She didn't have to have children of her own, but she couldn't want to have children with me. Certainly I had to find her attractive. Okay, beautiful. She had to be free to travel with me. She had to have a big sense of humor. And she had to truly love horses. It was an impossible list, I knew, I could never find anyone like that. I was resigned to spending the rest of my life alone. That was hard for me to accept because I had all the desires and the passions and the physical ability that I'd always had.

After Nerine's death I had received hundreds of letters from people offering their condolences or advice or sympathy. Eventually I read them all. One of them attracted my attention, mostly because the calligraphy on the envelope was so striking. It was from a woman named Elizabeth Martin, whom I knew vaguely from the horse world. Elizabeth and her husband, Mike, had owned and operated a very successful saddlebred stable in Montecito, near Santa Barbara. They were well-respected trainers and had won several championships. I knew them from competing against their horses. I remembered having thought in passing that she was a beautiful woman, but I don't think we'd ever said more than a few words in passing. I had heard that her husband had gotten cancer and she'd nursed him for several years until his death. The last time I'd seen her I'd been with Nerine at a horse show. Elizabeth had been one of the judges.

Her letter was a surprise. "My husband died of cancer two years ago," she wrote. "Since then I've been through all the stages of grief. I know what it is. And if there is anything I can do to help you get through this period, I'd be delighted." When I read the letter I thought fate had handed it to me: you gave me the list, here's the woman who fulfills that list. I remember telling some friends, "There's a girl in Santa Barbara that I think I've got to meet."

Other women were sending me letters with their pictures in them. This was a lovely letter offering what I most needed, understanding of what I was going through. It was a sincere letter of sympathy and the message that eventually you heal; she didn't even include her phone number. She had trained a horse owned by my business manager's wife, so I got her phone number from him. And I called. We became friends on the phone. We spoke every day for several months, but she just didn't have time to meet me. She was too busy; in addition to running a large business she was helping her mother deal with her father's Alzheimer's. Her parents were staying with her and, as she explained, she had learned enough about loss to know how to make the most of the time you have with the people you love. All she wanted to do was help me get through this period. I was so fearful of being alone that I wanted to cling to someone right away. As often as I told myself I didn't want to get married again, that it was too painful, I also admitted to myself I needed to be with someone. Somehow that seemed logical at the time.

Finally we made plans to meet for dinner. I'd spent that day in San Francisco, interviewing scientists for a show we were planning about the Human Genome Project, which fostered a competition between the government and private industry to map out the entire human genome. Fascinating stuff, and as I was listening to these brilliant people discussing the very matrix of life I was thinking, I can't wait to see her tonight.

I was exhausted when I got home; I drove up to Santa Barbara in the last stages of sleep deprivation. We met on the pier in Santa Barbara. I got out of my car and immediately saw this beautiful lady standing beside her car, looking so elegant and dignified. We had dinner that night in a quiet restaurant on the pier, a place she had often gone with her husband. She sort of knew I was an actor, but had never seen a full episode of *Star Trek* and knew nothing about the show. In fact, many months later we went to dinner with Patrick Stewart and his wife, and Elizabeth was listening to our conversation and interrupted, "I'm not sure I understand. How can you be the captain," she said, pointing to Patrick, "if he's the captain?"

So it became obvious she wasn't after me for my *Star Trek* action figures — which, by the way are still available at The Store on Shatnervision.com. In fact, it quickly became even more obvious that she wasn't after me at all.

During dinner I had asked her if she would ever come to L.A. Absolutely not, she said. She was much too busy. So instead a few days later I called and invited her to the South Pole.

I had been invited to accompany a world-renowned nature photographer on a camera safari to Antarctica. They were going to fly me to Patagonia and we would sail from there. It was a two-week trip and I could bring someone with me. "You can have your own cabin," I said. "It'll be a great adventure." Then I added, "An opportunity like this may never again happen in our lifetime."

Of course I was talking about the trip to the South Pole. Of course.

She said, "I have to figure out the pros and cons. I'm going to write them down." Well, that was efficient. And she called me back and said, "The cons have won. It's just not practical."

She was talking about the trip to South Pole. Actually, she really was.

Eventually I turned down the offer. The prospect of being alone in the Antarctic, perhaps the most isolated place in the world, was a lot more than I was ready to face. But perhaps a month later I had to go to New York for a long weekend. Again I invited her, and I used those very special words, "separate rooms."

While I was there my New York agent, Carmen La Via, asked me to participate in a fund-raising event for a young girl with cancer up in Albany, about a three-hour drive from the city. I suggested Liz spend the day at a spa in the hotel, but she volunteered to come with Carmen and me. Our conversation in the car that day was about life and death, and she expressed such empathy and humanity, and by the time we got to Albany we knew each other. The rest of that day was equally magical. The fundraiser was held at a bowling alley. There were three hundred bowlers there and several thousand bowling alleys across America participating on some sort of closed-circuit network. I hadn't bowled in fifteen years. I picked up a ball and threw a strike. It was amazing. Then they auctioned off my bowling ball for several thousand dollars. After the event Liz and I walked around and found a toy store that had stayed open later than normal. We'd heard that this little girl was not permitted to see her dog and missed it terribly. She had shown us pictures of him. In that toy store we found a stuffed dog that looked just like her dog. We bought it and went back to the hospital.

Carmen did not come back to New York with us. It was a cold night and the heater in the limo didn't work, so we snuggled in the backseat. As we passed an open field I asked the driver to stop. The field was covered with fresh snow just glistening in the moonlight. We walked into the middle of the field and I kissed her for the first time.

It all seemed too perfect. Liz wondered if it was some sort of elaborate setup. And then she realized it didn't make any difference because she was freezing. On the ride home she slept in my arms.

From New York she went with me to Belle Reve, my horse farm in Kentucky. I knew she was confused. As she explained, she had never been with an actor before and she was scared, because she didn't know how to determine whether an actor is acting or telling the truth. If I was really a good actor, she said, she couldn't know that I was being truthful.

How could I respond to that? Convince her I was a bad actor?

Incredibly, I had found the woman who fulfilled all the criteria on my list. It was some sort of miracle: I'd made a list of all the qualities I needed in a companion and suddenly there she was in front of me. I had been describing her without knowing her. I had to convince myself not to be fearful. I had to grasp this opportunity and I had to urge her to grasp it too, because it was not going to happen again. While we were in

Kentucky I asked her, "Have you ever thought about getting married again?"

Not that I was thinking about it, of course. Not me, not really. It was just conversation, what movies do you like, pass the salt please, you interested in getting married? Okay, perhaps I was rushing things a bit; I was talking about marriage and she was still wondering whether or not she should be going out with me.

But I couldn't resist. Since Nerine's death I hadn't been able to regain a foothold on life. I'd been drifting through the days and the nights . . . the nights were dreadful. Thoughts of death and loneliness visited me every night. I was angry and remorseful; I was frustrated and even afraid. Ironically, though, it was not death that I feared, I was afraid of life. My health was deteriorating and my doctors were extremely concerned that the stress was slowly killing me. And then I met this woman. This intelligent, funny, wise, compassionate, and loving woman named Elizabeth Martin.

Was it truly possible? Were there really happy endings in life? To meet a woman as young and vital as Elizabeth Martin at this point in my life, to have all the mutual interests: movies and literature and poetry and dance and horses — and to be available for the possibility? Didn't I make that movie years earlier?

Six months after we'd begun dating she agreed to marry me. She told me that her fantasy was to be married by the author Marianne Williamson. As she explained, during her husband's terminal illness they had been reading her book *Illuminata,* and as he died she had been reading a prayer for a peaceful death. Marianne Williamson is a Jewish woman who is a minister in the Unity Church, which emphasizes love and common sense. The religious aspect was not particularly important to me and if it meant that much to Elizabeth then I wanted to do it. "This is William Shatner," I said when I reached Marianne Williamson in Detroit. "We'd like you to marry us."

"That's what I do," she said. Well, this was great. Marianne Williamson agreed to perform the ceremony, but wanted to speak with both of us together to confirm the arrangements. We set a date and time to speak about a week later.

I was making Elizabeth's fantasy come true. This was just great. Unfortunately, the day before this appointment Elizabeth and I had a terrible argument. Just terrible. At 9 p.m. the following night we were on the phone with Williamson. "Hello . . ." Elizabeth said, and then started crying. Not just crying, bawling, loud uncontrollable bawling.

"What's wrong?" Williamson asked.

And Elizabeth cried even louder.

"You two need work," Marianne Williamson said. "I'm sorry, I can't marry you."

We had been rejected by Marianne Williamson.

For the next hour we debated what was more important, being right or wrong, or spending the rest our lives together. Everything cleared up; both of us gave up our need to immediately fulfill our anger and spite and all those negative emotions in exchange for the other person's love.

Eventually we called Marianne Williamson back and again she agreed to marry us. The ceremony was to be held at Elizabeth's father's farm in Indianapolis, Indiana. A few days before the wedding Marianne Williamson called — she had laryngitis and her doctor wouldn't let her fly. So again we weren't going to be married by Marianne Williamson. We decided to go ahead with it. It was going to be a very low-key ceremony; no publicity, no media, just family. It was going to be beautiful. We got our marriage license at the town hall in Lebanon, Indiana. Nobody recognized us. We took a nice walk around the town square and as we got back in the rented car my cell phone rang. It was my manager, Larry Thompson, calling from Los Angeles. "Congratulations!" he said. I had signed the license about ten minutes earlier — and the story was already on the news in L.A. To evade the media — in Indiana — and protect Elizabeth's father, we secretly moved the ceremony to her sister's home about fifty miles away.

For almost a year we believed we'd gotten married that night. Then we discovered that because we'd moved the ceremony to another county, our license wasn't valid. So we had to get married again in Los Angeles.

I was legally married, but for the first time I had to learn how to be married. And that was not particularly easy for me. In my past, marriage had been relatively simple — I earned the money, my wife ran the house. It was very traditional. And to a point, those marriages were successful. That point came when my wife wanted more than I was capable of giving emotionally. Then the relationships changed — and I was not flexible enough to understand that or deal with it. So I had to learn that a lopsided relationship doesn't work. The exercise of power is inevitably self-defeating. What happens is that the person without power loses their self-respect, their whole entity becomes less, and the reasons their partner fell in love with them disappear.

So Elizabeth turned out to be the culmination of all my relationships — all the people I've known, and all the women of my life. She gets to experience both the good and the bad, and fortunately there's a lot more good than bad now. I hope. I like to believe I've raised the quality of my ability to relate to other people; it's not that I was a terrible person but admittedly almost always I put my responsibilities ahead of the relationship. I could justify it in my mind; my career financed the relationship. But I've learned; oh I've learned.

Elizabeth is a strong, independent woman — and a very talented one. She was a wonderful trainer, and the energy that once went into that now goes into our life together and her painting. She's discovered her creative talents. And because she brought with her into our marriage her confidence and her pride, I know that when Elizabeth sacrifices herself in an argument to come over to my side, which she does much of the time, she's not doing it from weakness, but rather from love. And that matters.

And we do have our arguments. But there

is one argument that does rise above the others. Now, there are certain invitations a man receives in his life that he just doesn't turn down. I was invited to fly in an F-16. How could I turn that down? I was allowed to ride along in the back of a police cruiser. There was no way I could turn that down. I was asked to dance with a killer whale. Of course I couldn't turn *that* down.

And then I was invited by *Playboy* to photograph a naked Playmate. Now, really, was I going to turn that down? Did I dare risk being known forever as William Shatner, the only guy in history who turned down the opportunity to photograph a beautiful naked Playmate? There was really only one problem with the offer: I knew Elizabeth would ask me not to do it. If I insisted it would lead to an argument and I certainly didn't want to have that argument. So given the circumstances and loving my wife very much and not wanting to have an argument I did the only realistic thing possible: I didn't tell her about it.

This was one of the most difficult decisions I'd been forced to make in many years. Truthfully, it *didn't* seem like a good idea at the time. I admit it — I don't know what I was thinking. This photograph was going to appear in *Playboy,* a magazine with one of the largest circulations in the world. They were going to promote the fact that I took the shots. I didn't believe for a moment that Liz wouldn't find out about it. Instead I figured, well, I'll just mention it to her when it's about to come out. *After* I'd photographed the beautiful naked Playmate.

Every married man understands this. And agrees with me. Would I have objected to Liz photographing a naked Playmate? Of course not, I'd probably even want to go with her to the shoot to be supportive. Actually I was completely innocent. My concept was that rather than simply photographing a beautiful, completely naked Playmate alone, I would use a wide-angle lens and include in the picture all the technical people required to make this completely naked Playmate look as sexy as possible. I'd include lighting people, assistants, makeup people, costume peo . . . well, there wouldn't be any costume people in this particular shot, as the beautiful Playmate would be naked. But I would show the viewer all the people required to make this hot work. Shot work, make this *shot* work. Liz couldn't really object, I was never going to be alone with the naked Playmate. It was very technical, just work. So I did it and I didn't tell her.

As months went by I expected to be notified by *Playboy* when my photographs were going to be published. But I didn't hear a word. That was actually fine with me; I'd already taken the photographs. If they weren't published and I never had to just sort of casually mention it to Elizabeth, I could live with that. But one morning I was in New York and I appeared on Barbara Walters's wonderful program (that I hope she has me on again to promote this book), *The View.* Liz was waiting for me in the guest room, the green room. And so I was very surprised when Joy Behar asked me, "So what does your wife think about you doing a *Playboy* bunny shoot?"

Apparently my photographs were being shown on *Playboy*'s Web site. I hadn't known anything about it. But thinking quickly, proving my ability to respond to a crisis, I said smartly, "Oh, she didn't worry about that. She's far more beautiful than any of the *Playboy* bunnies." Which is true, by the way, but when I said it there was an element of self-protection in it.

Elizabeth wasn't buying that particular bridge. "You lied to me," she said.

Technically, I pointed out, I didn't lie. I just didn't say anything.

Technically, smecknically, she was furious.

That precipitated an argument about exactly what is a lie. Let me hazard a guess that we were not the first married couple to debate that question. The best way to describe the outcome of that argument is I got my lawn trimmed. I got my shingles nailed down. I got my car waxed. I was wrong and, maybe not right away, but I admitted it.

I have learned that the definition of exactly what is a lie is quite different to men and women. Let me give you another example. When Elizabeth and I were dating we went to a several-days-long horse show. She was riding in the competition, which meant she brought five or six different riding outfits with her. As is common, she left those expensive outfits hanging in the tack room. Usually what happened was that after each performance I would take the wardrobe that she'd worn off the rack and put it in the trunk of the car, so we would have the minimal number of costumes to carry home at the end of the competition.

But after the first day she noticed that one of her suits was missing. "I think somebody took it," she said. "I know I brought it with me." After her second ride another suit was missing. "Somebody is definitely taking them," she said. "We have to lock this place up."

Three expensive riding suits were missing. I said to her, "Look, it has to be someone who's tall and slim, like you. Probably an adolescent girl. There just aren't too many people who can fit into your outfits. I'll look for that person. I'll find her."

When the competition ended I was standing by the car with several of Liz's friends, packing the final suit into the trunk — and that's when I realized what I had done. Rather than simply taking the outfit she'd worn each day, I'd carried off two of them. Nothing had been stolen. And as I realized this I saw Liz walking toward me. "Liz!" I shouted at her. "Great news. I got your garments back. I saw that girl and I followed her and I found them. I wrestled her to the ground, I got her in a headlock, and I took the wardrobe off her. Everything is here. I'm your hero!"

Unfortunately, she believed me. She started crying. "I've never had a hero in my life," she said. "I love you so much."

I was just about to tell her I was joking and we would have a big laugh at my stupidity — but how could I tell her? I was her hero! I thought, I'll tell her tomorrow.

The next day I was just about to tell her that I'd made up the whole story when I heard her tell one of my daughters, "Do you realize your father is a hero? He found the person who stole my clothing. I so admire him."

How could I tell her I was joking? Or, as she would have put it, lying. I decided to tell her . . . the following week, assuming she would have forgotten about it by then. It would be our little joke. Hey honey, remember that time . . . Next week, yeah, or maybe the week after. But as time passed she continued to tell the story to every single person that we meet. She told old friends, new friends, people she was on line with at the market, even in an interview we did together. "My husband is a hero!"

And there was nothing I could say. Months later we were at another horse show and one of the women who had been standing by the car when this all began asked me when I was going to finally tell Liz the truth.

"You mean that I was joking?" I asked. "Maybe I don't have to. You know, a lot of time has passed . . ."

Her friend responded just like a woman. Actually, she was a woman. "You have to tell her. If you don't, I will."

The next day I sat down with Liz. "Darling," I began. "I have a funny story to tell you."

"You lied to me."

"It wasn't a lie. I just got stuck in a story. Hey, it's really pretty funny when you think about it. I took these outfits by mistake and we thought . . ."

"You lied to me."

"I was desperate. I'm not a liar, but you were telling everybody I was a hero. What was I going to do? I'm not a hero . . ."

To this page, as you read this, whenever you are reading this, you can be certain about one thing: Liz has never seen the humor in it.

I don't think I'll ever successfully answer all the questions I have about Nerine. But with Elizabeth I have learned that the healing power of a human being is amazing. Both of us grieve for the people we loved — but we found each other and a wonderful, strong new love. As she has taught me every day for all the years we've been together, life is for the living.

I'm an extraordinarily lucky man. To have met someone like Elizabeth at that point in my life is probably about as unlikely as suddenly being cast into a brand-new hit television show and creating a character as popular as Jim Kirk. Or collaborating with major musical talents to make a hit record. Those kinds of things just don't happen in real life. Except that they did. I'm an extraordinarily lucky man.

By late 2003 I was again beginning to wonder if my career was ending. I was still receiving offers, but basically they were all a variation of the same theme: William Shatner poking fun at himself. I missed the excitement of creating something new, something different. I was actually sort of resigned to working less often, and the prospect of being free to travel the world with Elizabeth was exciting to me. I thought my career was washed up. I thought, I've had my run. Nothing's going to happen.

And in some odd way, that was okay with me.

What I did not know was that producer-writer David E. Kelley's legendary legal show *The Practice* was in its last season and he was looking for a way to use the final few episodes to create a new show. *The Practice* was a gritty and serious drama, but according to producer-director Bill D'Elia, Kelley wanted to do a show that was "bigger, bolder, and funnier." This would be a show about a major law firm that generally worked huge cases for a lot of money. Unlike most legal shows, in which noble defense attorneys fight in sometimes unorthodox ways for truth and justice, the lawyers in this firm wanted to make a lot of money.

Another reality show. At the center of it all was a character named Denny Crane. Kelley told D'Elia that he wanted Denny Crane to be "a legendary attorney, an extremely vain man who makes no bones about his vanity. A man who believes he's the greatest attorney who ever lived. A man who believes he is kind of above the law, even above traditional morality." He had to be pompous and sometimes brilliant. He needed someone who could carry all of that — and do it with a sense of humor.

Get me Shatner.

I've been told that David E. Kelley had seen me doing my Priceline.com commercials and had begun thinking about me for this role he was creating. Eventually David and I and my Hollywood agent Harry Gold had breakfast together. And there David E. Kelley began describing a character he had written for me. A pompous, eccentric, unpredictable, outrageous attorney. Denny Crane. Now, why would he think of me for that role? His plan was to introduce the character in the final few episodes of *The Practice* to see if there was any chemistry with the existing characters. If it worked he wanted an option for me to do the new series.

I called David E. Kelley's office a few

hours later. "I don't want to do it," I said.

Sound effect: The phone drops onto the floor. "What?"

I'd thought it through, I explained. "If it works it's going to get picked up for a series and I don't want to do another series. I'm not going to work every day. I know, you're going to tell me it's an ensemble and I don't have to work every day, but let me tell you something. Every time I've done a series I've lost a wife. I'm not going to lose this wife. I'm not going to spend the rest of my life sitting around a set. I just don't want to work that hard anymore.

"Look, if you want me to do the six episodes of *The Practice* I'll do that. But I'm not going to give them an option for a series."

Eventually I was convinced that if the show did move forward it would be an ensemble piece. Each actor would have a week to star. It meant that I wouldn't have to work five days each week and I wouldn't be responsible for the success of the series. So we negotiated a mutual option that would allow me a limited work schedule if it became a series. And I put on Denny Crane's immaculately tailored suit for the first time.

In my first episode of *The Practice* I was

hired to defend James Spader's character, the intense, socially conscious Alan Shore, who had been fired by his law firm for his somewhat dubious ethical practices in defense of truth and morality. "What's with the red tie?" were my first words to Shore. "Around here we wear cold ties. Blue. Black. Hard colors. Tough colors. Red is soft. Soft does not work around here."

After I walked away an associate explained to Shore, "That's Denny Crane."

"*The* Denny Crane?" Shore said, impressed. And so a character — and a relationship — was born.

Crane's brilliance became obvious in the very next scene. After Spader had explained his legal problem, Crane considered the options for a moment and then asked, "You Jewish?"

Shore was confused. "Am I Jewish?"

"Best bet we argue they fired you because you're a Jew. No defense against that."

"Well, I would ordinarily agree," Shore responded. "But they didn't fire me for that. And I'm not Jewish."

I lowered my Denny Crane eyes. "I didn't hear that."

Our conversation was interrupted by a young attorney from another firm who was in our offices to try to work out a settlement in a negligence case. Unfortunately his firm was not offering enough money, so I had been delegated to convince him to increase his offer. "Did Mr. Billings explain that Marie Sennet is one of my oldest and dearest friends, and I'm like a brother to her late husband?"

The associate calmly corrected me. "It was actually her brother who died. Not the husband."

I put my hand on his shoulder and corrected him. "Really? You know what? Medical records aside, if *Denny Crane* tells the jury it was the husband, they'll believe it was the husband." Denny Crane's huge ego was immediately defined as he told this young associate, "I'll bet later tonight you'll be on some barroom stool trying to finesse your way into some legal secretary's panties. You want to get there faster, son? Tell her, earlier you held court with . . . Denny Crane." I paused and repeated in an urgent whisper. *"Denny Crane."*

Seconds later Alan Shore was standing outside my office complaining to another lawyer. "He's a whack-job . . . He's asking me to plead Jewish."

"I promise you," this lawyer said, awe dripping from his voice. "Once he stands up in court . . . he's Denny Crane." And then he repeated it, *"Denny Crane."*

Alan Shore wasn't convinced. After the first courtroom hearing he complained to me that he didn't want Denny Crane to speak. Denny Crane corrected him. "You want Denny Crane to talk. When Denny Crane talks, E. F. Hutton listens."

The story arc continued in the next episode. I was walking across a lobby in the first scene, and I saw Alan Shore. "Denny Crane," I said, shaking hands.

"Why do you always tell me your name? Is it so *you* won't forget?"

And here Denny Crane described completely his unique character. "Let me tell you something, soldier. I've learned from experience that people can't actually believe they're in the room with Denny Crane. They think it can't be true. So I let them know it is true. I look them in the eye, Denny Crane. Gives them something to tell their grandkids. Denny Crane."

Beautiful, just beautiful. What an extraordinary character to be permitted to play. Denny Crane is an actor's amusement park; you can find anything you want there. For my work in *The Practice* I was again nominated for an Emmy, this time as Outstanding Guest Actor in a Drama. Oh, I wanted to win. I'd always professed not to have felt slighted that I wasn't even nominated for *Star Trek,* but I was. We often did some very good work on that program. So this time I wanted to win as strongly as anything I'd ever wanted in my life. It's my time, I thought, I'm older now, this isn't going to come around again. I wanted to win so badly that I managed to convince myself I wasn't going to win, that way it would not be so painful when I didn't win. I didn't dare write a speech because if I did, it would mean I thought I might win. So as long as I didn't think I could win, there really was a chance I could win.

Liz and I were sitting in the audience when my category was announced. A camera was focused on each of the nominees. Believe me, I was as aware as a pinprick that a camera was right on my face. Don't show any disappointment, I told myself. Don't dare frown.

I focused my eyes on the lips of the presenter. This is absolutely true. I was looking for the pursed lips of a "W." And when I saw his lips purse I squeezed Liz's hand. "William Shatner!"

The audience cheered. Literally cheered. I received a loud ovation. It was obvious the people in that room were genuinely happy for me. I was so moved because I've always felt like an outsider in this business. I've never felt like I belonged. This was a vote from my peers and it was so incredibly meaningful to me. As I walked onto the stage I had absolutely no concept of what I was going to say. I wanted to express my gratitude, I wanted to tell these beautiful people who had so honored me how deeply I was indebted to them for their love and support. So I opened my mouth and said honestly, "What took you so long?"

Denny Crane. Denny Crane!

After the successful introduction of Denny Crane on *The Practice,* ABC bought David E. Kelley's spin-off, *Boston Legal.* My reluctance to commit to the series had changed so drastically that rather than being reticent, I was very upset when I was offered a 7/13 contract, meaning they would only guarantee that I would appear in a minimum of seven of the first thirteen episodes rather than an all-shows-produced deal. That didn't seem right. I was Denn . . . William Shatner. Emmy Award–winning William Shatner.

Denny Crane is a brilliant, outrageous, unpredictable, funny, sexist — "A hundred women there and you didn't invite me? That's two hundred breasts and you kept them all to yourself" — courageous, occasionally looney character. Creating Denny Crane was a collaboration between the producers, the writers, and me. He is an extraordinarily complex character, capable of moving almost instantly from serious drama to the comedy of the absurd, without ever acknowledging to the audience which aspect of that is real. When he confides to Alan Shore, "I'll tell you what I'm afraid of . . . I think I have mad penis," it has to be said with such honesty, such fear, that the audience will wonder how much he believes that and how much he is playing with Shore. Is he truly crazy, with moments of laserlike insight or is he absolutely brilliant, using absurdity to control his terrain? It took us several shows to clearly define the character as indefinable.

Denny Crane was described as a man whose great financial success as a litigator is visible. He wears only expensive suits, he's always perfectly dressed, smokes the best cigars, and drinks the best scotch — and knows the difference. Apparently in early meetings F. Lee Bailey's name was mentioned. The sets were designed before the first script was written, which was somewhat unusual. Basically, it takes place in the plush offices of a respected Boston law firm, one of those places where the carpet is so thick the only sound you hear is the perfect-tone chime of an arriving elevator. In one show, for example, Denny Crane admits, "I'm so far up the ass of big business that I view the world as one great colon."

The most difficult aspect for Kelley was finding just the right balance between drama and humor in the scripts. So after we shot the pilot David E. Kelley decided it wasn't substantial enough and rewrote it. He asked one of the producers, "What if we made it *One Flew Over the Cuckoo's Nest* set in a law firm?" The second version of the pilot was much funnier than the initial script. Then he wrote another version which was extremely serious and tended to minimize the relationship between Denny Crane and Alan Shore. The draft was, it was finally agreed, a very good episode of *The Practice* and would disappoint those people expecting it to be a truly new show. Then he rewrote it again and that was the version we finally shot.

That balance between drama and comedy was extremely difficult to find and it took some poking around to get there. We struggled with it for several shows. As brilliantly as the shows were written, there was a lot about Denny Crane that wasn't on the page. In one of our very first scenes, for example, Alan Shore asks Denny Crane, "What are you, homosexual?" The way it was written I didn't respond. I had to say something. Why are you asking? Nice of you to care. So's your old man. Anything, but I had to respond. Yet there was nothing written to indicate Denny Crane's reaction. And I had to stop and think about it. How would this character react? He's a tough guy, a former military officer, always calling people "soldier" and fixing their ties, and sexual harassment be damned — he's never afraid to tell a woman how sexy she looks. And what he would like to do about it. I was left completely on my own to develop this character, which is right because that's why they hired me. So my first reaction to it was to laugh. Denny Crane a homosexual? Now that's funny, soldier. I had no idea how to play it. I didn't know how to deal with it and that kind of scared me. Do you like this guy or not like him? Is he sardonic or not sardonic? I needed an emotion to color my words and I didn't know it yet, I didn't know Denny Crane well enough to know how he would react. But I learned. As Denny Crane went through a variety of sometimes very unusual experiences, from being caught in a passionate embrace with a blow-up doll made up to resemble his

568

partner, played by Candice Bergen, to falling in love with the midget daughter of a former girlfriend, I learned who he is. Denny Crane was once a great lawyer and at times is still at the top of that game. He is a great reader of human nature, which gives him a great advantage. And he reads people with the skill of a great poker player.

Each decision we made further defined the character. In the first episode an old friend sadly told Denny Crane that his wife was having an affair and he was asking Denny to investigate. "I want you to find out what's going on," he said.

As it turned out Denny Crane knew exactly what was going on — because he was the one with whom she was having the affair. When this friend found out he pulled a gun on Denny Crane and threatened to kill him. Rather than pleading for his life, or warning the man of the consequences, Denny Crane became the aggressor. "Go ahead, pull the trigger. Because that's the way Denny Crane should go out. It'll be front-page news in *The New York Times*." Great writing, strong character definition — but my question was, how do I play it? I knew what Kirk would do, and Hooker. I wanted to walk around my desk and confront this man; I wanted to be bold, get up right in his face. I wanted to show him that a mere gun doesn't scare Denny Crane. That seemed the right response to me. But our director, Bill D'Elia, strongly believed Denny Crane would sit behind his desk defiantly and say quietly and resolutely, "Go ahead and pull the trigger . . ."

We argued about it. Voices got raised. We stood toe-to-toe. Mano a mano. Actor-to-director. The creative process at work. Loudly. He followed me back to my dressing room, both of us defending a position that we knew might not even be the best answer. Finally I agreed to do it his way. It worked, and further colored the character.

Although certainly it didn't work as well as walking around the desk and confronting him.

Scene by scene Denny Crane was shaped. David E. Kelley's writing fed my performance which further fed the writing which enhanced my performance which was reflected in the writing . . . Everything I'd learned in my career went into his creation, so when I read a line the underlying emotion had to come from the life I'd invented for him, rather than from my own life. When Denny Crane is asked by Alan Shore if he's lonely, for example, I could say no and mean it or I could say no and mean, yes, I am desperately lonely. But in order to do that I had to say it with the conviction of an arrogant lawyer whose attitude is, I can convince a jury that anything I say is true. An actor's choice is to say the lines as he or she thinks they should be said, or say them through the filter of their character's life. And the more I learned about Denny Crane the more he was able to speak for himself. Although, truthfully, Liz believes that sometimes I experiment with Denny Crane at home. And as he is a broad exaggeration of what I am, and she knows me so well, it's difficult for her to separate Shatner from Crane.

But there was one thing that I insisted Denny Crane was not — Captain James T. Kirk. In one of our first scripts I had a line in which I insisted members of the firm call me "Captain." I told D'Elia, "If you don't mind, I'd prefer not to say this line. I don't want to be called Captain."

D'Elia agreed. "I bet I know why." I smiled and nodded, and then he asked, "Okay, so how about Commander?"

Admittedly, by the end of our second season I was feeling so comfortable in Denny Crane's expensive suits that while talking to my partners I did describe myself as "the captain of the ship." And in another episode Alan Shore did refer to sealice as "cling-ons," to which I responded, somewhat startled, "Did you say 'Klingons'?"

I think what surprised everyone was the intensity of the relationship that developed between Denny Crane and Alan Shore. Their friendship has been called the best love affair on television. Certainly there has never been a stronger bond between two men portrayed on a series. David E. Kelley had planned for them to be law partners, close friends, and confidants, but what developed organically from these two characters has far transcended those original intentions. What has become a hallmark of *Boston Legal* is the final scene, in which Denny Crane and Alan Shore relax on the balcony outside Denny Crane's office, overlooking Boston, smoking their cigars, often sipping an aged scotch, and talking honestly and intimately in a way very few television characters have ever related to each other. At the conclusion of an episode in which the two of them had engaged in a charity wrestling match, for example, Alan Shore says, "You cheated."

"I did not." And after a thoughtful pause Denny Crane remembered, "Y'know . . . the first time I had sex with Shirley . . . it went exactly like that. I flipped her on her back and sat on her head."

Alan took a long drag on his cigar. "I hope it was better for her than it was for me."

"Better for me. It also lasted about four seconds."

On the balcony at the end of another episode, in which Alan had defended a man who had been charged with allowing his terminally ill wife to die so he might be with his lover, Alan quotes a witness who testified, "Families often act to end their own suffering." Then he wonders, "Is that what happened with your father?"

I rolled Denny Crane's cigar in his fingers and remembered his father, and possibly my own, although Denny Crane's had suffered from dementia and had lost his awareness. "He wasn't exactly in pain. His appetite was good. In fact he was actually smiling more in the end than he . . . On the day, the day we told the doctor to up the drip, he was blissful. We put him out of our misery. And I often wondered, did that life belong to the man with the brain of a two-year-old? Or to the life of the man who preceded it? It certain . . . it didn't belong to me . . ."

"How'd you get the doctor to do it?"

"Denny Crane. I was still the real thing then."

"Denny, I'm gonna say this right now and then I'm going to memorialize it in my living will. If I ever end up with the mind of a two-year-old . . ."

"I'll have Bev sit on you . . . My day is coming, Alan. We both know that."

"It's a long ways off. And in the meantime, live big, my friend. Live big."

The always-humorous, usually poignant, amazingly popular, reflective balcony scenes were created by accident. David E. Kelley's first script ended with Alan Shore on the balcony with his then-girlfriend, Sally Heath. On our balcony with a woman! That cad! But after several rewrites a romantic ending just didn't work anymore, so instead Alan Shore ended up there with Denny Crane. It was not intended to be the kicker for each episode; in fact several of the initial shows didn't end that way. But the feedback was enormous; people, men mostly, responded to their friendship. I've had to play some very difficult scenes on *Boston Legal* — believe me, it's not easy to look good dressed as a pink flamingo, but one of the most intense balcony scenes ended a show in which Denny Crane had caught Alan being friendly with another man. Denny Crane was piqued, he was terribly jealous. It was a very fragile moment, I had to express the emotions of a woman who had caught the man she loved cheating on her — but in a very nonsexual way. If I went too far it became broad comedy; if I was too intense it became anger rather than hurt. When people talk to me about *Boston Legal,* this is the show they often cite. More than any other moment, this is the balcony scene that most accurately describes their relationship. "I don't know whether you know this," Denny Crane admits to Alan Shore, "but not many men take the time, every day, to have a cigar, a glass of scotch, to talk to their best friend. That's not something most men have."

"No, it isn't."

"What I give to you, what I share, I do with no one else. I like to think that what you give to me you do with nobody else. Now that may sound silly to you. But here's what I think is silly, the idea that jealousy or fidelity is reserved for romance. I always suspected there was a connection between you and that man. That you got something you didn't get from me."

"I probably do. But gosh, what I get from you, Denny. People walk around today calling everyone their best friend. The term doesn't have any real meaning anymore. Mere acquaintances are lavished with hugs and kisses upon a second or at most third meeting, birthday cards get passed around offices so everybody can scribble a snippet of sentimentality for a colleague they barely met, and everyone just loves everyone. As a result when you tell someone you love them today, it isn't heard much. I love you, Denny, you are my best friend. I can't imagine going through life without you as my best friend. I'm not going to kiss you, however."

The relationship between Denny Crane and Alan Shore never could have worked if James Spader and I hadn't become friends. I mean, him I don't love. But certainly I like him and respect him greatly. I remember the day we met, I extended my hand. "Hi. Bill Shatner."

We shook. "James Spader."

I asked, "Is it James or can I call you Jimmy?"

And he replied firmly, "No. It's James."

My kind of guy. "Well, in that case," I told him, "perhaps I should be called William."

Among the many things I enjoy about . . . James, is that he makes me appear much closer to normal than might otherwise be true. Like me, he's a sensualist; especially about food and drink and other people. He's self-taught and extremely knowledgeable about a great range of subjects. On the set we have great rapport — and of course I enjoy teasing him. And perhaps he'll tell you what I tease him about in his autobiography.

James is a very precise person. When planning a vacation in Europe, for example, he'll book a reservation in a restaurant weeks in advance and actually decide what he will order. Unlike me, who simply goes into a restaurant when I'm hungry and eats . . . something.

But as far as I'm concerned it's the very best something anybody has ever had at any time. Really, you have to try this something, I promise you you've never tasted something like it before. You have to try it, you must.

He's a wonderful actor, an award-winning television and movie star known for the quirky parts he has played. What makes our onscreen relationship work so well is that the way we approach a script reflects the way we experience life. James's desire is to set his performance, usually at home. By the time we start rehearsing he has already decided how he wants to read a line and what he wants to do physically. If he sets a move he doesn't want to vary it: this is where I'm going to stand, this is where I'm going to be looking, this is how I'm going to read that line. And I'm going to do it that way every time.

Or so I thought. But one day James and I sat down — although not on the famous office balcony where we conclude each show — and discussed the technique of acting. It was fascinating for me to see how we both got to the same moment. "I meticulously prepare the text," James explained. "I go over and over and over it for hours at a time. I don't have to think about the words at all.

"Therefore, when I get to the set, because I'm so familiar with the character, I'm ready for anything my character might want to do. Anything."

What James was saying, or perhaps what I heard him say, is that he spends a tremendous amount of time preparing to be spontaneous. That preparation allows him to inhabit the character. But the character is on his own.

I like to ad-lib. Not with the words — especially not with the words on *Boston Legal* because of the quality of our writers. Generally there is nothing an actor can do that will benefit those words, except say them exactly as they are written. I have noticed that when I do change a word or two it does make a difference; the lines are so beautifully crafted that if I say "we" instead of "I" I might change the rhythm. Maybe the joke is not quite as sharp or the timing is slightly off, so I learn the exact words and I say them exactly as they have been written. So my improvisation is in the emotion; in the way I recite the lines. Once I have the lines down I'll experiment with variations. That's the way I examine a role, I hear all the possibilities and within each one a slightly different meaning. For me, that's the fun of acting. The words aren't ad-libbed, the intent is. The way a person says something that reveals not only the true meaning of their words, but the essence of their character.

For example, on the page the words "Don't do this to me, Bill" are cold. But to hear Nerine begging me not to leave, "Don't do this to me, Bill" as she exposed her very soul to me, has a hugely different meaning.

James and I also approach our roles with very different energy. He is low energy, he takes his time to ponder each word, and he's very slow to respond. Me? High energy. Bust it out there.

Somehow it works. At the end of our first season James received the first of the two Emmys he would win as the Outstanding Lead Actor in a Series — the second and third Emmys of his career — while I would win my second Emmy.

There is at least one other very important thing I like about James — in some ways he reminds me of Leonard. We had a scene in which James was in a conversation with several other people. The action of the scene required me to go to one of those people and lean over. It occurred to me that while leaning over I could stick my ass in James's face. The value of all my experience is that I recognize an opportunity to stick . . . to provide a prop for a fellow actor. I thought I was giving to James perhaps the single greatest straight line one actor can bestow on another: I was presenting him with the butt of the joke. There were many options; he could play it broadly for laughs, "Ah, I see there is a full moon on the horizon." Or he could be acerbic, "Congratulations, Denny, you've finally gotten a bigger part." He could be angry, "Denny, do you know you're a bigger lawyer than you've ever been?" Or he could wax philosophical, "There is nothing like a man's posterior in close proximity to make you consider your own mortality." Instead, he chose to tell me, "You can't do that."

I was offended by his attitude, but I said nothing because I had instigated it and didn't want to cause a problem. Instead I just stayed away from him for the rest of the morning. I was eating lunch in my dressing room when James knocked on the door, "Can I come in?" En-terrrr! "You're offended, aren't you? Let's talk about it."

"There's nothing to talk about." I knew he was there to put my behind behind us. As Leonard had responded when I threw his photographer out of the makeup room, James insisted we talk about it. "What was the big deal? I leaned over."

"Yes, and when you did your ass was in my face."

"Well, why didn't you play off it?" There, another great straight line for him.

"I couldn't," he began, and explained why. I listened, and then I said, "You know, James. What you just did is something I can't do. Face a person. You got a problem, deal with it directly. I don't do that, I let it fester for a day and then it's gone." James had opened it up, aired it out, smoothed it over. "That's a quality I admire in someone. And I wish I could do more of it." And in fact, I have learned that from James, and that honesty is a huge part of our relationship. "But what I get from you, James. People walk around today calling everyone their best friend . . ."

Candice Bergen plays my partner and

former lover. The really interesting thing about Candice is that the qualities she projects through the character of Shirley Schmidt are her own qualities. She is a beautiful woman of great style and intelligence. She has more class than almost anyone I know, and has become a good buddy. But then there is that famous sex-doll scene.

Denny Crane has never lost his deep lust for Shirley Schmidt. In one episode, Alan Shore caught him in a storage closet humping a blow-up sex doll made up to resemble her. I remember reading that script for the first time, and thinking, "Well. Well. This could be . . . interesting." On *Boston Legal* perhaps the most important point on which we've all agreed is that no matter how absurd the scene, how ridiculous you have to act, we will play it like it is absolutely real. Truth matters.

Fifty years as an actor and I had to hump a blow-up sex doll.

Me. Oh, believe me, I could play sex scenes. I definitely could play sex scenes. I'd done a classic sex scene with Angie Dickinson, I'd worked with some of the most beautiful actresses in the business. But this was the first time I had to make love to a blow-up sex doll. As with all the other absurdities we are directed to do on *Boston Legal*, I knew that the only way I could make this work was to make it absolutely real. I remembered being a kid more than seventy years ago and watching a boy masturbating. I'd never seen anything like that before; his eyes were turned inward and he was totally self-absorbed. I can't remember that kid's name or the circumstances, but I've never forgotten that look. And so I tried to do that with the doll. I became totally absorbed in that doll, and anything else — the closet door opening and the one of us being discovered together — came as a shock.

What makes Denny Crane such a wonderful character to play at this point in my life is that we share so much. When Denny Crane talks about his own mortality and his recognition that he is older now and has lost some of his powers, there might be some of my life sneaking in. I do think about those things, I wonder about them. I'm never far from the fear of old age or senility or being incapacitated by a stroke. I've tried to bring the realities of my life into my performance. Fortunately, my ability to focus allows me to learn my lines as easily now as I did when I was twenty. So I don't have any problem memorizing lines

— although I do wish the producers would use cards or a prompter. For some of the other actors, of course.

There is a scene I had with Candice Bergen during which this once legal lion showed . . . well, at least hinted at his vulnerability. Denny Crane and Shirley Schmidt were in her office, sitting on her couch. Shirley just happened to ask me about the fishing waders I was wearing. "I may not be the lawyer I once was," I explained. "But I can still fish circles around all of you. Sometimes I just like to wear them to —"

She interrupted me, interrupted Denny Crane! "When I was in high school I was captain of the debate team . . . and miserable over being cut from the cheerleading team. I went out and bought my own outfit, complete with pom-poms. Sometimes I'd dress up, look at myself in the mirror . . . it somehow made me feel better.

"Years later, after I became a lawyer, even a partner, every once in a while if I was feeling particularly low, I'd pull out that costume. And put it on."

"I did exactly the same. Not with a pom-pom, but —"

Shirley shook her head. "You're just determined not to let me have a vulnerable moment, aren't you? You want to hog them all for yourself." She paused, maybe even sighed. "Denny, we're getting older, we can no longer fit into our outfits. But we're not over. Not by a long shot. You're not over."

With each line another layer of Denny Crane gets peeled away. "You know what used to make me feel better than anything? . . . It was back when we were . . . us. And you'd put your head on my —"

"Denny!"

"I was going to say shoulder. That felt better than anything."

"Oh. I remember you'd sing, 'You Are My Sunshine.' "

Sing? There are sentimental sides of Denny Crane that get revealed at the oddest times. Perhaps that's one reason he's become so popular. "Could you do that for just a minute? Put your head on my shoulder?"

"Denny."

"I just want . . . to remember." She pauses, and then lays her head gently on my shoulder. It's a beautiful moment. And then I say softly, "This feels . . . can you put on the cheerleader . . ."

"Don't push it."

And the ending, of course, is perfect. I get to sing. "You are my sunshine, my only sunshine. . . ." Fade to black.

There was no specific direction for that moment, just a suggestion in the script that it be meaningful. But as we did it I realized it was coming from the longing the character had for Shirley, for their past together, as he held her. And at that moment, without meaning to, I had slipped into not the suit, but the skin of the character.

There is one trait I've given Denny Crane that no one has recognized. Many years earlier, when I was having dinner with Edward G. Robinson, I asked him, "Are you aware that you go . . . *nyeh?*"

He wasn't. "I go *nyeh?*"

"Yes, you go *nyeh.*"

So every so often, as a paean to my hero Edward G. Robinson, Denny Crane will throw in a little, *"Nyeh."*

I love the thought that David E. Kelley had decided to write the character for me after seeing me doing a Priceline.com commercial. Remember, one of the primary reasons I was hired to do those commercials was because a copywriter remembered — and loved — my 1968 album, *The Transformed Man.* And now, probably because of the attention I was getting from playing Denny Crane, after thirty-five years I was asked to record a second album. My career had made a full, singing circle.

Several years ago I listened to *The Transformed Man* and I had to admit that parts of it aren't very good. In my memory it was much better than it actually was, but at least it was an attempt to do something interesting. It was a concept album. For it to work you had to listen to the entire six-minute cut, which consisted of a piece of literature tied to a song; on radio they played the three-minute song and it sounded mostly like me screaming and yelling. What I had intended to be drama had emerged as comedy. People mocked it and it was somewhat humiliating. I had smiled and tried to carry it off with some sort of grace, but I felt bad about it.

But had it been even slightly better it probably would have been quickly forgotten. Instead it has lived on in legend. Some people believe my version of "Lucy in the Sky with Diamonds" is the worst musical rendition of all time. Apparently George Clooney picked it as one of the few things he would want to have with him if he were marooned on a deserted island. As he explained, "If you listen to this song, you will hollow out your own leg and make a canoe out of it to get off the island."

Comments like that kept the album alive

by creating curiosity. How could anything be that bad? So people wanted to hear it. And because of it, I've been given the opportunity to talk-song in movies, on television, and on other records. On the 1992 MTV Movie Awards I performed all of the Best Movie Song nominees. On the animated science-fiction show *Futurama,* for example, I talk-sang Eminem's "The Real Slim Shady," proving it was possible to do a spoken-word version of a rap song.

Surprisingly, some of the people who took the time to listen to the long versions of the songs actually appreciated it. One of them was the well-respected musician Ben Folds. "I got *The Transformed Man* at a yard sale as a kid, and that's how I got a little Shakespeare burned into my head. And hearing that next to Bob Dylan, that was pretty interesting. Maybe it was laughable to older people or people who thought they had it all figured out, but I just locked onto his voice and his timing."

In 1997 he wrote and asked me to participate in an experimental album he was making, *Fear of Pop.* One of my daughters loved his music and convinced me to do it. As a result Ben and I became friends and worked together on several other projects.

The company that made the most money

from *Transformed Man* was Rhino Records, who used several cuts from that album on a series of very popular albums called *Golden Throats: The Great Celebrity Sing Off.* Not to take all the credit for the great success of that album, several of Leonard's songs were also used, including his version of "Proud Mary."

In 2003 the Foos brothers, who had produced *Golden Throats,* came to my office and sat on my couch and asked me to record another album. And they did it with straight faces. They had sold Rhino Records and were starting a new label, Shout! Factory. Now, I knew they were hoping to produce another album that people would mock. I probably would have turned them down, but as they were sitting there my phone rang. Ben Folds was calling from Nashville, a coincidence too amazing to ignore. Literally, Ben called me while they were in my office. He was coming to L.A. to do a live show, he explained, and wanted me to perform with him.

Boy oh boy, did I have a great idea. I put my hand over the speaker and asked the Foos brothers, "Can I do anything?" Anything I wanted to do, they said.

Although I'm quite certain the last thing

that they expected me to do was a good album.

I asked them, "Would you take Ben Folds as my producer?" They agreed instantly. "Ben," I said, "the two guys who used to own Rhino Records are in my office right now. They want me to do another record. Would you produce it?" Ben agreed. It was amazing, I was going to do another album!

Only after the Foos brothers had left my office did I realize I didn't have the slightest idea how to do an album. I called Ben back. "Now what am I gonna do?"

Ben had a simple answer. "Tell the truth. You write it down, I'll make the music."

With Ben's advice I sat down and started writing songs about my life. I tried to distill the important events of my life into a few songs, focusing on those things I wanted my loved ones to understand. I managed to get it down to only about one hundred different songs. Then Ben and I went to work rewriting and editing them.

I flew to Nashville to record the album. Ben had bought the studio in which Elvis Presley had recorded some of his music and we were going to work there. As I was getting on the plane I saw my name on the cover of one of the tabloids and picked it up. And then I hid it until all the passengers were seated so no one would see me reading it. It is sort of embarrassing. The story quoted an actress who was complaining about working with "that has-been." Has-been? What? I'd always resented that phrase. It's an oxymoron. How can you be a has-been unless you've been something? Big deal, you're not that now. The fact is you're not what you were a split second ago. People are constantly changing. I never understood why it is considered a derogatory term to have been something. Is it better to never be than to be and eventually become a has-been? The only people who stay the same are minuscule talents who earn their livings writing about other people who are busy living real lives, people who think "has-been" is an insult.

I got it! That's the title! *Has Been.* We were searching for a title and there it was, right in front of me, on the front page of a tabloid. I loved it, it was turning a phrase in upon itself. It was the last thing anybody could have expected, which is why it was my first choice.

Ben recruited great musicians for the album; Joe Jackson, the British group Lemon Jelly, punk star Henry Rollins, Aimee Mann, and country icon Brad Paisley. Novelist Nick Hornby wrote a song for us. We worked every day and night for two weeks and eventually put down — that's music industry insider talk — eleven cuts, the story of my life from *It Hasn't Happened Yet* to *Has Been*.

Has Been received wonderful reviews. Absolutely wonderful. Modesty, and my editor's instructions, prohibit me from including the top fifty or sixty. So please Google *Has Been,* read them for yourself. Then order it — and I'll just bet you can figure out where you can find it!

After the album was released Ben and I did a live show in Los Angeles. I had to relearn the songs and then, in front of several thousand people, for fifteen minutes I was a rock 'n' roll star. Without the tattoos, of course. At the end of the concert all the lights in the hall were turned off. And then the band started playing "Lucy in the Sky with Diamonds." When the song started I raised my arm high into the air — and stuck out my middle finger. Just that one finger. The spotlight caught it and remained focused on it. And I kept it there as I sang "Lucy in the Sky" exactly as I'd done it decades earlier on *The Transformed Man*. That young audience, Ben's audience, got it immediately. They started screaming — and laughing. I performed the song almost exactly as I had done it so many years earlier. This time though, instead of being mocked, we got a long, long standing ovation. The audience stood cheering for a half hour. Literally, a half hour. We would have done an encore, but we had nothing else to play. They got it. Maybe it took thirty-five years, but they got it.

A few nights later Ben, Joe Jackson, and I appeared on the *Tonight Show* and did a song from the album titled *Common People*. Again we got an enormous response. I was flying! I was pumped! When I got in my car to drive home I turned the radio to a local music station. Suddenly I heard the male host say to his female co-host, "We've got William Shatner's new record here." They're going to play my record on the radio! This was thrilling; within hours I'd sung on the *Tonight Show* and I was about to hear my record being played on the radio for the very first time!

"Yeah," the female host responded. "What an asshole."

"You're right," the male host said. "He really is an asshole."

Here's what I did *not* think: I've got the title for my next album. Instead I got my cell phone and called them. "This is William Shatner," I said. "And I am not an asshole!" Then we started arguing about whether or not I was an asshole. Finally I asked them, "Listen, would an asshole call a radio station to complain that he is not an asshole?" I stumped them with that one.

We spoke for about five minutes and then hung up. The female asked, "Was that really Shatner?"

And her partner responded, "Yeah, it was. And he's still an asshole."

Well, that started a whole discussion. People kept calling the station to state their opinions. "I don't think he is an asshole." "Well, sometimes he can be an asshole." "It depends on your definition of the word 'asshole.' " For the entire segment the topic of discussion was, is William Shatner an asshole?

Has Been eventually rose to number twenty-two on *Billboard*'s Top Heatseekers chart.

A few weeks later a woman named Margo Sappington called me from the Milwaukee Ballet. She loved the album, she told me, and wanted to create a ballet around six cuts. As a man who takes pride in supporting the arts I asked her what I perceived to be the key question, "Any money in it?"

"This is ballet," she explained. "Ballet depends on the kindness of strangers."

Of course I gave them the rights for free — but then I made a documentary on the making of a ballet, titled *Gonzo Ballet.* I have to admit that when I told certain members of my family — and they know who they are — that I'd decided to record another album they were a bit dubious. More than anything, they didn't want to see my feelings hurt again. So you can just imagine how they responded when I gave them the news, "Guess what? They're doing a ballet from the album."

Knowing me so well, one of my daughters felt compelled to remind me, "Dad. You can't dance."

I can't? Of course not, but just the thought that this idea would be interpreted into an entirely different art form was exciting to me. And I'd never previously been involved with a ballet. It's new to my life, and I like that a lot. I believe new challenges are essential in life.

At this point in my life it's amazing that my career is growing. Go figure that one out. I don't believe I've ever been busier. Or, thank you very much, more popular.

I now wonder if I'm working too much. Perhaps I should experience other things? But I'm having such a good time it's difficult to say no to anything. In fact, my daughter Lisbeth and her husband play a game: Can they get through an ordinary day without hearing my name mentioned or hearing my voice on the radio or television? Mostly they lose.

Ironically, the one part I might have enjoyed playing I wasn't even offered. The producers of the movie *Star Trek XI* — which apparently focuses on the early life of our characters — did not ask me to appear in that film. Spock lives in that film, but I guess that because Kirk had been killed they felt they couldn't find a place for him. Many people wondered if I was upset or angry not to be offered a role. I wasn't; I was sad, though, and I was slightly mystified. It just seems like a poor business decision not to bring back Jim Kirk one last time.

I recognize that I'm getting older. And I do think about my own mortality. And what I now know is that there are so many questions to which I'm never going to know the answer. We are born into mystery and we leave life in mystery. We don't know what transpired before and we don't know what's coming ahead. We don't know what life is. We don't even know the truth behind the assassination of JFK. Is there a God? What is time? There's everything we don't know.

I love a good mystery. I love wondering

and speculating and guessing. I love looking at the stars and imagining what's out there. I love closing my eyes and trying to visualize a day three thousand years ago. Mysteries simply are a feast for an active mind. And while in my lifetime I've seen science make extraordinary inroads into solving the most complex questions of life, after all this time I admit that I am thrilled that there are some things that forever will remain a mystery.

For example, do I wear a toupee?

ABOUT THE AUTHOR

David Fisher is the author of more than fifteen *New York Times* bestsellers. He is the only writer ever to have works of fiction, nonfiction, and reference offered simultaneously by the Book of the Month Club. He lives in New York with his wife, two teenagers, one dog, and one cat.

We hope you have enjoyed this Large Print book. Other Thorndike, Wheeler, and Chivers Press Large Print books are available at your library or directly from the publishers.

For information about current and upcoming titles, please call or write, without obligation, to:

Publisher
Thorndike Press
295 Kennedy Memorial Drive
Waterville, ME 04901
Tel. (800) 223-1244

or visit our Web site at:

http://gale.cengage.com/thorndike

OR

Chivers Large Print
published by BBC Audiobooks Ltd
St James House, The Square
Lower Bristol Road
Bath BA2 3SB
England
Tel. +44(0) 800 136919
email: bbcaudiobooks@bbc.co.uk
www.bbcaudiobooks.co.uk

All our Large Print titles are designed for easy reading, and all our books are made to last.